W9-ALA-653

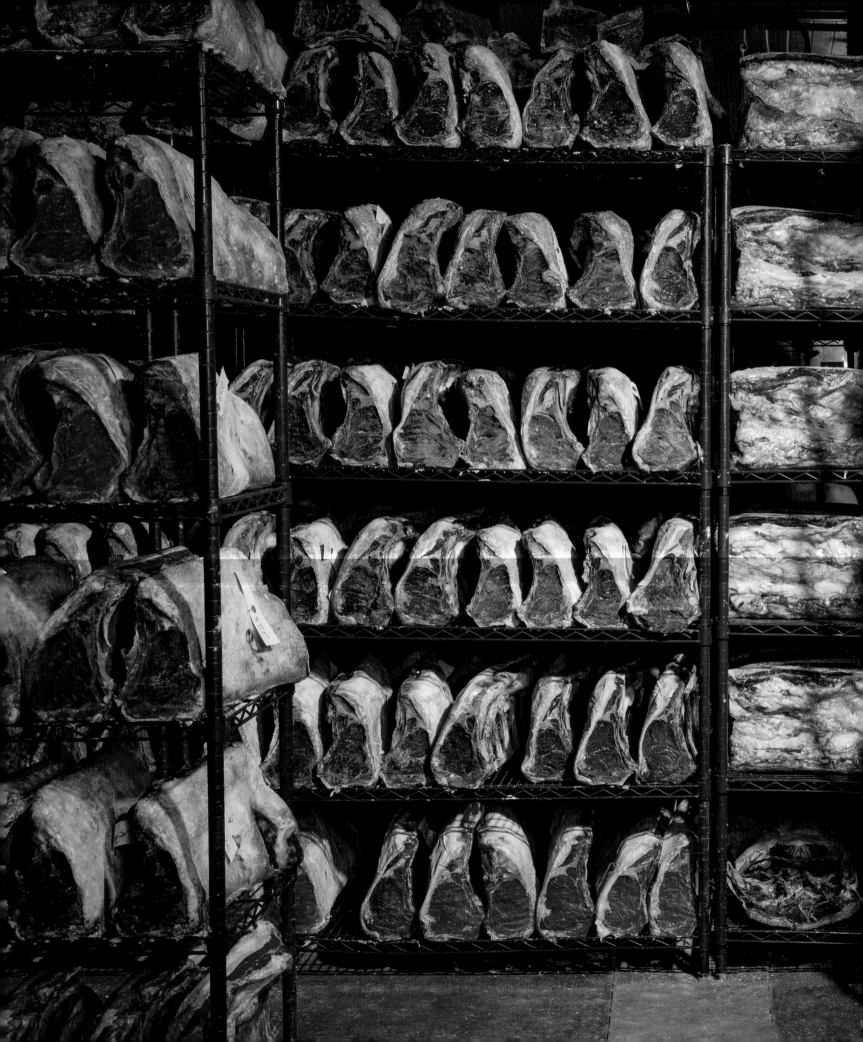

MEAT

EVERYTHING YOU NEED TO KNOW

Pat LaFrieda

AND Carolynn Carreño

PHOTOGRAPHS BY EVAN SUNG

ATRIA BOOKS

New York London Toronto Sydney New Delhi

ATRIA BOOKS

A Division of Simon & Schuster, Inc.
1230 Avenue of the Americas
New York, NY 10020

Copyright © 2014 by Pat LaFrieda
Photographs © 2014 by Evan Sung

All rights reserved, including the right to reproduce this book or portions thereof in any form whatsoever. For information, address Atria Books Subsidiary Rights Department, 1230 Avenue of the Americas, New York, NY 10020.

Photo on page 66: author with chopped meat, and photo on page 219: LaFrieda's steak sandwich, courtesy of Nick Solares. Photo on page 222: Black Angus Cattle in field/on farm courtesy of Creekstone Farms Premium Beef LLC Photography.

First Atria Books hardcover edition September 2014

ATRIA BOOKS and colophon are trademarks of Simon & Schuster, Inc.

For information about special discounts for bulk purchases, please contact Simon & Schuster Special Sales at 1-866-506-1949 or business@simonandschuster.com.

The Simon & Schuster Speakers Bureau can bring authors to your live event. For more information or to book an event, contact the Simon & Schuster Speakers Bureau at 1-866-248-3049 or visit our website at www.simonspeakers.com.

Interior design by Jason Snyder
Jacket design by Jeanne Lee

Manufactured in China

10 9 8 7 6 5 4

Library of Congress Cataloging-in-Publication Data

LaFrieda, Pat.
  Meat : everything there is to know : recipes and stories from America's greatest butcher / Pat LaFrieda and Carolynn Carreño.—First Atria Books hardcover edition.
    pages cm
Includes bibliographical references and index.
1. Cooking (Meat) I. Carreño, Carolynn. II. Title.
  TX749.L224 2014
  641.6'6—dc 3
                    2014000898

ISBN 978-1-4767-2599-4
ISBN 978-1-4767-2601-4 (ebook)

This book is dedicated to our restaurant
customers and their patrons who eat our meat
and allow us to do what we love to do.

CONTENTS

Pat Sr., Pat Jr., and Mark

PROLOGUE

It's Saturday around midnight and I'm dressed in a suit, sitting in the back of a Lincoln Town Car with my wife, Jennifer, coming home from a fund-raiser for our son's school, when my cell phone rings. It's the organizer of an enormous, meat-heavy food event that is taking place in Prospect Park in Brooklyn. It's the first of the two-day event and the organizer is telling me that a good number of the vendors have run out of meat. There was such a shortage of food that earlier in the day riots broke out. Two people got stabbed in the hand with skewers over who would get the last chicken breast. So now the organizer is with the New York Police Department, who were brought in because of the fighting. The police are refusing to open the event the next day unless the event organizers can guarantee there will be enough food. Which is why they are calling me: I'm a butcher.

I run a business—along with my father (also Pat LaFrieda) and my cousin, Mark Pastore—that my great-grandfather put in motion almost one hundred years ago. Back then we were one of many small butchers in Greenwich Village, many Italian American like us, and all of them vying for their little piece of the pie. Twenty or thirty small restaurants in and around the neighborhood—that was our piece. Today, we supply more than 1,200 restaurants from New York to Las Vegas with the best meat in America: dry-aged steaks, milk-fed veal, Colorado lamb, and custom chopped meat blends.

My men and I have been busy all week getting meat ready for our customers participating in this event. But everyone ordered short. They braced for five thousand or ten thousand people over the course of the weekend, but instead, they got hit with thirty thousand on the first day. Now the NYPD is refusing to let the show go on unless LaFrieda Meats will guarantee that there will be food.

I'm a guy who likes to make the impossible happen. In fact, even though it's interrupting my evening, there's a part of me that loves a call like this. I look at it as a challenge. Can you help? Can you deliver? Can you and your company operate in case of emergency in ways that nobody else can? We supplied our customers when the blackout happened in 2003 and we did it again when Hurricane Sandy hit.

The organizer has me on speakerphone so the police will know what my answer is, and if it's "no," the event will be canceled. I tell them I can do it.

Our plant is open through the night six days a week. We are closed only from Saturday afternoon until Sunday evening, and that's where I am now: right in the middle of that time. So after dropping my wife at home, on my way to the plant I call up a couple of my regular guys who meet me there, and together we work through the night cutting and packing beef ribs, St. Louis ribs, skirt steaks and hanger steaks, some chicken items, and all kinds of meats for burgers. In addition to supplying their vendors, I'm also serving a whole 875-pound steer—this was planned—and my guys have been at the festival cooking since early that morning, but the festival organizers have now asked me to open a burger stand for which I must make four thousand 8-ounce patties myself. By 8:00 a.m., I've packed my Escalade to the roof with meat and am headed to Brooklyn with another packed truck behind me.

My guys and I have barely set up in Prospect Park when the festival-goers start pouring in. We split our burgers in half and make eight thousand portions. The steer is another two thousand portions. Still, by 6:00 p.m. we don't have a bite of food left. But the day is over and the crowd is happy.

At the end of the day, Mark and I are sitting back to back, leaning against each other on top of a picnic table. We're both exhausted. He's worked all day serving burgers, and I have blisters on my hands from slicing two thousand portions of steer as quickly as I did. We're talking about the day, and how great the event turned out. He laughs that we're the only ones who didn't make any money, and it's true. It costs a lot to get your guys to work on a Saturday night at the last minute. But that's not what this day was about for me. It was about being needed and being able to come through against all odds. It was the perfect execution of a Doomsday plan and it was definitely one of the best days of work I've ever had.

I know. It's only meat. I'm not saving the world. But people need to eat. And getting meat to people is my business. This is what I do. Being a butcher in New York City—this is who I am.

PAT LA FRIED
QUALITY MEATS
WHOLESALE DISTRIBUTOR
212 929-2420

INTRODUCTION

My father never wanted me to be a butcher.

When I was growing up, he had a restaurant supply butcher shop in a 1,500-square-foot space on the corner of Bleecker and West 10th Streets, in Greenwich Village. It was a business that he ran with his father, the first Pat LaFrieda. My grandfather Pat and his older brother Lou learned the trade from my great-grandfather Anthony LaFrieda, who had opened a retail butcher shop in Brooklyn in 1922, thirteen years after he and his son Lou landed on Ellis Island from Naples, Italy. During a meat workers' strike that made it difficult for restaurants to get meat in New York City, the two boys opened their own shop, the original LaFrieda Meats, in a sawdust-covered space on 14th Street, in the 14th Street Meat Market (today's Meatpacking District), a chaotic, congested congregation of over 250 meat purveyors in an oddly shaped, 44-acre corner on the far west side of lower Manhattan. The area was bordered by 14th Street to the north and extended seven blocks south, where guys split lambs heads in their shops on pretty cobblestoned streets right next to Village brownstones as far down as Jane Street.

Top left to right: My grandfather Pat LaFrieda the first; my grandfather, my great-uncles Tom and Frank, my father; my great-uncle Lou; my great-uncle Lou, his wife, and two apprentice butchers; my father in the '70s; Mark, my father, and me; my aunt Lisa; our delivery truck in the '90s.

Until those businesses started to dwindle and the area turned into one of fancy hotels, expensive boutiques, and trendy restaurants and nightclubs, the streets surrounding it were backed up for blocks, especially in the early morning hours, with trucks carrying every kind of meat that the people and restaurants of New York City wanted.

When my father came to work for his father and Uncle Lou, he was twelve years old and my grandfather had moved three blocks south to a second-floor space on Little West 12th Street, a wobbly, cobblestoned street near the entrance to the West Side Line, a branch of the New York Central Railroad line. Today, it's the High Line park, but until 1980, it was a working train line that brought beef, veal, and lamb. Chickens came by truck in wooden crates—sometimes with the feathers still on them. As the trains came in, my dad, still a young kid, and not a very large one, would be sent to buy the meat. He'd climb the stairs and meet the train right where The Standard, High Line hotel is now located. He would pick out the meat, buy it, throw a quarter of a steer weighing close to two hundred pounds over his shoulder, haul it back up the flight of stairs to the shop, and then go back for more. Sometimes the guys in the market would swipe grocery carts from the A&P, he remembers. "You used them to push the meat through the market. Even though it was cobblestones, it was easier than carrying it. Once you found a cart, you guarded it with your life because everyone else was looking to swipe it from you."

Today, because of how closely we are scrutinized by the USDA, we have to work their hours so their inspectors can be at our plant at all times. But back then, before Lyndon Johnson passed the Wholesome Meat Act in 1971, there were no regular inspections. This meant that guys in the meat business, like my father, grandfather, and Uncle Lou, worked as late as they had to. My father started work with his uncle at 3:30 a.m. and worked straight through until night. "One time I got off work," he says. "My uncle told me, 'Look, it's a nice day. The sun is out. Go enjoy yourself.' By the time I got to the train a few blocks away, it was dark. He'd tricked me into thinking we worked a half day but it was already night." In the winter, when it was cold, the men would toss chicken crates, and the fat that they'd trimmed from meat they were cutting, into metal trash cans and light them on fire. Up until as recently as ten years ago, you'd see guys in long white butcher's coats standing around those fires to stay warm.

Working with his father and uncle, my father learned how to buy meat, how to cut it, and everything there was to know about the business. And the one thing he definitely learned was that he didn't want to be a butcher. "I knew from the first day I went to work with my uncle that I was not going to do this," he says. "That was fifty years ago. I still know I'm not going to do it." He laughs, but it's no joke. Cars were his passion; he had some automotive innovations that he wanted to bring into being. But by now he knew the meat business inside and out. Of three siblings and thirty cousins, my father was the one chosen to take over his family's business. He put his dreams aside and did what was expected of him. But when it came to his own kids, he wanted the opposite.

I'm the oldest of four. I have two brothers, Joseph and Christopher, and a sister, Michele. We grew up in a three-bedroom, three-family home in Bensonhurst, Brooklyn, with a family above us and a family below. Bensonhurst was, and still is, a very tough neighborhood. When I was there, it was divided: mostly first- and second-generation Italian Americans, with a large African American population as well. Everyone was always beating up on everyone: Italians on Italians, Italians on blacks, blacks on blacks, blacks on Italians. The local public school was so violent that it had a police station right on campus. Because he'd been forced into the business, our father wanted to make sure my brothers, my sister, and I got out of it. He saved his money and sent all of us to private schools. We were reminded often that our dad's money was going toward our educations and we were expected to take studying very seriously and to go to college. He made it very clear: Education was our way out of the meat business. It was how we would save ourselves, or how he would save us, from being butchers.

By the time I was born, my father and grandfather had moved from Little West 12th Street to a space on Bleecker Street, now the Village Apothecary, where my earliest memories are of sweeping the floors—I must have been eight or nine years old—and of the *Playboy* magazines that I would find in the bathroom that belonged to the guys that worked there. Today, that same stretch of Bleecker Street is lined with

In 2003, the stretch of Leroy Street where LaFrieda Meats was located was renamed Pat LaFrieda Lane. Here my Aunt Lisa receives the award for the renaming from councilmember Christine Quinn.

expensive boutiques, but back then, Greenwich Village really was a village. On Bleecker Street, there was Zito's bakery, which sold nothing but long crusty loaves of bread and some canned tomatoes and other Italian canned goods that looked like they'd been on the shelves for a hundred years. Uncle Frankie, my dad's older brother, used to go there at 3:30 or 4:00 in the morning when the bread was coming out of the oven; he'd pick up a few loaves and bring them to us still hot. We knew all the other shopkeepers, some of whom are still there: Ottomanelli & Sons, another Italian American–owned butcher shop on the opposite side of the street from us; Murray's, an artisanal cheese store; and across from them, Faicco's Pork Store, which specializes in fresh and cured pork products.

We've always been a wholesale butcher, meaning we supply meat to restaurants, not the general public. But, as the shop was on a street with a lot of foot traffic and mostly retail shops, occasionally customers would walk in wanting to buy from us. My father thought, "We have the meat. Why not sell to them?" But it did not go well. Customers would often ask for two slices of a ten-pound calf's liver leaving my father stuck with the rest, which he couldn't sell; he would have to then bring it home to my mother. Then someone else would come in and want four chicken wings. "I'm supposed to stop what I'm doing to get four chicken wings? And what am I gonna do with two chickens with no wings?" He soon

went back to only supplying restaurants in and around the neighborhood.

As the oldest son, my father often took me to work with him. He got to the shop at 3:30 in the morning—the same hour his father arrived to work and the same hour my dad had been coming to work since he was a boy—five days a week, to get the meat ready to deliver to his restaurant customers for that day's lunch and dinner service. It would be dark out when we left the house, and I would sit in the front seat alongside him as we drove through the sleeping streets of our neighborhood listening to 1010 WINS, the AM radio station that was the only place to get information in those days, and talking. My father would tell me what we had to do that day. And we'd talk about if we got done early enough, how we would go fishing. Where did we want to fish that day? What did we want to fish for . . . ?

My father has had a boat his entire life. That was his favorite pastime. The boat was parked in the Marine Basin Marina in Bensonhurst, and my father's lifelong best friend, and my godfather, Jerry Albers, had a boat parked a few down from ours, so it was a boys' camaraderie kind of escape. My brothers and I grew up on that boat. In the summertime, we'd fish every day, or as often as we could. Over the course of my childhood, we fished the waters from the Verrazano-Narrows Bridge to the Rockaway jetty and across to the New Jersey Highlands and the waters of Jamaica Bay. We'd catch porgies or snappers and herring, then we'd use those as bait and clean up with striped bass, bluefish, and fluke. At the end of the day, we would take our catches home and get them ready to cook. (I was filleting fish long before I started cutting meat.) My dad didn't care to eat fish, but he would grill it up for us while my mother and sister cooked inside and my brothers and our friends and I jumped in the aboveground pool. Before dinner, we would pull the cooler full of fish out in front of the house and the Italian ladies from the neighborhood would come over in their housecoats, ten or twelve of them lined up with their pots and pans in hand, and we'd take the fish out of the cooler and put it in their pans to take home. Sometimes, before there were regulations on how many you could keep, we'd catch so many fish, my father would drive back to Manhattan and sell it to restaurants.

My father smoked back then, and he always had a pack of Marlboro reds on the seat between us. As we drove through the Brooklyn-Battery Tunnel into lower Manhattan, talking father to son about meat and work and fishing, I would pick up the pack, open it up, and inhale as deep as I could. I loved the smell of unlit tobacco, and still do. That to me is the smell of being a boy, being with my father.

There were no computers then, at least not in our business. A few hours after my father and I got to work, my mother would come in and the first thing she would do was listen to the customers' orders that were left on our answering machine throughout the night. She would write them by hand in an order book—each customer had his own—with carbon paper behind the order slips, and the other guys and I would take a book to see what we needed to do for each customer. My father didn't extend any preferential treatment to me. I was expected to do what all the other guys did, and I answered to them, not to him. Once we got an order, we went into the walk-in cooler, grabbed what we needed, cut what needed to be cut, wrapped everything in brown butcher paper, and boxed up each restaurant's order. Each got labeled, which consisted of scribbling the restaurant's name on the side of the box with a Magic Marker, and then loaded onto one of two vans we had back then. When the van was full, a driver jumped in and started making deliveries.

In the early days, my father took me to work just to spend time with me, and to show me what he did the way any father might do with his son. But by the time I was about twelve years old and I'd graduated from sweeping floors to cutting and tying top rounds of beef, he took me to work to show me how hard it was, to show me what I'd be doing, day in and day out, for the rest of my life if I didn't do well in school. "Don't do what I do," he told me on a regular basis. "You'll never make any money. You'll be rubbing pennies together your whole life. You'll work yourself to death and then in the end you'll kick yourself in the ass for it."

But no matter how much my father tried to discourage me from being a butcher, I remember always thinking that it didn't seem as bad as he made it out to be. And in fact, secretly I loved it. I loved the rides to work. I loved working with the other men. I loved the work itself. Sometimes, when making chopped meat, and nobody was looking, I would take it in my hands and smell it just like I did with my father's cigarettes. I loved that smell and the only way I can explain it is to say it's like it was a part of me; it was in my blood.

On every delivery van there were two guys: the driver and the helper, who rode in the passenger seat and jumped out when the driver made his stops. As often as I could, I was the helper. The drivers loved having me along because I didn't mind getting in and out of the van and flying down steep, often slippery steps carrying boxes into restaurant basements while they sat listening to the radio and eating a sandwich or smoking a cigarette until I hopped back in and they drove to the next place. If a chef had a problem with something we were delivering to him, he'd explain to me what was wrong, or he might draw me a picture of what he wanted in the future. I loved being inside the mind of a chef.

While my dad did not succeed in convincing me to hate butchering, he did succeed in keeping me out of trouble. All during my teenage years, while my friends were out smoking cigarettes, drinking, and stealing cars, I was working. If I didn't have school, I was at LaFrieda Meats, which meant all through Christmas and spring breaks, every summer, and any other school holiday from the time I was eleven until I graduated from high school. As a result of my dad's insistence, I did pretty well in school, and after graduating I went to Albright, a private college in Reading, Pennsylvania.

By this time, my father had convinced me that I wasn't going to be a butcher, so I started college with the mind-set of being premed. I did this for my father. For him, my becoming a doctor was the ultimate sign of success—not my success so much as his.

But as much as I wanted to please my father, I was just not cut out to be a doctor. I really struggled with science, and by the time I got to the more advanced classes, I couldn't keep up. The summer after my sophomore year, I found out I'd failed organic chemistry and I could not fool myself any longer. I changed my major to finance, which my father was not happy about, but business was obviously my forte. I aced my classes. Two weeks after I graduated, I was wearing a suit and reporting to a job on Wall Street. Not long after, I passed my Series Seven exam, which made me a certified stockbroker.

But from day one, I absolutely hated it. The company I was working for—a fairly large company with offices up and down the East Coast—was doing some really shady things. Even though I was new at it, I could still tell that what we were doing wasn't right. We were dumping worthless stocks on innocent people. It really put a bad taste in my mouth, and after ten months, I quit my job and told my dad, "I don't know what I'm going to do next, but in the meantime, I'm going to come work at LaFrieda Meats. Just for a little while . . ."

What else was I going to do? I honestly didn't have another idea. I always wanted to be a butcher. Even in college, when I was pursuing premed and then finance, whenever anyone outside the family asked me what I was going to do after college, I always said the same thing, "I'm going to take over my dad's business." They all knew what that business was because whenever my dad came to visit, he would bring me ten-pound bags of chopped beef and a five-pound package of sliced American cheese, and I would make hamburgers for all my friends.

My grandfather had passed away about five years before I left my job on Wall Street, and my dad had been running the company with his sister, my Aunt Lisa. They had moved the business into a building that they'd bought on Leroy Street, in the West Village, about ten blocks south of the 14th Street Meat Market. My Aunt Lisa is the real reason I was able to come into the business. My father resisted, but Lisa, who had recently retired, told him, "Give Pat a shot. Let him try growing the business." My dad was not happy with the idea, and without a doubt he was disappointed in me. But my aunt was a stronger person than my father (and believe me, my father is himself a very strong person). She really pushed for it, and eventually my father had no choice but to give in.

There was a little two-bedroom apartment on one side of the building on Leroy Street above the butcher shop. My aunt had lived in that apartment, but had since moved to New Jersey and only slept there a couple of days a week. After I'd graduated from college, I tried moving back home, but my brothers had taken over my room, and I was on the couch, so Lisa let me live in her apartment. At twenty-five, I was now living upstairs and working as a butcher in my father's company, which, looking back, is really the only path my life could have taken.

When I took over my father's business in 1994, we had forty restaurant customers and, in addition to my mom and dad, three employees and that included me. The 14th Street Meat Market was slowly diminishing; the meat industry—how meat was bought and sold in this country—was rapidly changing and industrializing. It was a time when small businesses of all kinds were being taken over by large impersonal corporations. But despite those factors, LaFrieda Meats went on to be enormously successful. We grew out of the Leroy Street space a few years later and moved to a 35,000-square-foot facility in New Jersey, and we're now looking to open a second facility nearby. I have more than 140 employees, deliver over three hundred thousand pounds of meat a week, and make more than nine hundred deliveries to restaurants and select retail shops every day.

In this book, I'll tell you everything I know about meat— how to buy it, how to cook it, where it comes from, how it's broken down. . . . But for me, the personal story that I will tell here—of how, against all odds, I took a struggling family business and built it into a national brand—that is the one that is closest to my heart. Even though this particular narrative is about something I accomplished, I think of what I've done as part of something bigger: I think of it as a Great American Success Story.

TOOLS

When I give butchering classes and demos, one of the questions people most often ask me is what kind of knives they should buy. People love looking at their knife blocks on their kitchen counters and they love an excuse to buy a new knife, so they're disappointed when I tell them that, from a butcher's point of view, you only need two, neither of which is very expensive.

A **scimitar** is a long (10- to 12-inch) knife with a curved blade. This is what you want to use to slice steaks or any other long, smooth cuts. It ensures one clean cut, not a sawed, stair step–type effect on the meat.

The second knife I use is a 5-inch **boning knife**, a slightly smaller knife. It's flexible, so when the knife hits the bone, you're able to steer the blade around and down the bone to cut off the meat.

In order to keep knives sharp, it's important that you hone them on a **sharpening steel** in between uses. Despite the name of the tool, "honing" a knife doesn't actually "sharpen" it. Honing a knife reshapes the blade by removing the imperfections and stray bits of steel from the blade's edge, which is why I recommend that after you hone a knife, you rinse it off before using it. A sharpening steel can take a knife from dull to sharp again, but there's a limited amount of time before you will need to take it to a professional knife sharpener. We do this weekly, but for the home cook once every six months will be enough. To hone your knife on a sharpening steel, hold the steel perpendicular to your work surface and place the knife blade, facing down, against the steel at a 15- to 20-degree angle. Pass the blade of the knife across the steel, pulling the blade slightly toward you in downward strokes and making sure the knife does not touch the work surface. Do the same to hone the other side of the blade. After you do four or five strokes on each side of the knife's blade, wipe down the knife to remove any microscopic bits of steel that remain on the blade. People often ask me: How can you tell if your knife is sharp enough? The way I was taught by the butchers in my dad's shop was that if you held the knife on your thumbnail, so the blade is at a right angle to the nail, and you were able to slide it easily across the nail, it needs to be sharpened. If you feel resistance, as if the knife is digging into your nail, you're in good shape. You may think this sounds crazy or dangerous or both, but I have never cut myself doing it. There is no better way to see if a knife is sharp, and if you're going to cut meat, you need to get comfortable with a knife.

A **butcher's needle** is a long, large needle used to sew meat.

Butcher's rope, often sold as "kitchen twine," is thin cotton cord used to tie roasts, and sew up pockets for stuffed roasts and chops.

A **butcher's saw** is a butcher's version of a hacksaw. It's used for cutting through bone. If, for instance, you wanted to cut porterhouse from a short loin, this would be the tool for the job.

I use a **meat mallet** at home to pound out veal cutlets. It has one texturized side and one flat side. The texturized side tenderizes the meat and the flat side flattens it. When I make cutlets, I start with the texturized side to break down the meat, and then finish it with the flat side (see "Pounding a Veal Chop or Cutlet," page 16), which won't tear up the meat.

I use only **plastic cutting boards**. Wooden cutting boards get nicks in them; bacteria can get in those nicks and it's not safe. Plastic boards also get nicks and cuts, but the cuts are not as deep, and plastic is not as porous as wood. When you put plastic boards in a very hot dishwasher to sanitize them, they come out completely clean; that doesn't apply to wooden boards.

There is no better way to know when meat is done than to use a **meat thermometer**. Chefs often say that you can tell the doneness of meat by comparing its firmness to that of various parts of your hand. I have never been able to do this. Instead, I use two types of thermometers. One is a probe that goes directly into the meat. The other has a long cable atttached to the probe, so I can read the temperature of the meat even if the oven or grill is closed. Checking meat for doneness using a thermometer is foolproof. There's no guesswork. I don't cook meat without one. I've ruined too many good steaks trying to do it any other way.

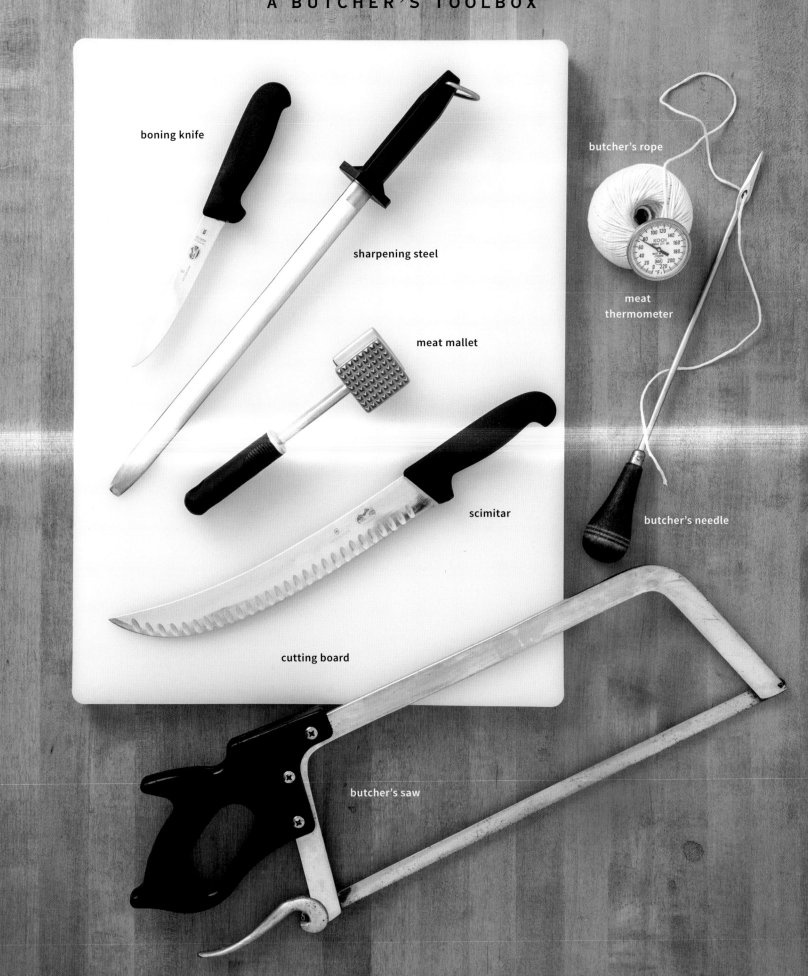

A BUTCHER'S TOOLBOX

boning knife

sharpening steel

meat mallet

scimitar

cutting board

butcher's rope

meat
thermometer

butcher's needle

butcher's saw

MEAT QUALITY AND SAFETY

FRESH VS. FROZEN

Avoid freezing meat or buying frozen meat. When you freeze meat, you break the muscle cells; and when you defrost it, you'll notice what we call "purge." Purge is the blood and water that comes out of the meat when it defrosts, which, had it remained in the meat, would have translated into moisture and flavor. With certain cuts of meat, such as those used for braising, you can get away with freezing because you make up for the moisture loss in the braising process. But when it comes to steaks or burgers, forget it. Buy fresh meat.

RINSING MEAT

Do not rinse meat of any kind before cooking. If there are any pathogens on the surface of the meat, they will be destroyed during the cooking process. The only thing you'll succeed in doing by rinsing it is spreading those pathogens around your sink and kitchen. Also, wet meat will not brown, and a good sear on the external surface is the goal when you're cooking any kind of meat.

HOW YOU KNOW IF MEAT IS BAD

The best way to know if meat is bad is to smell it. Meat of any variety should have almost no odor. If meat has even the slightest off-odor, it's bad (unless we're talking about aged beef, which has a slightly funky, corn-like smell). Another sign of meat that has gone bad is an iridescent or greenish hue on the surface. Lastly, meat that has spoiled will have a sticky texture. In order to avoid any doubt, use large cuts of meat such as roasts or thick steaks within three or four days of purchasing them from a reliable source, and use chopped meat and stew meat within a day or two of buying it.

BRINGING MEAT TO ROOM TEMPERATURE

Since I'm constantly concerned about food safety, I am always confused to hear chefs talk about bringing meat up to room temperature before cooking it. Their theory is that meat at room temperature will cook more evenly; for instance, you would have to cook a cold pork chop until the edges were dried out in order to get the inside cooked enough, because the inside is cold. While this may be the case, the pathogen growth rate on meat that is left out at room temperature is out of this world. The most common pathogen is staph (*Staphylococcus aureus*), a food-borne bacterium that, even when the meat is cooked at high temperature, leaves enough toxins behind to give you food poisoning. Even if you cook the meat to the temperatures recommended by the USDA (which in my opinion means overcooking it), this won't help, as this recommendation assumes that the meat has been handled properly, which means it's been kept below 40°F until the time of cooking. I'm not saying you're going to get sick as a result of bringing meat to room temperature. Obviously people do it and they live to tell the tale. But if you are feeding small children, the elderly, or anyone else who may have a compromised immune system, don't take the risk. Keep your meat cold. I do, and the recipes in this book call for meat to be kept cold before cooking it. Controlling pathogens is a part of my daily life and that doesn't change when I am at home cooking for my family and friends. If you want to bring your meat to room temperature before cooking it, of course do so, but note that the cooking times could be slightly different than they would be if you were starting with cold meat. Those cooking methods were very carefully developed with cold meat and you will not get the best results if you start with anything different.

COOKING FROM THIS BOOK

This book is divided by varieties of meat. In each chapter, I tell you what you need to know about that kind of meat, from what to look for when you buy it to some basic principles as to how to cook it. Each chapter also contains a section defining all of the cuts of meat on the animal. By familiarizing yourself with some of the more unusual or lesser-known cuts, and with the recipes here, you'll be able to venture away from traditional chops and steaks and move into cuts of meat that you might not have tried before. It includes many of my family recipes. Some are mine. And some are from our chef customers that showcase our meat in an unusual way.

Recently many restaurants have begun to talk about "large format" cooking, which refers to big roasts and other cuts that have to be served family-style, rather than individual portion cuts, and you'll see a lot of that here. I am a fan of large format cooking, in part because I grew up with it. We are a big family, and we didn't have a lot of money. Large format cuts, like fresh ham (see Fresh Holiday Ham with Tangerine and Cloves, page 152), veal breast (see Grandma LaFrieda's Braised Stuffed Veal Breast, page 20), and leg of lamb (see Roasted Leg of Lamb with Garlic, page 61) are economical relative to other cuts on the same animal. These cuts allowed my mother and grandmother to feed large crowds with the money they had. I also like these cuts for the presentation. There's something really special about bringing a magnificent whole roast to the table.

VEAL GOING TO THE SOURCE

When I came to work with my father in 1994, he had just started selling to Il Mulino, an Italian restaurant in Greenwich Village. New York City has many hot restaurants at any given time, but back then, none was hotter than Il Mulino. It was and still is a place where the city's most powerful and influential people go to make deals, to celebrate, and to eat really well; it was rated the number one Italian restaurant by Zagat for twenty years in a row. Limousines were lined up for blocks every night, waiting for patrons inside. Among other things, Il Mulino was known for their impossible-to-get reservations, their high-profile clientele, their enormous portions, and their stuffed veal chop. Il Mulino was the most prestigious restaurant to sell veal to in the city, so it was important that we get it right in terms of getting them exactly what they wanted: milk-fed veal where the meat was very white, and with a large loin or "eye" muscle. The eye is the muscle that makes up a substantial portion of the chop, and since Il Mulino was charging an astronomical price for theirs, it had to be big, and it had to be perfect.

Around the time I came on board, one of Il Mulino's owners, Gino Masci, began complaining that he wanted better veal than what we were giving him. There were no two more demanding people in the industry than Gino and Fernando, his brother and business partner. We respected the fact that they were as discerning as they were, and when they asked for something, we did it. We wanted to meet their request for veal, but there wasn't a lot we could do because we were limited to whatever was offered by either of the two veal suppliers at the 14th Street Meat Market.

At the time, the way the meat business worked was that butchers like us would go to the 14th Street Meat Market where there were various brokers from whom we bought meat. My dad and I would get in a van and fight our way through traffic to get to the veal and the lamb suppliers first, then beef, then pork, and then poultry. We'd pick up all of what we needed for that day, and then head back to our shop to cut it.

Il Mulino on West Third Street in the Village is still an institution.

But Il Mulino was an account we could not afford to lose. My dad and I had to really think about what we could do, and we decided to go on a spying mission. There was one veal house in particular where we were getting our best veal. The next time we got a delivery from them, we looked on the box for the USDA number of the meat processor who had delivered it. Every meat processor in the country has a USDA number that identifies them, and every meat delivery is required to have that number on it. There was no Google back then, but we had a yellow pages–size USDA directory and we were able to take the numbers off that box and look up the source of the veal. It turned out the veal was coming from a processor located in New Jersey. The very next day my dad and I jumped in the car and drove out there. We just showed up and introduced ourselves. We told them we were butchers, that we supplied restaurants in Manhattan, and that we'd like to start buying from them directly. We assured them we would pay all our bills within seven days. In our business, credit is everything—if you can't pay your bills, you

can't get product, and if you can and do pay your bills, there's a lot of power in that. We also promised them exclusivity: We would buy only from them, and in return, we wanted their best product. We already knew this veal to be very good because we had been buying it through a distributor; we just wanted to know that we would get the cream of the crop. We asked for the top 10 percent they had to offer. And we had a deal. Once we made that agreement, we went downstairs into the processing facility where the calves were being split. Just as a precautionary measure, to make sure we really *did* get the cream, my dad pulled aside one of the gentlemen who oversaw the production line, slipped him an envelope containing $500, and told him, "I need the best veal coming off the line." When my father and I went back to New York, we gave two days' notice to our veal purveyor and began getting our deliveries straight from this processor.

Cutting out the middleman and going directly to the source was a very significant change for us. It wasn't about saving money; if we saved anything, it would have been pennies, and in more instances, we paid more for our product because even though we had the first right to it, we were still bidding against other meat companies to get the best available. What was important was that we now had control over the quality of the veal we were buying. Veal was just the first meat we did this with. Today, we don't use any middlemen; we get all of our meat directly from the grower. This is how we completely changed the way meat had been brokered up until that point in New York City, and also the way my dad had been buying meat since he was a twelve-year-old boy.

When the truck with our first delivery pulled up in front of our plant on Leroy Street, it was a truly exciting moment. We now had something none of our competitors had—a direct line to the source, and a promise to offer the best there was to be had. We were very proud of what we had done. We knew it was going to change the way we did business, and it did.

Because we had Il Mulino as a loyal customer, we were

now the go-to guys for veal. Every chef with a good restaurant in New York City wanted to buy veal from us. Back then veal was very, very popular. The demand has diminished since then, but in the 1990s, veal was what set a restaurant apart. And it's how we relaunched our identity.

To give you an idea of how small we still were at that time, my mother used to do all of our marketing, which consisted of her walking into restaurants in Greenwich Village and giving them our business card or a T-shirt. My mother had dropped a card at Pó, a tiny place on Cornelia Street owned by Mario Batali. This was before Mario was "Molto Mario," and before he was a household name. I had never heard of the guy until the day he called asking for a veal loin. It was about 2:00 in the afternoon and all the other shops were closed; butchers start early and most of them end their day by 1:00 p.m. Mario asked if we were still open and if I had a veal loin I could sell him. I said, "No problem. I'll bring it over." When I got off the phone I told my dad I was going to package the veal and bring it over to this chef, and my dad started yelling. "Are you crazy!? It's Friday! We don't start business with new customers on a Friday!"

I said, "Why? What are you talking about?"

And he yelled, "If it's Friday and someone you don't know is calling you for meat, it means they didn't pay their meat purveyor—and we're gonna get beat out of that money."

I told my dad, "I like this guy. He sounds really cool."

My dad said, "I'm telling you. Don't do it. Call the guy up and tell him to forget it."

I told my dad, "Put it on me. If he doesn't pay, I'll be responsible for the money." And I sent one of my men to deliver the veal loin to Mario.

As it happens, the reason Mario had called me for that veal loin is that he'd ordered it from his regular butcher, who was our biggest competitor. But instead of delivering a veal loin, this butcher gave Mario a veal rack. When Mario said, "Hey, I wanted a veal loin," the guy said, "This is what I've got. Take it or leave it." This kind of attitude, like my dad's rigid attitude toward taking new business on a Friday, was rampant in the meat business. Adjusting that attitude and making customer service the priority is one of the reasons we started to pull ahead of the competition. If it sounds basic, it is. I guess you could say that the bar was set pretty low in that department.

The Monday after I delivered the veal loin to Mario, he called me up and gave me his entire meat order. I went to meet him and I gave him my pager number and my home number. My dad and I shared our numbers with everyone. It has always been important that our customers have access to us. For them to be able to reach us whenever they needed was vital to them, and we welcomed it.

A few weeks later, on another Friday evening, Mario called and said that he needed a veal breast right away for a television appearance the next morning. This was before it was a normal course of events for chefs to be on TV, so I asked, "Mario, what the hell are you going to do on a TV show with a veal breast?"

Mario said, "Pat, enough with the questions. Can you get me the veal breast?" I told him of course I could. I opened up the shop, got the veal breast ready for him, jumped in a cab, veal breast tucked under my arm, and took it across the Village to Pó. When I handed the veal breast to Mario, he was so grateful. From that day on, I couldn't ask for a more loyal friend or customer. The show he was doing was called *Mediterranean Mario.* That was the beginning of his television career, and for us it was the beginning of a whole new chapter for LaFrieda Meats and the way we would come to work with chefs.

I made my television debut on Mario Batali's Mediterranean Mario, *which appeared on the Food Network in the early 1990s.*

ALL ABOUT VEAL

Veal, the meat from unweaned dairy calves, is the star of many of the Western world's most luxurious dishes, including veal tournedos in France, osso buco and veal Milanese in Italy, Wiener schnitzel in Austria, and, among Italian Americans, veal Parmigiana. Veal is prized for its supreme tenderness and mild flavor, but as wonderful as it is to eat, veal is also the subject of heated controversy.

In order for veal to have its characteristic tenderness, mild flavor, and pink color, not only do the calves have to be fed a specific diet, but their movement also has to be restricted. If not, iron is produced in the calves, which is what can make their meat red. In the 1970s, you heard reports of farmers restricting calves' movement in inhumane ways. Much of that has changed. In 1990, the American Veal Association implemented guidelines, which are strictly enforced, as to how veal calves are raised. These guidelines also require that veal sold in America be all natural, meaning that the calves have never received antibiotics or growth hormones.

Another important note about veal is that it is a natural by-product of the dairy industry. In order for dairy cows to produce milk, they must give birth at least once a year. The females will be raised to be dairy cattle; the males are not very salable as beef because Holsteins, the favored breed for dairy cows, do not produce the best beef so they are raised and sold as veal.

We get most of our veal from Amish and Mennonite farmers in Pennsylvania. Having heard all the reports about the mistreatment of calves, my dad and I took a trip to see how the veal that we were buying was being raised. What we saw was very reassuring. It's true, the animals were confined in large pens; they have to be. But at this particular farm, their living quarters were clean, well lit, ventilated, and climate controlled. The animals stood around eating all day long; you could see that they were comfortable and healthy.

BUYING VEAL

There are three types of veal on the market: nature veal, grain-fed veal, and bob veal. Nature veal—also called "special-fed," "milk-fed," or "formula-fed"—comes from calves that were fed either milk or a formula of milk and whey, and that were slaughtered at under twenty weeks. Traditionally, veal calves would have fed on mother's milk, but as veal production has become a big industry, mother's milk has been replaced with a milk formula that includes milk proteins such as whey isolate. (In recent years, veal has gotten more expensive because whey isolate is also used in the protein bars and drink powders that have become so popular.) Nature veal has a pale color, delicate flavor, and an almost velvety appearance, with little or no visible fat. Nature veal is the only veal we handle; it is the best there is, and it accounts for 85 percent of the veal on the market. Bob veal is from animals younger than three weeks, and often just a few days old. Whereas nature veal has a mild flavor, bob veal has *zero* flavor, because it has not been fed anything; it's essentially a newborn. You might be served bob veal in low-end or chain restaurants, where the priority is on the bottom line, but you will rarely see it sold in grocery stores or butcher shops. The last type of veal on the market is from grain-fed calves, which are slaughtered at five to six months. Their meat is dark pink, almost red; it is less tender than nature veal, and has a more pronounced flavor, similar to beef.

Unlike in the beef industry, there are no regulations in the veal industry in terms of labeling, so when you buy veal, it might just say "veal," and not specify which classification. Ask for "nature veal" and look for meat that is light in color and has little or no odor.

COOKING VEAL

I like to be creative in the kitchen, so for me the subtle flavor of veal is its best characteristic. You as the chef get to bring the flavor to the meat. I love seeing veal on restaurant menus because I'm always curious to see what creative things chefs are doing with it. What I don't like to see is veal listed simply as something such as a "grilled veal chop." Because even if you start with the best veal and you are the most skilled chef and grill that veal chop to absolute perfection, it's still not going to have enough flavor to be a great dish. Veal needs something—sauce or breading or stuffing—to give it flavor. The other consideration when cooking veal is that since it has so little fat, it will go from moist, delicate, and melt-in-your-mouth, to flavorless and dry in minutes. The solution is to not overcook it. Unless you're braising it, veal needs to be cooked to medium, or 145°F.

The beauty of veal is that its flavor is nearly neutral, allowing chefs to dominate the dish with their own flavors, sauces, and stuffing.

Veal is a natural by-product of the dairy industry in that every milking cow must give birth annually to at least one calf, of which half will be raised for milking and the other half, the males, will be raised for veal production.

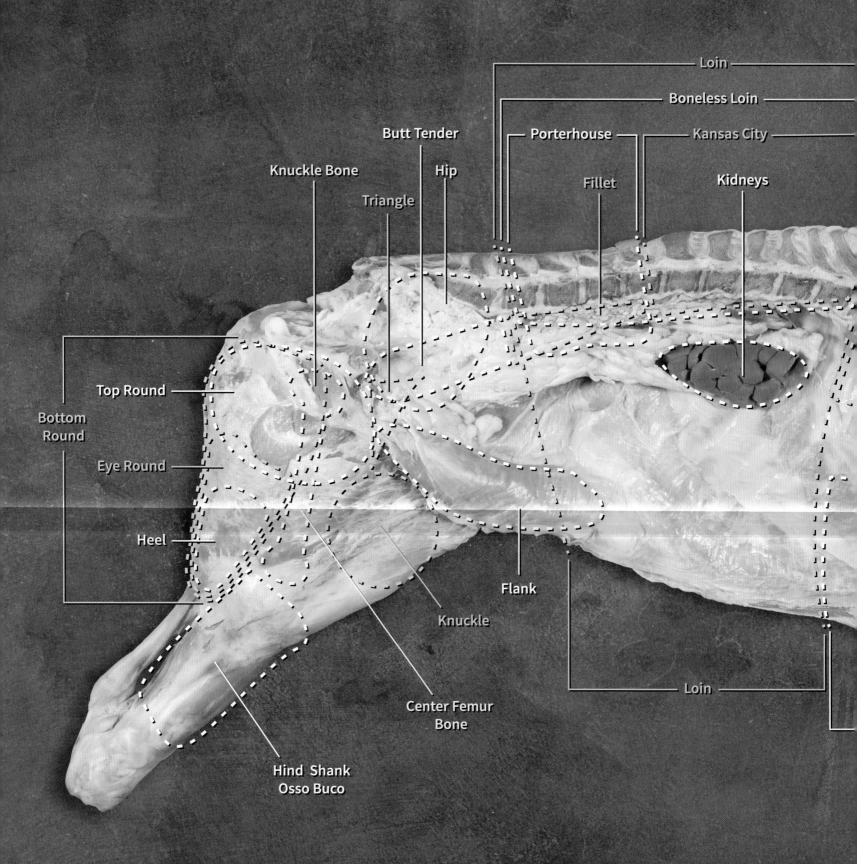

Loin

Boneless Loin

Butt Tender

Porterhouse

Kansas City

Knuckle Bone

Hip

Kidneys

Triangle

Fillet

Top Round

Bottom
Round

Eye Round

Heel

Flank

Knuckle

Center Femur
Bone

Loin

Hind Shank
Osso Buco

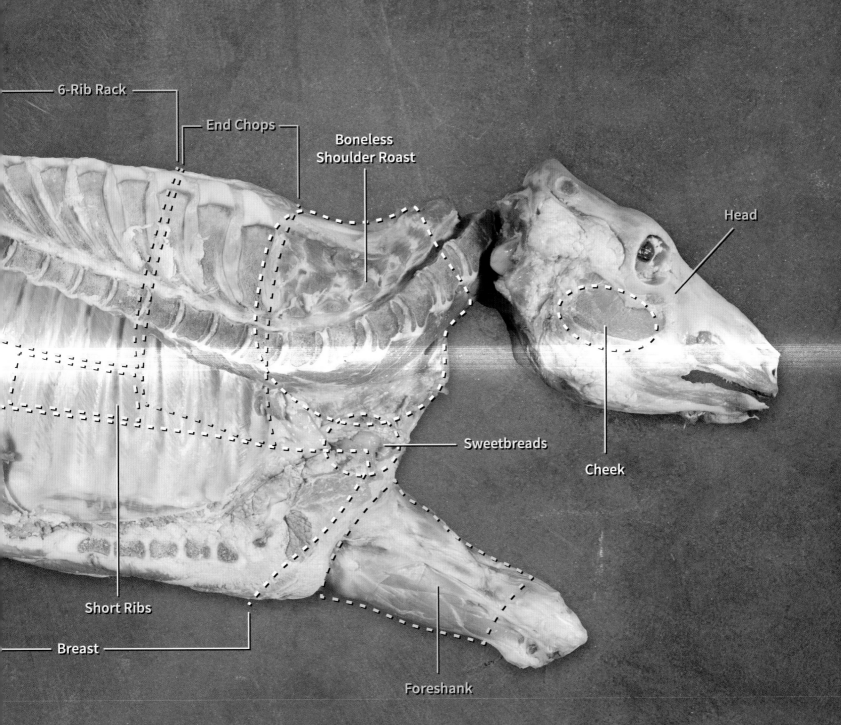

6-Rib Rack

End Chops

Boneless
Shoulder Roast

Head

Sweetbreads

Cheek

Short Ribs

Breast

Foreshank

VEAL CUTS

Grocery stores and even butcher shops usually offer only the most popular cuts of veal. But there are many lesser known, less expensive cuts that are delicious if you know what to do with them. By familiarizing yourself with the various cuts on the whole animal and their cooking and eating characteristics, I'm hoping you might venture away from cutlets and chops at least once in awhile.

A **6-rib rack** consists of six rib chops. You could use two of them frenched, as shown here, to make a crown roast (see "Making a Crown Roast," page 54), but you rarely see such a thing. On a retail level, this rack is almost always cut into chops.

The **rib chops** are the most flavorful and expensive cut of veal there is; these are the best twelve ribs (six on each side of the full rack) on the animal. You'll often see veal rib chops in restaurants stuffed with rich ingredients and seared (see Veal Rib Chops Valdostana with Foie Gras Mousse, page 23). They are often frenched, as shown here.

Veal end chops are the two ribs in front of the 6-rib rack from which rib chops are cut. They aren't as pretty, or as tender, as rib chops, but they have great flavor and are much less expensive. Because of their uneven shape, they're almost always pounded out to make Veal Milanese (page 24).

Kansas City chops, the veal equivalent of a bone-in New York strip steak, consists of the tender and flavorful loin meat. Veal **porterhouse chops** consist of tenderloin on one side of the "T" bone that divides the chops and loin meat on the other. Both types of chop are best seared or grilled over high heat. Although these cuts contain the same loin meat as the rib chop, they are about 20 percent less expensive because they don't have the long rib bone, which restaurants like for presentation.

A **boneless loin** is a long, cylindrical cut consisting of the same meat you find on Kansas City chops. A boneless loin can be tied, and cooked as a roast, in which case ask your butcher to keep the belly flap attached and wrap it around the loin meat; the fat in the belly protects the meat and keeps it moist while it cooks. Even better, roll and tie the roast yourself (see "Tying a Roast," page 145), so you can season the meat all the way through. It can also be sliced into **boneless loin chops**.

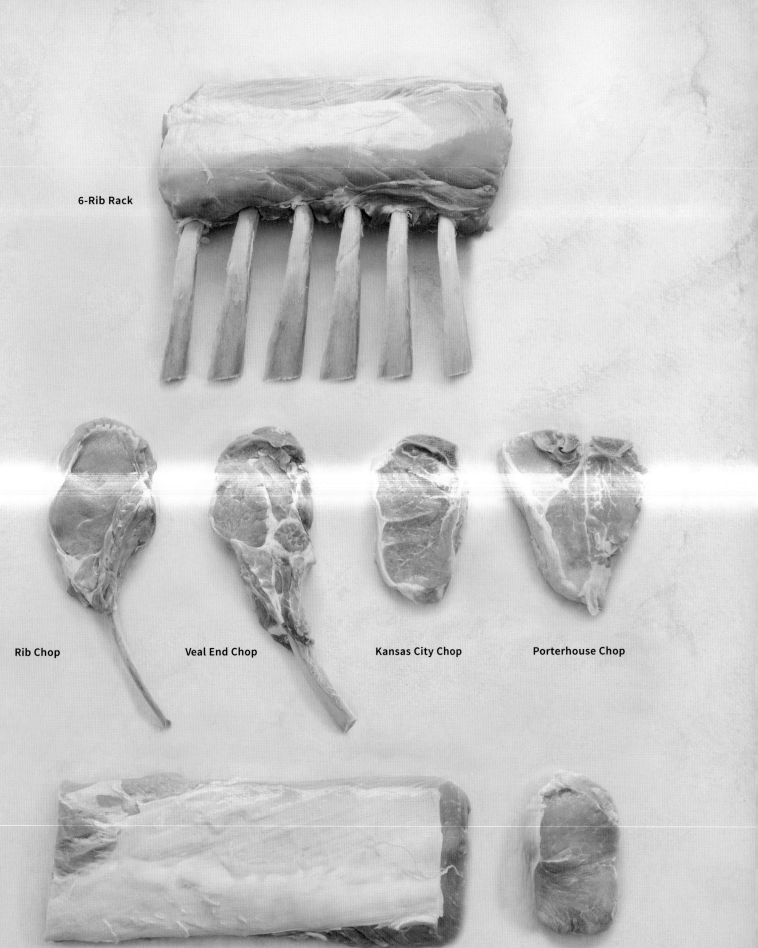

6-Rib Rack

Rib Chop

Veal End Chop

Kansas City Chop

Porterhouse Chop

Boneless Loin

Boneless Loin Chop

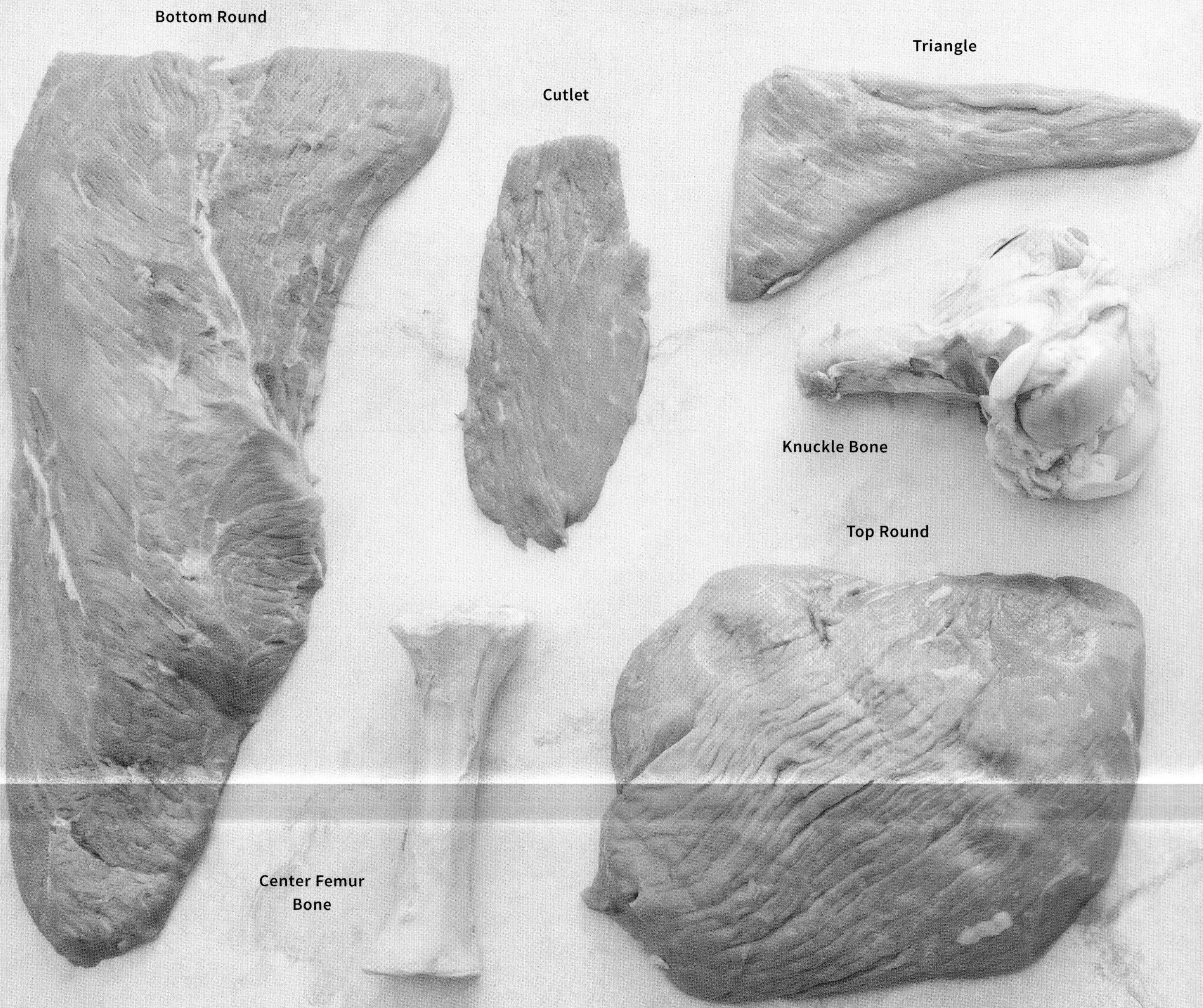

Bottom Round

Cutlet

Triangle

Knuckle Bone

Top Round

Center Femur Bone

LEG

The **bottom round** is slightly larger than the top round. It is composed of two major sections, with sinew that needs to be carefully removed, dividing them. It is made up of tightly bound muscle and is thus not as tender as the top round. It is generally sliced into cutlets.

Veal **cutlets** are also called scallopini or schnitzel. The meat, generally derived from the leg, is sliced thin against the

grain. Although any leg cuts can be used for cutlets, each has slightly different characteristics.

The **center femur bone**, used to make stock (see Brown Veal Stock, page 31), is filled with marrow that melts into the stock, giving it a gelatinous, silky quality.

The **triangle** is attached to the hip. Once the exterior sinew is removed, you can slice it into five portions of veal cutlets.

Knuckle bones are used almost exclusively to make stock.

The **top round**, the most expensive of the leg cut, is the largest muscle in the leg that's uninterrupted by sinew. It's also the most tender cut from the leg, so it doesn't need to be pounded to tenderize it; you may still want to pound it to thin it out a bit.

Knuckle

Hip

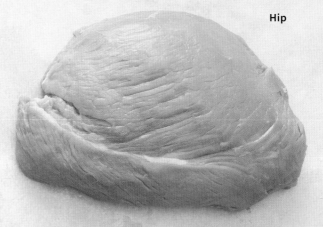

Butt Tender

Flank Steak

Heel

Eye Round

The **knuckle** consists of three sections of tightly bound, fibrous meat that makes for great cutlets. It's a bit laborious for the butcher because he or she has to cut around a lot of sinew, but the end product for the cook is tender veal cutlets that are less expensive than, say, cutlets from the top round.

Butt tender is the head of the tenderloin, the most tender cut. The butt tender and the tenderloin are often cut into medallions. Because the tenderloin has

virtually no fat and an even milder flavor than other cuts of veal, the medallions are usually covered in a rich sauce.

The **heel**, the outer part of the hind shank calf muscle, is a tough but flavorful cut that needs to be braised to tenderize it; it's usually used for stew meat.

The **hip** makes an economical alternative to top round. It has a section of sinew running through it that needs to be removed, but the muscle fibers are loosely bound, which makes for tender meat.

Flank steak is very lean; it can be sliced into two cutlets. It has long striated muscles, so it needs to be tenderized by pounding or marinating it.

The **eye round**, a long cylindrical cut from the leg, and one of the least expensive on the animal, is a good choice to slice and pound into evenly shaped cutlets (see "Pounding a Veal Chop or Cutlet," page 16) or medallions. It is a little tougher and requires more pounding than other leg cuts.

Boneless Shoulder Roast

Boned, Rolled, and Tied Veal Breast

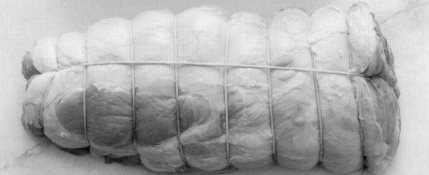

Bone-in Veal Breast

BREAST AND SHOULDER

A **boneless shoulder roast**, a tough cut, can be either roasted or braised whole, or cubed to make stew. A whole shoulder roast weighs about 12 pounds; relative to other cuts of veal, it's very inexpensive.

For a **boned, rolled, and tied veal breast**, ask your butcher to remove the rib bones and cartilage and have him save them for you to make Brown Veal Stock (page 31).

The **bone-in veal breast**—a long, narrow cut from the animal's chest—is one of the biggest, cheapest, and most delicious cuts of veal available. It has nine rib bones and weighs about 15 pounds.

SHORT RIBS, SHANKS, AND FEET

Veal **short ribs** are a very flavorful cut; they need to be braised to tenderize the meat. They have a milder flavor than their beef counterparts. You don't see them very often, but they can be used in any recipe that calls for beef short ribs, or to make osso buco.

Because of their cylindrical shape, hind shanks are preferred ten to one to **foreshanks**, which are therefore much less expensive. But what the butcher knows is that although they don't look as nice, the meat on foreshanks and their cooking properties are exactly the same as those of hind shanks. The meat on both is extremely flavorful and tender when braised.

Less expensive than veal bones, calves' **feet** or ("trotters") make a thicker, more gelatinous stock (see Brown Veal Stock, page 31). Before using the feet, your butcher needs to split them to access the marrow. There is no way to do this at home without a band saw; it would be like trying to open a coconut with your fingers.

Veal **osso buco** is a crosscut round ideally from the hind shank. It is one of the most popular cuts of veal there is because of its role in the classic Italian dish by the same name (see Pat's Whole Shank Osso Buco, page 26). The name *osso buco* literally translates as "bone with a hole," referring to the hole, which is full of marrow, that runs through the bone.

Stew meat can be cut from any of the shoulder cuts, but my favorite is cut from the foreshanks.

The **hind shank**, which comes from the lower part of the animal's rear leg, is one of the most popular and expensive cuts of veal because of its use in osso buco. When the shanks are braised, which they must be in order to break down the tough meat, the collagen in the muscle and the marrow makes a thick, gelatinous sauce.

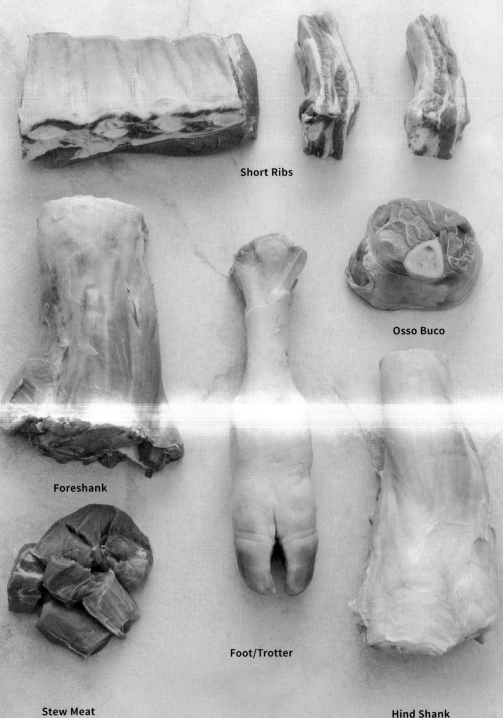

Short Ribs

Osso Buco

Foreshank

Foot/Trotter

Stew Meat

Hind Shank

HEAD, HEART, AND OFFAL

Although roasting a whole **calf's head** is something you see often in countries such as Mexico or Italy, it is virtually unheard of here. That said, with the current nose-to-tail dining trend, expect to see more of it (see Roasted Calf's Head alla Perla, page 34). Besides the tongue and brain, which are removed and cooked separately, the only edible part of the head are the cheeks. The head contains an abundance of gelatin, so it is often used to make veal head terrine, aka "headcheese."

Veal **heart** has a mild, delicate flavor, and it can be very tender if it is seared to medium-rare or braised—nothing in between. Before you get started cooking you have to trim off the excess fat, tissues, and valves, which is no small task.

Veal **brains** have a mild, sweet flavor and a creamy texture. In the United States, most veal heads are exported whole to Mexico, where the brains, called *sesos,* are fried and eaten in tacos. At the Greenwich Village restaurant Perla, the brain is roasted in the skull, and then whipped with mascarpone; it's hands down the most delicious way I have ever eaten brains (see Mike Toscano's Whipped Brain Puree, page 36).

Veal **sweetbreads** come from either the pancreas or thymus gland of the animal. When you see sweetbreads as a main course, such as for my mom's Veal Sweetbreads with Lemon-Caper Sauce (page 32), they are from the main lobe of the thymus gland. Smaller, marble-size pieces of the thymus, as well as the pancreas, are used when the sweetbreads are secondary to a recipe, such as when they are tossed in pasta. Cooked properly, sweetbreads have a soft, custardy texture and a mild, delicious flavor. When they're overcooked, they have the flavor and texture of chalk.

Because the **cheek** does so much work, the muscle is dense and tough, which means it needs to be braised to break down the meat. Cheeks of any species were relatively unused here until about fifteen years ago, when chefs began using the braised meat to fill ravioli. As I started needing more and more cheeks, the processor I order them from complained that their customers in Mexico, where they serve the heads whole, were getting upset that they were receiving heads with no cheeks.

Tongue is a dense, fibrous muscle that can be very tender when cooked properly, which generally means poaching it before you do anything else (see Grilled Calf's Tongue, page 36).

Veal **kidneys** have a rich, mushroomy flavor and are used in British steak and kidney pie, which also utilizes the kidney fat (or suet) that surrounds the kidneys to make the crust. In recent years, as American chefs have started cooking more offal, kidneys are more in demand. Before you start cooking, remove the visible fat and clean out the tough core inside each kidney; they should be cooked quickly over high heat.

Calf's **liver** is milder and more tender than the liver of any other animal. When shopping for liver, you want it to be firm, not mushy, and you don't want liver with any dark spots. Liver is best quickly seared to medium-rare in a very hot pan as it is in Lidia Bastianich's Seared Calf's Liver with Caramelized Onions and Balsamic (page 30).

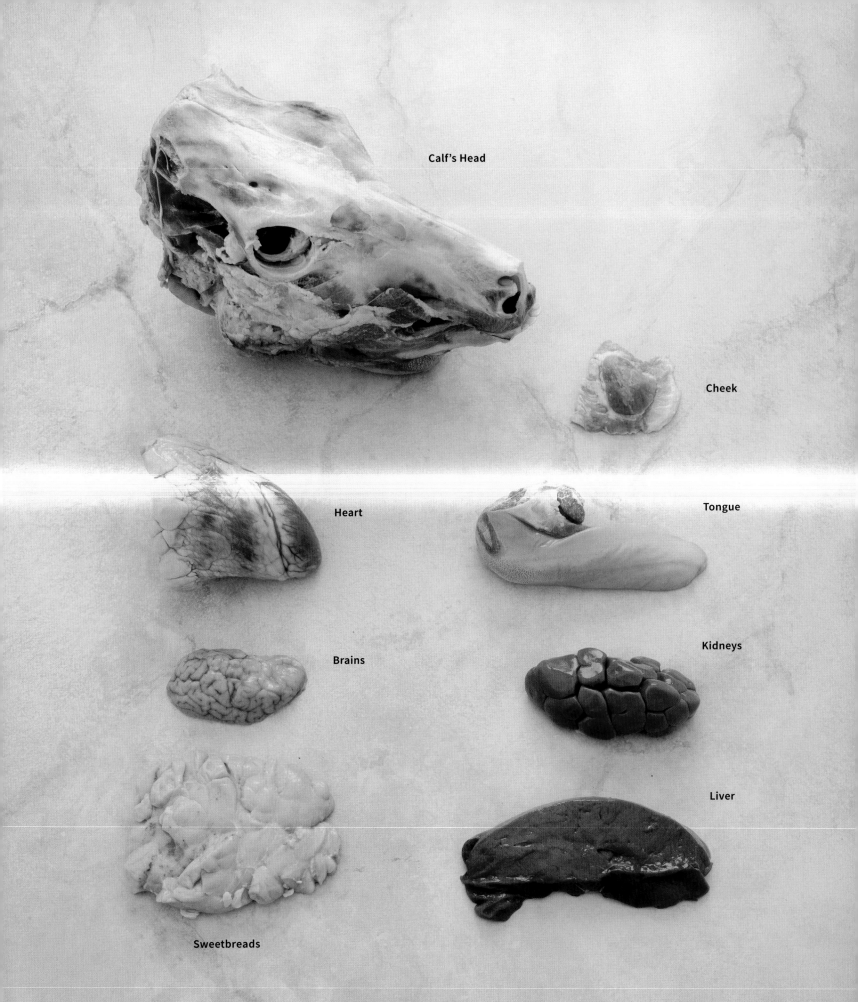

Calf's Head

Cheek

Heart

Tongue

Brains

Kidneys

Sweetbreads

Liver

BUTCHERING TECHNIQUES
POUNDING A VEAL CHOP OR CUTLET

Pounding out a veal chop the way it's done for veal Milanese is a true art form. When pounded out correctly, the diameter of the chop is roughly the size and shape of a dinner plate and with Italian American chefs it's like a competition to see who can get their chop the thinnest and the biggest. In many restaurants, to make life easier, they cut off the bone before they pound out the meat and then just thread it back in before frying it. With the correct side facing down, the customer would never know the bone had ever been removed. I've seen Milanese served without the bone, but for many chefs serving the chop with the bone attached is a point of pride. Use the same pounding technique below to pound veal, beef, or pork cutlets to the desired thickness, just skip any references to the bone. Note that chicken cutlets will fall apart more easily so they must be treated gently.

To pound out a veal chop, you need a cutting board, boning knife, meat mallet, and parchment paper.

1. Set the chop (or cutlet) upright on its bone (or boned side for the cutlet) on a cutting board. Using a boning knife, slice through the center of the chop.

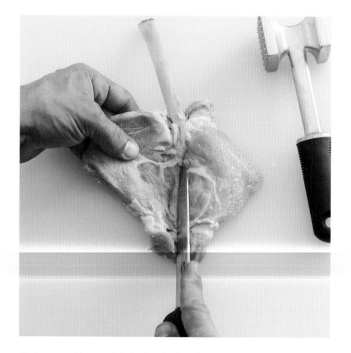

3. Open up the meat to butterfly the chop.

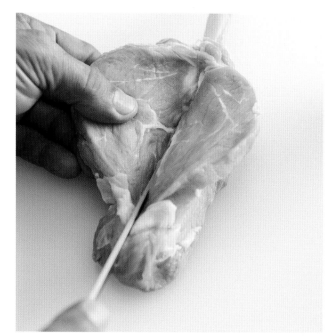

2. Do not cut all the way through the meat.

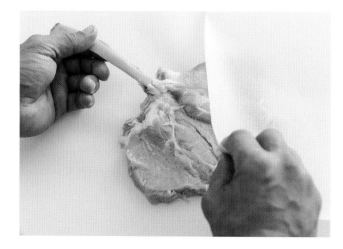

4. Lay the chop between two sheets of parchment paper.

5. Using the smooth side of a meat mallet, gently pound the chop starting from the center and working out toward the edges. If the meat needs a little help flattening, start with the texturized side of the mallet for the first few poundings, then switch to the smooth side so you don't tear the meat.

7. Pounded rib chop ready to be breaded.

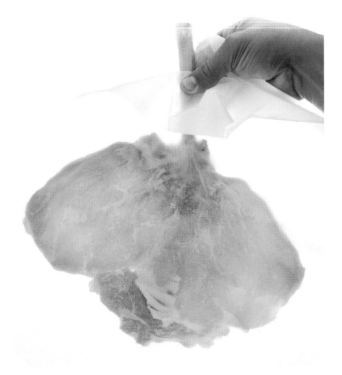

6. Flip the chop and parchment to pound the meat from both sides until it is ¼ inch thick; it will be translucent when you hold it up to the light.

NOTE: As you are pounding the meat, it's going to look like you're destroying it. Small pieces of meat may even tear off. If this happens, lay the stray piece of meat on top of the main piece of meat. Hit the unattached piece with the mallet to adhere to the chop. In Italian American restaurants, this is how it's done; they just keep taking those torn-off shreds and mending them back onto the chop. In the end, the chop isn't actually one piece of meat, but a bunch of small pieces that have been grafted together. If the meat falls off the bone entirely, set the bone aside until you've finished pounding the veal. Then, starting with the narrow side of the bone, thread it into the meat on the side where it originally lived.

CUTTING A POCKET

The reason to create a pocket in a veal or pork chop is to be able to stuff it. You want the opening to be as small as possible, so the stuffing doesn't fall out when the chop is cooked.

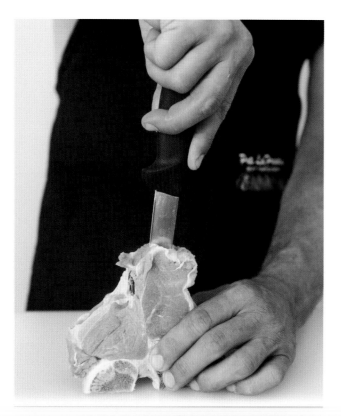

1. To cut a pocket in a veal or pork chop, set the chop up on the bone parallel to you. With your knife parallel to the chop, make an incision on the loin (not the tenderloin) side of the bone; insert the knife into the chop as far down as it will go.

2. With the knife still inserted, turn the chop so it's lying flat on the cutting board and the sharp side of the knife blade is facing away from you. Move the knife back and forth in a windshield wiper motion to cut a pocket in the meat.

3. Use your index finger to check that the pocket is as open as possible. You want the pocket as big as you can make it without puncturing the meat.

4. Stuff the pocket through the small hole left by the knife blade.

NEEDLING

Needling is a butcher's technique used to close a pocket after it has been stuffed.

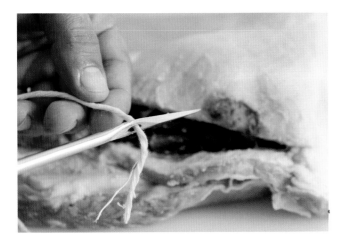

1. To close a pocket in a chop or roast, thread a butcher's needle with butcher's rope leaving a 6-inch tail of rope.

2. Start at one side of the opening that is to be sewn shut, pierce through both layers of meat that are going to be connected.

3. With the needle going through both sides of the meat, pull the rope out of the needle and remove the needle from the meat.

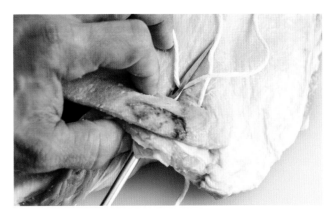

4. Pierce the needle through the meat on the same side where you made the first piercing. Rethread the needle and begin to pull back through the meat.

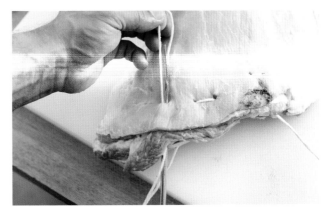

5. Thread the needle again, and pull the rope through the meat to the other side.

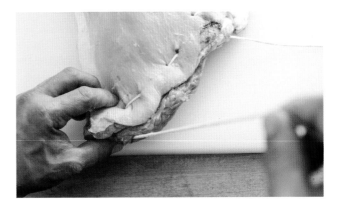

6. Continue this process along the length of the incision to close the pocket. Cut the butcher's rope, leaving a 6-inch tail. Tie knots on both sides to secure the pocket shut.

GRANDMA LaFRIEDA'S BRAISED STUFFED VEAL BREAST

1 veal breast (about 4 pounds),
    with pocket

Utica Greens (page 22), at room
    temperature

Kosher salt and freshly ground
    black pepper

2 cups white wine

1 cup low-sodium chicken stock,
    or as needed

1 large shallot, finely chopped
    (about ⅓ cup)

1 bay leaf

¾ teaspoon finely chopped fresh
    tarragon leaves

BUTCHER'S NOTE:

Ask your butcher to remove the plate,
which is the cartilage and bone that
fuses into bone at the center of the
sternum, from the breast. This will
leave you with an evenly shaped roast
that will allow you to cut the cooked
roast into neat, even portions, each
containing one rib bone. You can also
ask the butcher to cut a pocket in the
breast unless you want to do it yourself
(see "Cutting a Pocket," page 18). You
will need a butcher's needle and rope
to make this.

Grandma LaFrieda was the matriarch and central chef of the greater LaFrieda clan until she passed away in 2000. Her husband, my grandfather Patrick, was one of seven: five boys (all butchers) and two girls. My grandfather was the most settled and structured of the boys, which meant that unlike his brothers, who were often out partying and womanizing late into the night, he was always home with his family. Because of this, and because he was the kind of guy who always greeted you with a warm smile and a kind word, his brothers and their friends would often stop by at late hours. And when they did, without hesitation, my grandmother would rise to the occasion and put out a spread of food for them. This braised stuffed veal breast was one of her specialties; it takes a long time to cook, but it's something she could easily warm up for my great-uncles. You can make this in advance and heat it up when you're ready to serve it.

SERVES 9

1. Preheat the oven to 250°F.

2. Stuff the breast pocket with the Utica Greens, using your fingers. Use a butcher's needle and rope to close the pocket (see "Needling," page 19), or use about eight toothpicks, inserted vertically, to keep the pocket closed. Season the breast all over with salt and pepper.

3. Put the veal breast in a Dutch oven (or another high-sided ovenproof pan). Add the wine, stock, shallot, and bay leaf. Put the lid on the Dutch oven (if you're using a pan without a lid, cover it with foil). Put the veal breast in the oven to cook until it is fork-tender, about 3 hours. Remove the veal breast from the oven and uncover. (You can cook the veal breast to this point up to a day in advance. Cool it in the braising liquid, then refrigerate the meat in the liquid until you're ready to proceed with the recipe.)

4. Turn the oven temperature to broil.

5. Remove the veal breast from the braising liquid and transfer it to a baking sheet. Put the veal under the broiler until the top is browned, about 5 minutes. Remove the veal from the broiler and transfer it to a cutting board to rest for 15 minutes before slicing it. Cut the breast between the rib bones into nine portions, so that each portion includes a rib bone. Lay the slices on a platter or individual plates. Stir the tarragon into the braising liquid. Ladle the braising liquid over the meat and serve.

UTICA GREENS

Kosher salt

2 heads escarole (about 1½ pounds total)

3 tablespoons extra-virgin olive oil

6 to 8 fresh or pickled hot cherry peppers (depending on how much heat you like), halved, seeded, and finely diced

1 cubanelle pepper, finely chopped

2 ounces prosciutto, finely chopped

1 large shallot, finely chopped

3 cloves garlic, minced

1 cup low-sodium chicken stock, or as needed

1 cup Italian-Style Breadcrumbs (page 94; or store-bought; use only ¼ cup if you are serving the greens as a side dish)

½ cup grated Parmigiano-Reggiano cheese (about 2 ounces)

Grandma LaFrieda grew up on a farm in Utica, about four hours northwest of New York City. Utica is home to a large Italian American population. Many popular Italian American dishes were born there. The most well known is Utica Greens, which consists of sautéed escarole with hot peppers, prosciutto, and breadcrumbs. Every Italian restaurant in Utica offers its own version. My grandmother used the greens to stuff her signature veal breast, but she also served them as a side dish. Traditionally, the cherry peppers used to make this are pickled, but I prefer to use fresh. You can use either.

MAKES ABOUT 2 CUPS/ENOUGH TO STUFF A VEAL BREAST

1. Bring a pot of salted water to a boil over high heat. Fill a large bowl with ice and water. Remove and discard the cores from the escarole. Coarsely chop the leaves and blanch them in the boiling water for 2 minutes. Drain and plunge the escarole into the ice bath to cool completely. Drain well.

2. In a large skillet, heat the oil over high heat until it slides easily in the pan, about 2 minutes. Add the cherry peppers, cubanelle pepper, prosciutto, shallot, and garlic and cook, stirring occasionally, until the peppers are soft and golden brown, about 5 minutes. Add the escarole and stock and bring to a simmer. Reduce the heat to low and cook until the liquid has thickened, about 10 minutes. Remove the pan from the heat and stir in the breadcrumbs and Parmesan. Set the greens aside to cool to room temperature before using them to stuff the veal breast. (If you are serving this as a side dish, serve it hot.)

VEAL RIB CHOPS VALDOSTANA WITH FOIE GRAS MOUSSE

CHOPS

4 veal rib chops (about 12 ounces each), frenched (see page 186)

1 teaspoon kosher salt

¾ teaspoon freshly ground black pepper

¼ cup plus 2 tablespoons Foie Gras Mousse (page 125)

2 ounces prosciutto, chopped

½ cup shredded Fontina cheese (about 2 ounces)

2 large eggs

½ cup all-purpose flour

¼ cup canola or another neutral-flavored oil plus more as needed

SAUCE

1 tablespoon canola or another neutral-flavored oil

8 ounces mixed mushrooms (such as cremini, shiitake, and white), wiped clean, stems discarded, and thinly sliced

½ teaspoon kosher salt

¼ teaspoon freshly ground black pepper

½ cup minced shallot (about 1 large)

1 tablespoon unsalted butter

¼ cup cognac

1 cup Demi-Glace (page 31; or store-bought)

¼ cup heavy cream

This recipe is an adaptation of the one Il Mulino was known for in the nineties, when we started working with them. It's from Val d'Aosta, the northernmost region of Italy, located in the mountains near Switzerland, which might explain why it seems like a French dish. I omitted a few ingredients to make it more realistic to make at home, but with all those expensive, rich ingredients, it's still a special-occasion dish. Black truffles are a seasonal item; if you can't find them, don't bother using those in a jar; just omit them.

SERVES 4

1. For the chops: Preheat the oven to 350°F.

2. Cut a pocket into each chop. (See "Cutting a Pocket," page 18). Season the chops on both sides with the salt and pepper.

3. Put the mousse in a medium bowl and stir in the prosciutto and Fontina. Put the mousse mixture in a pastry bag, or a plastic bag with a ½-inch hole snipped diagonally from one corner. Dividing it evenly, pipe the mousse mixture into the pocket of each chop until the chop becomes firm, like a water balloon, indicating that it is full of stuffing. Close the pockets using two toothpicks inserted vertically in each chop, or needle it shut with butcher's rope (see "Needling," page 19).

4. Put the eggs in a bowl big enough to dip a chop into and whisk lightly to break up the yolks. Pour the flour onto a plate. Working one at a time, dip each chop into the egg to coat it all over, then dust it in the flour.

5. In a large skillet, heat the oil over medium-high heat until it slides easily in the pan, about 2 minutes. (Depending on the size of your pan, you may need to cook the chops in two batches or two separate skillets, using more oil as necessary.) Add the chops and sear until they are deep brown, 4 to 5 minutes per side. Remove the chops from the pan, transfer them to a baking sheet, and bake for 15 to 20 minutes, until a meat thermometer inserted into the meat (not the mousse) registers 145°F.

6. Meanwhile, for the sauce, wipe out the pan you cooked the chops in, add the oil, and heat it over medium heat, about 2 minutes. Add the mushrooms, sprinkle with the salt and pepper, and cook, stirring occasionally, until wilted, about 5 minutes. Add the shallot and butter, reduce the heat slightly, and cook until the shallot is tender, about 2 minutes. Add the cognac and cook for 1 minute to burn off the alcohol. Increase the heat to medium and stir in the demi-glace and then the cream. Cook the sauce until it is thick enough to coat the back of a spoon, 5 to 7 minutes.

7. To serve, place one chop on each plate and spoon the sauce over the chops, dividing it evenly.

VEAL MILANESE

DRESSING

1 medium shallot, minced

2 tablespoons fresh lemon juice

2 teaspoons balsamic vinegar

½ teaspoon kosher salt

¼ cup extra-virgin olive oil

¼ teaspoon freshly ground black pepper

VEAL

10 ounces breadsticks

⅔ cup finely chopped fresh flat-leaf parsley leaves

1 large clove garlic, minced

5 large eggs

¼ cup whole milk

1½ cups all-purpose flour

4 veal end chops (about ¾ pound each), pounded ¼ inch thick (see "Pounding a Veal Chop or Cutlet," page 16)

Kosher salt and freshly ground black pepper

Extra-virgin olive oil for shallow-frying

SALAD

5 ounces baby arugula or baby mixed greens (about 4 big handfuls)

1 pint grape tomatoes, halved

Kosher salt

3 lemons, halved, for serving

Milanese is a classic dish for which veal chops are pounded thin, breaded, and fried. My favorite place to eat Milanese is a small restaurant, Scalinatella, on the Upper East Side in Manhattan. What makes theirs special is the crust, which is really flavorful and extra crunchy. Their secret is to use crushed breadsticks instead of traditional breadcrumbs for the breading, a trick that I have adopted.

SERVES 4

1. For the dressing: In a bowl, combine the shallot, lemon juice, vinegar, and salt and set aside for at least 10 minutes. Stir in the oil and pepper and refrigerate the vinaigrette until you're ready to use it, or for up to 2 days.

2. For the veal: Preheat the oven to 250°F. Line a baking sheet with paper towels.

3. Break the breadsticks into a bowl wide enough to dredge a chop and use a wooden spoon or a fork to crush them to the size of peas. (The reason I don't use a food processor is that I don't want the crumbs too fine.) Add the parsley and garlic and stir to combine. In a second wide, shallow bowl, whisk the eggs and milk. Pour the flour into a third wide, shallow bowl.

4. Working in an assembly line fashion, season the chops on both sides with salt and pepper and dredge the chops in the flour. Next, dip the chop into the egg mixture, turning to coat them evenly on both sides. Lay the chop in the breadcrumbs and gently press down to adhere the crumbs to the meat. Turn and do the same thing on the other side. Set the chop on a plate and continue breading all the chops in the same way.

5. Pour enough oil into a large skillet to come up ¼ inch and heat it over high heat for about 2 minutes, until a pinch of salt sizzles when dropped into the oil. Carefully slide one chop into the oil and cook until it's golden brown, 2 to 3 minutes per side. Transfer the chop to the baking sheet and place it in the oven while you cook the rest of the chops. (Putting them in the oven keeps them warm, but it also cooks the meat closest to the bone, which doesn't cook through in the skillet.) Cook the remaining chops in the same way. Add more oil to the pan as necessary and make sure it's hot before adding another chop. When you've cooked the last chop, put it in the oven with the others for 4 minutes to cook the meat closest to the bone.

6. For the salad: Put the arugula and tomatoes in a large bowl. Sprinkle the greens and tomatoes with salt and drizzle with ¼ cup of the dressing. Toss gently and add more dressing if desired.

7. Remove the chops from the oven and transfer each one to a dinner plate. Squeeze a generous amount of lemon juice over each chop. Serve on top of the salad to maintain the crust.

PAT'S WHOLE SHANK OSSO BUCO

1 whole veal hind shank (about 3½ pounds), knuckle cut flat by the butcher; or 2 veal foreshanks (about 5 pounds)

2 teaspoons kosher salt plus more for seasoning

½ teaspoon freshly ground black pepper

All-purpose flour for dusting

¼ cup extra-virgin olive oil

1 large yellow onion, cut into ½-inch cubes

1 large carrot, cut into ½-inch cubes

1 stalk celery, cut into ½-inch cubes

4 cloves garlic, smashed

5 sprigs fresh thyme

2 strips orange zest (removed with a vegetable peeler)

1 sprig fresh rosemary

1 bay leaf

½ cup white wine

¼ cup tomato paste

6 to 8 cups Brown Veal Stock (page 31) or chicken stock, or as needed

2 tablespoons finely chopped fresh flat-leaf parsley leaves

1 lemon or ½ orange for zesting

BUTCHER'S NOTE:

Make sure to specify a hind shank, which is considerably larger than a foreshank. If your butcher doesn't carry hind shanks, use two foreshanks. In either case, ask your butcher to cut off the top of the knuckle.

Osso buco is a classic Italian dish of veal shanks braised in white wine. We didn't eat it often when I was growing up because the hind shanks were in such demand by our customers there would never have been any left for us. These days, I make osso buco often, but rather than cutting the shank into disks as is traditional, I leave the bone whole and serve it standing vertically in its sauce because I like the presentation. I carve the meat off the bone at the table. If you want to make this using osso buco cut in the traditional way, keep in mind the cooking time will be shorter, so judge the doneness by when the meat is fork-tender, not by the cooking times given.

SERVES 4

1. Preheat the oven to 325°F.

2. Season the shank meat with the salt and pepper and dust it lightly with flour.

3. In a Dutch oven or other ovenproof pan just large enough to hold the shank (or shanks) resting on its side, heat the oil over medium-high heat until it slides easily in the pan, about 2 minutes. Add the shank(s) and sear until browned all over, about 15 minutes. Transfer the shank(s) to a plate. Add the onion, carrot, celery, and garlic to the pan you cooked the veal in. Season the vegetables with salt, stir to coat them with the oil, and cook until they begin to soften, about 10 minutes. Stir in the thyme, orange zest strips, rosemary, and bay leaf. Add the wine and cook until it reduces by half, 3 to 4 minutes. Add the tomato paste and cook for 4 or 5 minutes to caramelize it. Lay the shank in the pot (with the bone pointing to the side) and pour the stock around the meat, adding as much as needed so the liquid comes just to the top of the meat. Bring the liquid to a simmer over medium-high heat. Cover the pot with the lid (or cover it with foil if you're using a pan with no lid), put the pot in the oven, and roast until the meat is fork-tender and falling off the bone, about 3 hours. Let the shank cool in the braising liquid.

4. Remove the shank from the braising liquid and set it aside. Put the pot with the liquid on the stovetop and bring it to a boil over high heat. Reduce the heat to medium and simmer until the sauce is thick enough to coat the back of a spoon, about 15 minutes. Turn off the heat and stir in the parsley.

5. Put the veal shank on a platter with the bone standing straight up. Pour the sauce around it and zest the lemon (or orange) over and around the meat. To serve the shank, cut the meat down the length of the bone; it will begin to fall off in chunks.

Mom's Stuffed Veal Porterhouse with Marsala and Fennel

CHOPS

4 veal porterhouse chops (about 1 pound each)

Kosher salt and freshly ground black pepper

2 bulbs fennel (not cored), fronds reserved for garnish

6 tablespoons unsalted butter plus more as needed

1 stalk celery, diced

½ small yellow onion, minced

1 small clove garlic, minced

2 slices white sandwich bread (preferably stale), crusts removed, cut into ¼-inch cubes

2 tablespoons grated Parmigiano-Reggiano cheese (about 1 ounce)

1 heaping teaspoon finely chopped fresh flat-leaf parsley leaves

½ teaspoon crushed red pepper flakes

All-purpose flour for dusting

SAUCE

2 cups Marsala

3 cups Brown Veal Stock (page 31; or low-sodium store-bought)

¼ cup vegetable oil or other neutral-flavored oil

Veal chops, an expensive, much sought-after item, were not something we ate often at home when I was a kid. At that time, we sold veal chops as part of the entire loin. To get veal chops for my mother, my father would have had to sacrifice a twenty-eight-pound cut of the most expensive species there is. That was not going to happen. It would have been easier for him to buy veal chops from a grocery store or one of the nearby retail butchers than to get it from our own inventory. On the rare occasion that a mistake was made for an order, my dad would get stuck with an extra rack and my mother's prayers would be answered. She always prepared them in the same way: stuffed and covered in a thick, sweet Marsala reduction. Even with something as luxurious as a veal chop, each of us kids always got our own. I'm not saying we all finished them, but nothing went in the trash either. My mom always found a way to use leftovers. One of the things I like about this dish is that it offers another way to use Marsala wine. Marsala is a sweet fortified wine from Sicily; it's typically used only to make sauce for veal cutlets, which is a shame because it's inexpensive and delicious.

SERVES 4

1. For the chops: Cut a pocket in the larger (loin) portion of the chop (see "Cutting a Pocket," page 18). Season both sides of the chops with salt and pepper and refrigerate while you make the stuffing.

2. Cut one of the fennel bulbs into a ¼-inch dice. Stand the remaining bulb on its root end and cut it lengthwise into ½-inch-thick fanlike slices; do not remove the core, this way the slices stay intact.

3. In a large skillet, heat the butter over medium heat. Add the diced fennel, celery, and onion. Season with 2 teaspoons of salt and cook until the vegetables are very soft and translucent, about 15 minutes. Add the garlic and cook for 1 minute until it's fragrant. Transfer the vegetables to a medium bowl and toss them with the bread, Parmesan, parsley, and red pepper flakes. Work the ingredients together with your fingers and add more salt to taste.

4. Using your fingers, stuff 3 to 4 tablespoons of the stuffing into the pocket of each chop; you want it gently packed but not overstuffed, or the meat won't cook properly. Use a butcher's needle and rope to close the pocket (see "Needling," page 19); or use a few toothpicks inserted vertically into each chop to hold the chops closed.

5. For the sauce: In a large skillet, combine the Marsala and sliced fennel. Bring the wine to a boil over high heat, and boil until it reduces by half, about 5 minutes. Add the stock and return the liquid to a boil. Reduce the heat and simmer until the liquid reduces by half again, about 5 minutes to thicken it slightly.

6. In another large skillet, heat the oil over medium-high heat until it slides easily in the pan, about 2 minutes. Dust the chops lightly with flour on all sides. Add the veal chops to the pan and cook them until they are deep golden brown on all three sides, about 2 minutes on each side. (By the third side, I am referring to the top of the T-bone, standing the chops so the triangular portion faces up. Searing this side ensures that the meat near the bone will cook through.)

7. Pour the sauce and fennel over the chops, reduce the heat to medium, and cook the chops in the sauce until the sauce is almost syrupy and the chops are cooked through, or until a meat thermometer inserted into the meat (not the stuffing) registers 140°F, about 15 minutes, turning the chops once during cooking.

8. Remove the chops from the pan, remove and discard the rope or toothpicks, and place the chops on plates. Spoon the sauce over the chops, making sure each chop gets at least one slice of the fennel. Garnish with the reserved fennel fronds.

LIDIA BASTIANICH'S SEARED CALF'S LIVER WITH CARAMELIZED ONIONS AND BALSAMIC

POLENTA

3½ cups water (preferably Italian sparkling mineral water)

1 tablespoon kosher salt

½ cup polenta

2 tablespoons extra-virgin olive oil

LIVER

2 pounds calf's liver

1 tablespoon sugar

1 pound yellow onions (about 3), thinly sliced

4 bay leaves

3 tablespoons extra-virgin olive oil

½ teaspoon kosher salt plus more for seasoning

¼ teaspoon freshly ground black pepper

½ cup balsamic vinegar

1 tablespoon white wine

1 teaspoon all-purpose flour

¼ cup plus 1 tablespoon vegetable oil

In our family, my father strictly enforced a harmonious start to every meal. Nobody could lift a fork until everyone was served and our mother was seated. Liver night was the only exception. My mom served calf's liver once a month because she believed it would keep us healthy; calf's liver is loaded with B vitamins, zinc, protein, and all kinds of other things she thought we needed. My siblings, particularly my sister, weren't very happy about eating liver, but I loved it.

The way my mother made liver, only one serving would fit in the pan at a time. She would serve it to us straight from the skillet to the plate. When Mom put a plate of liver in front of us, we didn't have to wait for anyone. This recipe for liver and onions served over polenta, which our friend Lidia shared with us, allows you to more easily feed a family without making this break in table manners.

SERVES 6

1. For the polenta: In a large skillet, stir the water and salt and bring it to a boil over high heat. Gradually whisk in the polenta and then the olive oil and bring the liquid back to a boil. Reduce the heat to low and cook the polenta at a low simmer, stirring occasionally, until it's creamy, about 45 minutes. To make the polenta in advance, transfer it to an airtight container and refrigerate for up to 3 days. Just before serving, warm the polenta over medium heat, stirring often and adding enough water to loosen the polenta to a creamy consistency. Remove from the heat and cover to keep the polenta warm until you're ready to serve it.

2. For the liver: Peel the membrane off the liver and discard it. Trim the liver of blood vessels and any other blemishes. Pat the liver dry and cut it into 2-inch-wide slices, then cut the slices crosswise into ½-inch-wide julienne strips.

3. In a large skillet, cook the sugar over medium heat until it caramelizes, about 5 minutes. Add the onions and bay leaves and toss to coat well. Add the olive oil, salt, and pepper and cook over medium-high heat until the onions are golden brown and tender but not completely wilted. Add the vinegar and wine and simmer until the sauce is thick enough to coat the back of a spoon, about 2 minutes. Stir in the flour and continue to stir until it's blended in.

4. Meanwhile, season the liver all over with salt. In a large skillet, heat the vegetable oil over medium-high heat, until it slides easily in the pan, about 2 minutes. Add the liver and cook it for 1 or 2 minutes to sear it all over. With a slotted spoon, transfer the liver to the skillet with the sauce. Place the skillet over medium-high heat, and cook for about 1 minute to heat through, stirring gently to coat the liver with the sauce and onions.

5. Serve the liver immediately, spooned over steaming polenta.

BROWN VEAL STOCK

8 pounds veal (or beef) bones
(preferably shank, femur bones,
or trotters)

2 tablespoons extra-virgin olive oil

4 stalks celery (no leaves), cut into
3 or 4 pieces each

1 leek, halved lengthwise and
cleaned thoroughly

¼ cup plus 1 tablespoon tomato
paste

¾ pound yellow onions, peeled
and quartered

¾ pound carrots, cut into 3 or 4
pieces each

1 medium tomato, halved

8 large cloves garlic, halved

12 sprigs fresh flat-leaf parsley

2 sprigs fresh thyme

8 black peppercorns

1 bay leaf

BUTCHER'S NOTE:

When buying veal bones, specify
shanks, femur bones, or split calves'
feet; these contain the most marrow,
which melts into the stock; marrow
contains collagen, which becomes
gelatin when it's cooked, adding body
to the stock and any sauce the stock is
used to make.

I n classical French cooking, a rich veal stock is used as a base for many soups, stews, and sauces. To make brown veal stock, the bones are roasted before being simmered in water. You can also use this recipe to make beef stock by using beef bones in place of veal bones. Beef stock has a deep, hearty flavor, whereas veal stock is more delicate.

MAKES ABOUT 3 QUARTS

1. Preheat the oven to 450°F.

2. Arrange the bones in a single layer on a large baking sheet and roast them until they are golden brown all over, 1 to 1¼ hours, turning the bones once or twice during cooking time so they brown evenly.

3. In a large stockpot, heat the oil over medium heat until it slides easily in the pan, about 2 minutes. Add the celery and leek and cook until they are wilted and light golden brown, 8 to 10 minutes. Add the tomato paste and cook until the paste darkens in color slightly, about 2 minutes. Remove from the heat.

4. Remove the bones from the oven and transfer them to the stockpot.

5. Put the onions and carrots on the same baking sheet you roasted the bones on and toss to coat them with the fat on the baking sheet. Roast until golden brown, 35 to 45 minutes, turning the vegetables once so they brown evenly.

6. Transfer the onions and carrots to the stockpot. Add enough water to cover the bones by 2 inches and bring to a boil over high heat, skimming any foam that comes to the top. Reduce the heat to low, add the tomatoes, garlic, parsley, thyme, peppercorns, and bay leaf, and simmer for 3 to 4 hours, until the stock is a milky brown color, continuing to skim any foam or excess oil. Add more water if necessary to keep the bones covered. Remove the stock from the heat and let it cool to room temperature.

7. Strain the stock and discard the solids. Transfer the stock to an airtight container and refrigerate for at least several hours and as long as 5 days. Before using, skim off the fat and impurities that have hardened on the top.

DEMI-GLACE

Demi-glace, a rich brown sauce made by reducing veal stock by half, is both a sauce and also a base for many other rich sauces, such as Port Wine Reduction (page 214). To make 2 cups of demi-glace, bring 1 quart of Brown Veal Stock to a boil over high heat. Reduce the heat to a simmer and cook the stock until it cooks down by half, about 25 minutes. Use the demi-glace right away or turn off the heat and let the demi-glace cool to room temperature. Transfer to an airtight container and refrigerate for up to a week or freeze for several months.

VEAL SWEETBREADS WITH LEMON-CAPER SAUCE

3 pounds veal sweetbreads

Kosher salt and freshly ground
    black pepper

4 tablespoons olive oil

2 medium shallots, finely chopped

1 clove garlic, minced

⅔ cup white wine

Grated zest of 2 lemons plus 1 cup
    fresh lemon juice (about
    6 lemons)

⅓ cup capers, rinsed

1 tablespoon chopped fresh flat-
    leaf parsley

All-purpose flour for dusting

¼ pound (1 stick) unsalted butter

BUTCHER'S NOTE:
When ordering sweetbreads, specify
those from the thymus gland.

My mother fed us a variety of meats because she believed each had different health properties, and she thought veal sweetbreads to be among the healthier. It seems like every restaurant that serves sweetbreads prepares them differently—and I order them just about any chance I have—but my favorite preparation is still my mother's. She dusts the sweetbreads lightly in flour, sautés them quickly, and then tosses them in a lemon, butter, and caper sauce. It's the simplest preparation I've ever seen for sweetbreads—and also the most delicious. The key is to not overcook them. You will need to use two skillets simultaneously to make this, preferably one that is nonstick for cooking the sweetbreads.

SERVES 8

1. Put the sweetbreads in a large saucepan. Add enough water to cover and salt (about 1 tablespoon per quart). Bring the sweetbreads to a boil over high heat and cook for 2 minutes. Meanwhile, fill a large bowl with ice and water. Drain the sweetbreads in a colander and plunge them into the ice water to cool completely. Remove the sweetbreads from the ice bath and pat them dry. Peel off and discard the visible membranes.

2. In a medium skillet, heat 2 tablespoons of the oil over medium heat. Add the shallots and garlic, stirring often so the garlic doesn't brown, until the garlic is fragrant, about 2 minutes. Add the wine and lemon juice, increase the heat to medium-high, and boil until the sauce thickens slightly, 4 to 5 minutes. Turn off the heat and stir in the lemon zest, capers, and parsley. Season with salt and a few turns of pepper.

3. Season the sweetbreads with salt and pepper and dust them with flour.

4. In a large nonstick skillet, melt the butter with the remaining 2 tablespoons oil over medium heat until the butter stops foaming. Lay the sweetbreads in the pan in a single layer and cook, turning once, until the sweetbreads are browned all over, 3 to 4 minutes per side. Pour the lemon-caper sauce into the skillet with the sweetbreads and stir to coat with the sauce. Cook the sweetbreads and sauce over medium heat for about 5 minutes to marry the flavors.

MIKE TOSCANO'S WHIPPED BRAIN PUREE

1 calf's brain (about 6 ounces)

1 cup mascarpone

2 tablespoons champagne vinegar

1 teaspoon extra-virgin olive oil

1 teaspoon kosher salt

I'm not the biggest fan of brains, but the way Mike Toscano makes them—whipped with mascarpone—I could eat a bowlful. Mike serves it as part of a calf's head presentation, but you could also make this on its own and serve it with crostini.

MAKES 1¾ CUPS/SERVES 4

1. If you did not roast the calf's brain in the skull, preheat the oven to 300°F. Fill a bowl with ice and water.

2. In a saucepan of boiling salted water, blanch the brain for 3 minutes. Drain and plunge it into the ice bath. Drain the brain again and pat it dry with paper towels. Place the brain in a small baking dish, cover tightly with foil, and bake for 20 minutes, until the brain is firm to the touch and opaque throughout; the best way to test the brain is by cutting into it.

3. If you did roast the brain with the calf's head, look for the seam that runs down the middle of the skull at the back. Sometimes this seam will open on its own when the head is roasting. If not, use the heel of a knife to crack the skull open at that seam. Reach into the skull and remove the brain. Cut the brain into 1-inch pieces.

4. Put the brain, still warm, in a food processor. Add the mascarpone, vinegar, oil, and salt and process for about a minute, until the mixture is perfectly smooth. Transfer the brain to a bowl and serve warm.

GRILLED CALF'S TONGUE

1 calf's tongue

¼ cup kosher salt plus more for seasoning

¼ cup sugar

1 yellow onion, cut into 1-inch pieces

1 stalk celery, cut into 1-inch pieces

1 large carrot, cut into 1-inch pieces

1 teaspoon black peppercorns

1 tablespoon extra-virgin olive oil plus more for drizzling

Sea salt and freshly ground black pepper

Tongue has gotten a lot more popular in recent years since the nose-to-tail craze. This simple recipe, wherein the tongue is braised to tenderize it and then grilled, can also be applied to beef and lamb tongue, although the cooking times will vary.

SERVES 4

1. Put the tongue in a large saucepan and add enough water to cover by 1 inch. Add the ¼ cup salt, sugar, onion, celery, and carrot and bring to a boil over high heat. Reduce the heat to a simmer, cover, and cook until the tongue is very tender when pierced with a knife, about 1½ hours. Turn off the heat.

2. Remove the tongue from the braising liquid, reserving the liquid, and set the tongue aside until it is just cool enough to handle but still warm. Peel off and discard the outer layer of the tongue. Use a small knife to remove the fat on the underside. Return the tongue to the braising liquid to cool to room temperature. (The tongue can be prepared to this point up to a day in advance; put the tongue and the braising liquid in an airtight container and refrigerate until you're ready to grill it.)

3. Preheat a grill, grill pan, or skillet over high heat.

4. Remove the tongue from the braising liquid and discard the liquid and solids. Pat the tongue dry. Coat the tongue with the 1 tablespoon olive oil and season both sides with salt and pepper. Cook the tongue until charred on both sides, 3 to 5 minutes per side. Remove the tongue from the heat and slice it on an angle into ¼-inch-thick slices. To serve, drizzle the slices with olive oil and sprinkle with sea salt and a few turns of pepper.

Grilled calf's tongue (left), cheek meat (middle), and ribollita (right) over whipped brain puree.

LAMB

CORNERING THE LAMB MARKET

For a long time, beginning in the early 1990s, all of our delivery trucks bore the slogan: "Pat LaFrieda—The First Name in Veal and Lamb." When we began our transformation from small neighborhood butcher to supplying the vast majority of high-end restaurants in New York, the fact that we were known to have the best-quality product of those two meats was one of the ways that we set ourselves apart. We started sourcing our own lamb after we did so with veal, but what really put us in the game with lamb was a move that I pulled on the lamb market that I had learned from my days on Wall Street.

As background to the story, first I have to explain that there is an interesting situation in the lamb business in that the majority of processors and distributors are Jewish. This would not be relevant except that lamb is the traditional centerpiece of the Easter meal. And Easter frequently coincides with the Jewish holiday of Passover. Which means that on the Friday before Easter, when Americans are gearing up to eat five times as much lamb as they do at any other time of the year, lamb distributors throughout New York are completely unavailable.

By this time I had Joe Bastianich as a customer. Joe is now partners with Mario Batali, and together they have many restaurants in New York, as well as in Las Vegas, Los Angeles, and Singapore; but even back then Joe was up-and-coming as a prominent and highly respected restaurateur. He was the first customer I landed on my own, and I did it by chance. I didn't know who he was. I simply walked into his restaurant, Becco, one afternoon when I was trying to get new business. It's located on Restaurant Row, a stretch of West 46th Street between Eighth and Ninth Avenues lined with restaurants that cater to the theater crowd. I'd singled out Becco solely because I liked the restaurant's sign and their logo, a little line drawing of a bird. I just happened to come at the right time: Joe was sitting down having a pricing meeting with the chef. When I walked in and introduced myself, Joe told me that their biggest selling item was veal osso buco. He said they sold 250 orders a day. He told me what they were paying and asked if I could do better. I said I could and I gave him our price. He said, "Bullshit. Are you sure it's knuckle-off shanks?" I said yes, "I'm sure." He gave me a big order for the next day: twelve cases. When I left, Joe shook my hand. He said, "It's nice to meet you. I look forward to doing business with you." Joe is a very tall, intimidating guy. Then he said, "If I ever find out that you pay off any of my chefs, I'll make sure that I don't pay you whatever I owe you."

At that time, chefs often took bribes from their purveyors in exchange for buying from them, and the restaurant owner ended up paying for it in the form of higher food costs. Joe wanted to make sure that wasn't going to happen with me, and of course it didn't.

From that point on, the Becco account was my baby. I took care of Joe and he was happy with what we did. He started using us exclusively and he wanted his mother, Lidia Bastianich, to start using us as well. Lidia was partners with Joe in Becco, but she was really known and very respected for her own restaurant, Felidia, a fine dining Italian place in Midtown Manhattan. One day Joe called me and he said, "Hey, Pat. I've got a break for you. My mom wants to see a sample of a lamb rack. Can you bring one over this afternoon?" It had been a big deal to get Becco, and to get Felidia would be huge. I told him, "Of course!" I was all out of lamb racks at the shop, so I went about trying to get one.

It was late in the day for the meat industry—about one o'clock in the afternoon—and both my regular lamb suppliers were gone for the day. There was a third lamb distributor, so I went to him and asked if I could buy one lamb rack. His answer was, "No. You don't buy from me." Now, I understand that these guys are not in the business of selling one rack of lamb, but this guy knew me. He knew LaFrieda Meats. I sold to about one hundred restaurants by then, and I had the potential to be a repeat customer. I said, "Yeah, but I *can* buy from you in the future. We can start to build a relationship." If he was smart, he would have seen this as an opportunity. But instead he said, "Nah. Not interested."

I couldn't believe it. This was my big opportunity to impress Lidia, and I couldn't get my hands on a lamb rack. It's not something I could have gotten at retail. I needed to split it, chine it, french it, and present it to Lidia as something I had done. I gave it another try. I said to the guy, "What are you talking about? Charge me whatever you want."

"Nah," he said. "You don't do business with me the other fifty-one weeks of the year. You'll have to get it tomorrow from somewhere else."

Ultimately, I could not bring Lidia a lamb rack that day, and I was furious. I was able to find her one the next day and I ended up getting her account. But what happened with the lamb distributor really stuck with me. "We've gotta do something," I told my dad. "We can't let other people control our business. We can't be limited by this outdated way of thinking and doing business."

Not long after that, I was on the phone with a guy named Kevin at one of the two places where I usually bought lamb. It was about ten days before Easter, and I ordered some racks; this wasn't a holiday order yet, but Kevin told me they'd just made a huge deal with a national grocery store chain. "You should take a couple extra racks for the holiday because we're gonna run out. By the end of the week we're gonna have nothing but shoulders."

I got an idea. I said, "Kevin, let me do you one better. How much are lamb racks right now?" They were $6 a pound, so I said, "I'll give you $6.25. Give me every lamb rack you have from now until Easter." I did the same thing with my other supplier in the Bronx. I stacked LaFrieda with every lamb rack I could possibly get my hands on. We were still on Leroy Street then and the whole place was full of lamb, stacked so high you couldn't see anything else. I had so much lamb in that building, my dad went nuts. He walked in and said, "Jesus Christ! What is this?" My father is very, let's say . . . vocal. He was yelling throughout the warehouse, "What are we doing with all this lamb?" He does a similar thing every year before Thanksgiving when we have stacks and stacks of turkeys. "Where are all these going? We're gonna go out of business if we don't have all these sold!" About the lamb, I lied, "Dad, I have them all sold." I brushed him off and crossed my fingers that we *would* sell them all.

Easter was upon us and I had just about every lamb rack there was to be had in New York City. (When I say I had all the lamb, I am talking strictly about domestic lamb.) Word got out. Other butchers and meat distributors started calling me, but I wouldn't give it to them. I waited for the desperation to trickle down to the restaurant level, which it very quickly did. These restaurants were trying to order lamb racks from their regular meat purveyors, who had to tell their customers that they didn't have any. I had them all. The restaurants started calling other meat purveyors and eventually they found me.

At some point the same guy who wouldn't sell me a single lamb rack to show to Lidia Bastianich, called me. Evidently word had gotten around: LaFrieda bought thousands. He said, "Pat, I'm in a pinch here. It's Easter. And I'm in the lamb business. And I don't have a single rack of lamb to sell. I hear you've got a lot of lamb. Help me out. . . ." And I said, "I'm sorry. You don't do business with me the other fifty-one weeks of the year. You'll have to get it from somewhere else."

I got a lot of new business from that move. But the real reason I did it was out of frustration with this old-school, stubborn, shortsighted mentality that was very common in the meat business back then. If they knew supply was short on something, they'd raise the price. They knew you'd be desperate, and that they had what you wanted, and they'd kill you for it to the point where you didn't want to go back to them the next day, but you often had to.

We never did that at LaFrieda. That Easter when nobody could get lamb, I kept the price low. I knew that the restaurants that were calling me were desperate and I knew their regular purveyors didn't have what they wanted, and I knew that we were their only hope. But I charged the regular price and did whatever it took to get it to them. And people appreciated that. Sure, there's the basic idea of supply and demand. And sure, you can charge more money when the demand is high and you're the only guy that's got the product people are looking for. But we never thought you should care about that one sale, that one delivery. Our philosophy was to think about the next hundred deliveries. Because when a restaurant puts an item on a menu, that thing is going to be on the menu night after night, and it's going to stay there for months. If someone likes the product you give them and you give it to them at a fair price, that's going to become a daily delivery. We focused on those daily deliveries, and that stability has worked for us. Every day you come in and you've got a job and your men have jobs. You get another account, another person that trusts you, believes in you. Now you've got more work, more men. And like that, you keep growing. That's the way it happened for us.

I took a big risk, doing what I did. Lamb could have shown up from someplace else, another supplier in another city, such as Chicago, and we could have lost all that money. But it didn't, thank God. And the risk paid off. I sold every last one. The irony of that story is that I *truly* sold every last one. I got so into selling those lamb racks that I forgot to save some for myself. It was the only time in my memory that we did not have crown roast of lamb (see LaFrieda Family Stuffed Lamb Crown Roast, page 57) on our family table for Easter.

ALL ABOUT LAMB

Lamb is popular all over the world, but much more in other culinary cultures than in ours. It is central to the cuisines of Turkey, North Africa, and the Middle East. And it is the most prized choice of Mexican roasted meat, *barbacoa* (a preparation of meat stewed with chiles and other spices), though goat is more commonly used because it's a fraction of the cost. Lamb is also very common on dinner tables in England, in Australia and New Zealand (which together are the largest producers of lamb in the world), and now, with a growing Islamic population, in Canada. Lamb is much less popular in the United States, but those who like it, love it. And with good reason. Good lamb, cooked properly, is very tender, and probably the most flavorful meat there is.

I believe that one of the reasons lamb isn't as popular here as it is elsewhere (and as I wish it were) is that people are eating either poor-quality lamb, or that what they are eating isn't really lamb at all, but mutton. True lamb is classified as the meat of a domestic sheep that is under twelve months old. At a year they are classified as "yearlings," and most of these become breeding animals. Any older and the meat is classified as "mutton." This is the meat that has the intense, often unpleasant "gamey" flavor that can turn people off to lamb. (A lot of Europeans, especially Germans, don't like to eat lamb because in the years right after the war, mutton was all that was available in terms of lamb. That's what they ate, and they hated it.) The term "spring lamb" gets thrown around a lot but it's relatively meaningless these days. It used to refer to very young lambs that were born in the springtime. Today the more accurate term would be "baby lamb." This refers to lambs that are between ten and thirty days old; I don't care for this meat, as the flavor is too mild for me, but for someone who is wary of the flavor of lamb, this would be a good place to start. (You'll generally only find these sold whole, for those who want to cook the entire animal.)

The irony is that although Americans aren't the world's biggest lamb enthusiasts, we raise the best lamb in the world. About 50 percent of lamb in this country is imported from New Zealand and Australia, but domestic lamb, often labeled "Colorado lamb," because of where it is finished and processed, is by far the superior product. The main reason consumers and restaurants gravitate toward imported lamb is because it is much less expensive; the warehouse stores sell only imported lamb, which is why they can sell it at as low a price as they do. But imported lamb is not a comparable product to domestic. For one thing, imported lamb is almost always frozen, which compromises its quality (see "Fresh vs. Frozen," page xviii), where domestic lamb is available fresh. Domestic lamb also comes from significantly larger animals. The average dressed weight of New Zealand lamb is forty pounds; Australian lamb is fifty-five pounds; where the average weight of domestic lamb is seventy-five pounds. The larger animals yield more substantial loin chops, the most prized and expensive cut on the animal. New Zealand chops are so small that they refer to them as "lollipops." But most important, domestic lamb tastes better, and the reason for this has to do with what they're fed. In Australia and New Zealand, lambs are fed only grass; they are raised on state grasslands, so the feed is essentially free. Domestic lamb, by contrast, is raised on a diet of grains and legumes. At one time, Australian lamb farmers took some American lamb home to see if they could raise grass-fed lamb that tasted as good as ours. They couldn't.

The best lamb comes from animals between eight and ten months old that were raised on American farms—some in upstate New York but most in or around Colorado. This lamb is incomparably tender and sweet, and I have no hesitation telling you: It's the best lamb in the world.

BUYING LAMB

When shopping for lamb, ask your butcher for domestic lamb or look for a USDA label of either "choice" or "prime." Only domestic lamb is USDA graded. The grading of lamb takes into consideration a combination of age and marbling. The younger and the more marbled the meat, the higher the grade. The vast majority is rated "choice." Prime would be a rarity, but choice is a very close second. Either one will be great. Next look for lamb that is under a year old, as the older the meat, the tougher it will be and the gamier it will taste. One way to find out the age of the animal is to ask the butcher and hope that he tells you the truth. But also look at the color. The meat from young lamb will have a dark pink hue, where the meat from older animals will be a bit more purple.

If you're in the habit of shopping at an ordinary grocery store, you might think there are only four cuts of lamb: chops, steaks, kebab meat, and leg of lamb. But that is not the case. Many of the tastiest cuts, those most desired by chefs, are some of the lesser-known cuts, such as lamb neck and Denver ribs. Because lamb is on the pricey side (it's the second most expensive meat, after veal), use some of the less expensive, what we call "economy cuts," such as the shanks and leg steaks, as a way to enjoy great lamb flavor without spending the money you would on chops.

COOKING LAMB

Lamb is hands down my favorite meat to eat. Quality lamb has such a delicious distinct flavor of its own that, particularly when I'm working with a luxurious cut like loin chops, I keep it simple and season it with nothing but salt and pepper. Having said that, because lamb does have such a robust flavor, it also stands up to aggressive seasonings, such as those used in Mexican *barbacoa,* and in a traditional Greek "pie" made of ground lamb and a lot of intense seasonings, or in merguez, a Middle Eastern sausage loaded with cumin and red chile. In Italian cuisine, lamb is generally seasoned with garlic and rosemary, which I love. And we've all tasted (or at least heard of) lamb served in the English tradition—with bright-green mint jelly. I like lamb loin and rib chops roasted or grilled to medium-rare; those cuts are expensive, so cooking it any longer is a shame. As with any kind of meat, the tough, sinewy cuts of lamb, such as the shanks, neck, and cheek, need to be braised.

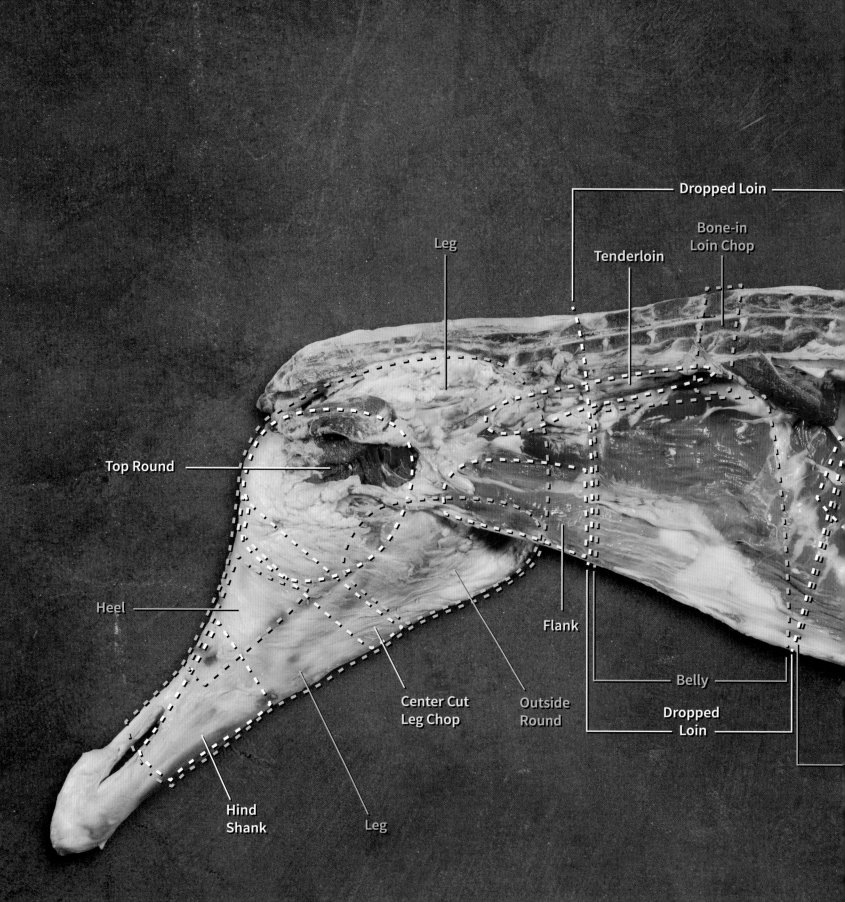

Dropped Loin

Leg

Tenderloin

Bone-in
Loin Chop

Top Round

Heel

Flank

Center Cut
Leg Chop

Outside
Round

Belly

Dropped
Loin

Hind
Shank

Leg

Head

Neck

Shoulder

Shoulder
Eye
Roast

8-Rib Rack

Cheeks

Tongue

Shoulder
Blade Chop

Shoulder
Arm Chop

Shoulder

Foreshank

Denver Ribs

Shoulder

Breast

Lamb is one of America's most prized meats because of its mild flavor, tender texture, and sweet profile, yet 51 percent of all lamb consumed domestically is foreign due to cheaper imported product.

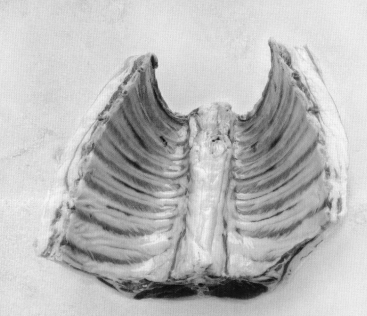

Double Rib Rack

Frenched 8-Rib Rack

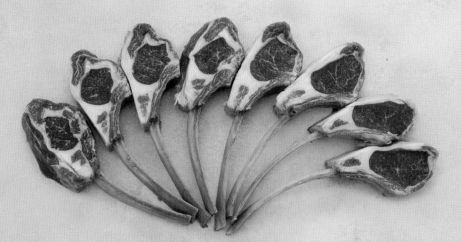

Rib Chops

LAMB CUTS

RACK

A **double rib rack** includes the ribs on both sides of the rib cage; it would never be sold at retail, but it's helpful to see it in order to understand where the ribs are on the animal.

A **frenched 8-rib rack** is the most prized retail cut from the animal. The rack has a pretty thick fat cap, which keeps the meat juicy even when it is cooked at high heat. You can also buy it not frenched.

Rib chops, which consist of the flavorful, tender loin muscle, are the most expensive cut on the animal. They're basically the steak of lamb. Single chops are great to serve at a party because they're luxurious and special; and they're also quick and easy to cook. They're also easy to eat.

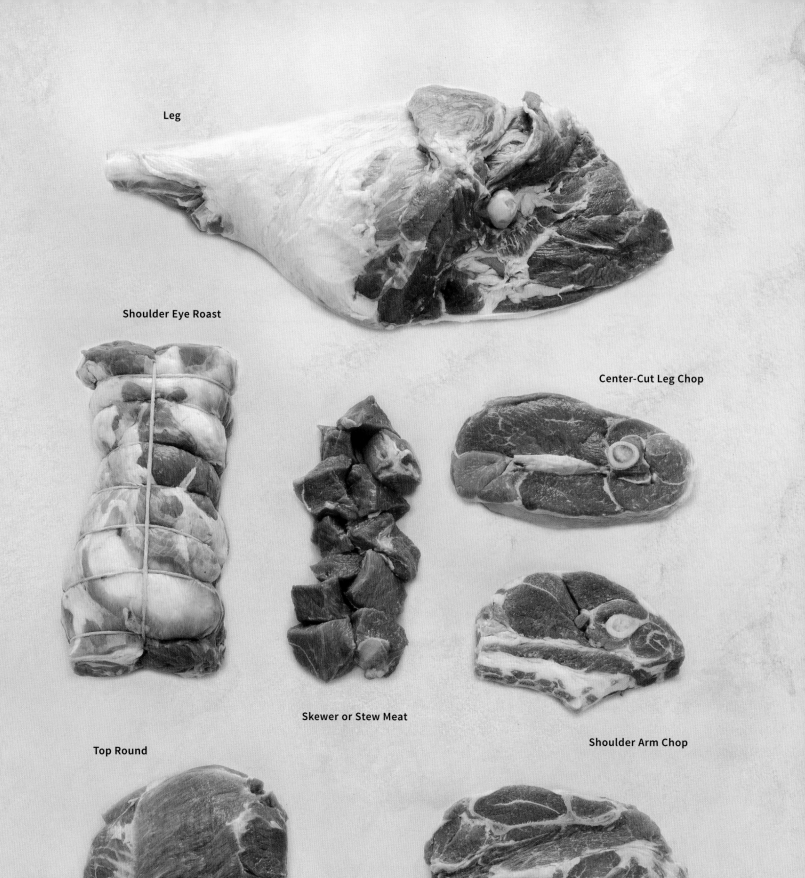

Leg

Shoulder Eye Roast

Center-Cut Leg Chop

Skewer or Stew Meat

Top Round

Shoulder Arm Chop

Shoulder Blade Chop

SHOULDER AND LEG

After chops, the **leg** is the most common cut of lamb. It's usually sold boneless or semi-boneless, which means the femur bone is still intact. Like any other bone, the femur retains its cold temperature, so having it run through a 10-pound roast makes it difficult to cook the meat correctly; the outer portions overcook while you try to get the center past raw. My preference is for a boneless leg, because when it's done, I like to be able to slice neatly through it, not carve around a bone like it's a spiral ham (see Roasted Leg of Lamb with Garlic, page 61). Most restaurants roast it or cut it into cubes to make skewers.

A boned and trimmed **shoulder eye roast**, or chuck eye roast, is cut from the shoulder of the animal; it makes a smaller and more economical alternative to a lamb leg, which is about double the size of the eye roast. Before being cooked, the eye roast should be rolled and tied into a cylindrical shape for even cooking.

The only way to tell the difference between **skewer** and **stew meat** is to ask your butcher which it is. Skewer meat needs to be high-quality and tender, because it is cooked quickly over a grill, whereas stew meat can come from lesser cuts, as it tenderizes as it slowly cooks. The best skewer meat comes from the leg because it's tender and relatively free of sinew. Skewer meat can be cut from anywhere on the leg: the outside round, heel, top sirloin, knuckle, or eye round. Stew meat comes from the shoulder and shanks because they are tougher due to the amount of connective tissue and collagen they contain. These cuts are very flavorful but must be cooked slowly at low temparatures to tenderize.

Center-cut leg chops are like steaks, cut by slicing directly across the leg, so each chop has a cross-section of the femur bone in the center. I am a big fan of this cut. There's not another cut of lamb that you can throw on the grill the way you can this one that isn't double the price. I also like the presentation. When you cook it on the grill, you can really see the bone in the center, which looks great in an old-school way.

The **shoulder arm chop** is cut from the lower portion of the front leg. It's a flavorful, economical chop but it's a bit tough.

The **top round** is a 2-pound roast from the leg. At one time it was not possible to buy it separately as it was sold as part of the leg. Today, the top round is usually cut out of the leg and sold separately, thus providing consumers with a smaller alternative to a whole leg of lamb and also reducing the size of the leg itself (see Roasted Leg of Lamb with Garlic, page 61).

The **shoulder blade chop** is cut from the top of the front blade. It is considered more tender and flavorful than the similar shoulder arm chop. Neither shoulder blade nor arm chops are as tender as loin chops, but they're still very good and they're much less expensive.

LOIN

Bone-in loin chops, the equivalent of beef porterhouse and T-bone steaks, consist of the loin eye muscle on one side of the bone and the tenderloin on the other. They are very tender and flavorful and, like other quality steaks, should be grilled or seared to medium-rare over high heat. Loin chops contain the very same meat as rib chops, just without the long rib bone for presentation, so they're about 20 percent less expensive. This is a favorite lamb chop at a lot of high-end New York steakhouses.

A **boneless loin roast**, which consists of the same muscle as that in loin chops, is a juicy, tender, and expensive roast that should be cooked to medium-rare. It is generally rolled and tied so it cooks evenly. When you order this, ask the butcher to leave the belly on and wrap it over the exposed meat where the bone was removed; the fatty belly is not only delicious, it will protect the meat when you roast it.

The advantage to **boneless loin chops** is that you can have them cut to any thickness you want; 1½ inches is ideal, because that way it's thick enough that after searing both sides, you still have juicy medium-rare meat—what lamb lovers look for in a chop—in the center.

Double boneless loin roast consists of the loin meat from both sides of the animal; the bone that separated them has been removed and the roast is rolled and tied with the belly flap wrapped around both loins. Cut into individual portions, double boneless loin chops are a favorite cut of mine. They are twice the size of a loin chop and they have a butterfly-like shape, so they look really impressive. I season them with salt, pepper, and fresh rosemary and then throw them on the grill.

The **lamb loin crosscut**, also called an English cut loin chop, contains two portions each of the tenderloin and the loin, as well as a flap of belly meat that is wrapped around the chop. One of the things I like about this cut is that you get three different textures in one chop, and I also like the way it looks, with the bone in the center. It's a difficult cut for the butcher, as his or her hands are really close to the band saw when cutting it, but the end result is very beautiful (see Lamb Loin Crosscut with Garlic Confit, page 61).

The **tenderloin** is the most tender cut on any animal and also the most expensive. A whole lamb tenderloin is an uncommon cut; the muscle is more commonly left attached to the loin and included in porterhouse chops, but very rarely you will see it sold whole or cut into medallions.

Bone-in Loin Chop

Double Boneless Loin Roast

Boneless Loin Roast

Lamb Loin Crosscut

Boneless Loin Chop

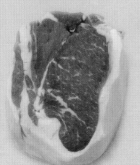

Tenderloin

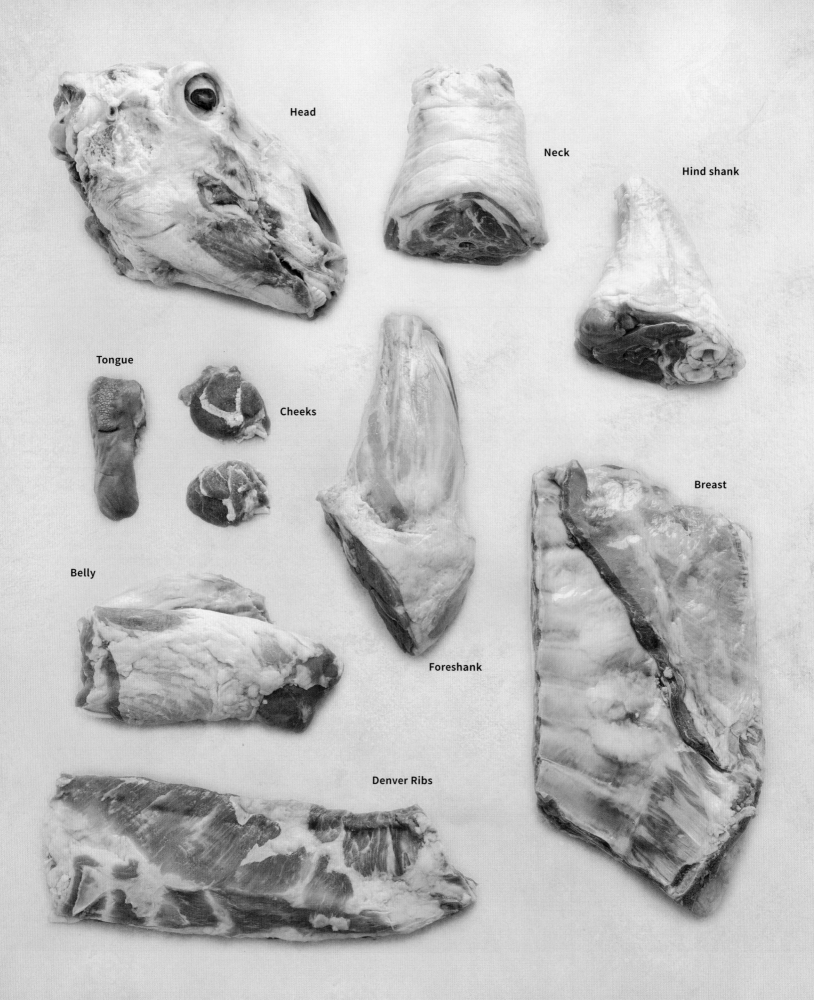

Head

Neck

Hind shank

Tongue

Cheeks

Belly

Foreshank

Breast

Denver Ribs

HEAD, NECK, BREAST, BELLY, AND SHANKS

In my father's and grandfather's days, a lamb's **head** was roasted whole to make *capozzelli di agnelli,* an old-school Italian dish where the head is split and roasted. Each person would get half a head and they would wrestle with it until they got all the meat out. I used to split the heads when I was a kid; I started at the back, and when the band saw hit the teeth, sparks would fly. I could do only a few heads before the blade was dead and I had to replace it. My grandfather's generation was the last to ask for lambs heads on a regular basis, but with the increasing popularity of nose-to-tail dining, you'll start to see more of them on menus. If you are daring enough to roast a whole head for your friends and family, use the recipe for Roasted Calf's Head alla Perla (page 34), but note that the cooking time will be shorter. Lambs heads contain an abundance of gelatin, so they are often used to make charcuterie.

Lamb **neck** is a very unusual cut. It is tough and needs braising (see Braised Lamb Neck Moroccan Style, page 65), but it is much meatier than other braising meats such as shanks, which are more bone than meat. It's totally underutilized because most people don't know about it, but it makes a delicious and economical alternative to veal osso buco (see Pat's Whole Shank Osso Buco, page 26) or Braised Beef Shank Bourguignon (page 204).

The **hind shank**, the shin portion of the back legs, consists of tough meat with a lot of sinew and connective tissue that must be braised for several hours in order for it to break down. The reward for your patience is fall-off-the-bone tender meat with hearty flavor.

The **tongue** is a dense, tough muscle; poached or braised, it becomes exceptionally tender. It's my favorite of all animal tongues.

Cheeks are extremely tough and fibrous, but braised, the meat becomes so tender it pulls apart; cheeks are most often used to make filling for ravioli.

The **foreshank** is the shin portion of the front leg and has the same cooking properties as the hind shank. Use the hind shanks or foreshanks in any braise recipe, such as Pat's Whole Shank Osso Buco (page 26) or Braised Lamb Neck Moroccan Style (page 65). The shanks can be braised whole or each crosscut into two round segments. In either case, count on serving one lamb shank per person.

Lamb **belly** is a very fatty, flavorful cut that can be incredibly tender if it's cooked right. It can be braised, cured, or smoked (to make lamb bacon); it is often rolled, stuffed with herbs, and then braised.

Lamb **breast** is a large, flavorful cut that consists of brisket meat and rib bones. If you cut the plate, cartilage, and rib tips off the breast, you are left with a neat line of **Denver ribs**; they are often referred and sold as spareribs, but if they were true spareribs, they would still contain a portion of the breastbone, which would prevent you from cutting the rack into individual ribs with just a knife. Cooked for a long time, as they are in Plum and Sesame Glazed Lamb Denver Ribs (page 58), the meat is fall-off-the-bone tender. Lamb ribs have gotten more popular in recent years, in part because they're inexpensive relative to other cuts of lamb, and also because people have discovered how good they are. I prefer them to the pork equivalent, St. Louis ribs, and that's saying a lot.

BUTCHERING TECHNIQUES

MAKING A CROWN ROAST

You can have your butcher tie a crown roast for you, but it's also a good skill to learn. And, if you don't have a broiler that will accommodate a crown roast standing up, you'll have to sear two rib racks individually and then tie them together to make the crown roast.

1. Start with two frenched racks and lay them side by side with the bone side up and the meat facing down.

3. Pull the rope to bring the two racks together.

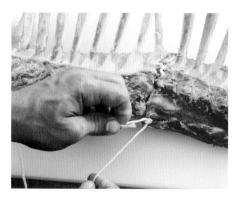

5. Pull the racks as close together as possible. Cut the rope and tie a slip knot.

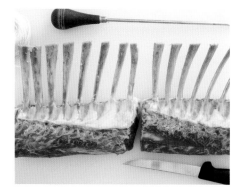

2. Thread a butcher's needle with butcher's rope and insert the needle between the first and second rib bones, in the intercostal meat just above the eye of the meat of the rack on the right side. Push the needle through the meat and out above the eye muscle of the first rib. Pull the rope through the meat; in the process you will pull the rope out of the needle. Rethread the needle and insert it into the exposed chop on the left rack, piercing through the meat just above the eye muscle of the first chop and pushing it to come out between the first and second ribs on that rack.

4. Mend the two eyes together so there is no gap in the circle when you have finished the crown roast. Cut the rope and tie a slip knot using the instructions in "Tying a Roast" (page 145). Thread the needle with a fresh piece of rope and insert it from right to left to pierce both racks at the bottommost point of the chops.

6. Make a third stitch between the first two bones and tie it off as you did the others.

7. With the bones still facing up, use a boning knife to score between each bone, making each score about ½ inch deep and 2 inches long. This gives the racks the flexibility you will need to curve them into a circle.

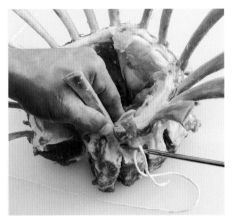

9. Thread the needle with butcher's rope and insert it between the intercostal meat on the first and second ribs of the rack on the right side.

10. Pull the needle through the eye of the first chop just as you did when you sewed the racks together on the other side; tie it with a slip knot. Pull the rope through, rethread the needle, and insert it into the exposed chop on the left rack, piercing through the meat so the needle comes out between the first and second ribs on that rack. and tie it with a slip knot. Make two more slip knots below the first, matching the way the racks were originally tied together. Loop the rope around the outside of the racks and tie the final knot of rope, securing the crown.

8. Stand the racks up and form them into a crown with the scored side facing outward.

11. Once the crown is secured, continue to form it with your hands, creating more space between each bone until the crown is in a perfect circle.

LaFrieda Family Stuffed Lamb Crown Roast

STUFFING

4 slices white sandwich bread (preferably stale), crusts removed, cubed (about 2 cups)

3 tablespoons whole milk

2 tablespoons canola or another neutral-flavored oil

1 cup finely chopped yellow onion (about ½ large)

2 teaspoons kosher salt

3 cloves garlic, minced

2¼ pounds chopped (ground) lamb

7 ounces aged provolone, cut into ¾-inch cubes (about 1¼ cups)

1 tablespoon finely chopped fresh rosemary

½ teaspoon freshly ground black pepper

LAMB

1 crown roast of lamb (from 2 frenched 8-rib lamb racks; see "Frenching a Rib Bone," page 186, about 5 pounds)

2 teaspoons kosher salt

½ teaspoon freshly ground black pepper

2 tablespoons canola or another neutral-flavored oil (only if searing the racks on the stovetop)

1 tablespoon finely chopped fresh rosemary

¼ cup Italian-Style Breadcrumbs (page 94; or store-bought)

When I started hosting our family meals about ten years ago, I made one crown roast. Today, as the headcount has crept up to around twenty-five people, I always make two. This is in addition to three aged New York strip steaks for those who don't eat lamb, pasta with Sunday Sauce (page 150), and a few other items that change from year to year. It's always an enormous amount of food and preparation, but it's well worth it. Serving food while my family sits around the table talking, laughing, and ribbing each other—these are the moments that make me satisfied with life.

SERVES 10 TO 12

1. For the stuffing: Put the bread in a bowl, sprinkle the milk over it, and toss to distribute the milk. Set the bread aside to absorb the milk.

2. In a large skillet, heat the oil over medium-high heat until it slides easily in the pan, about 2 minutes. Add the onion, season with 1 teaspoon of the salt, and cook the until the onion is lightly browned and soft, about 5 minutes. Add the garlic and cook until lightly browned, about 1 minute. Add the chopped lamb and cook until browned all over and cooked through, 5 to 6 minutes. Turn off the heat and pour the chopped lamb mixture into a fine-mesh sieve to drain off the excess fat. Add the drained meat, provolone, rosemary, the pepper, and remaining 1 teaspoon salt to the bowl with the bread and stir to combine the ingredients.

3. For the lamb: Position an oven rack in the lower third of the oven. Remove any racks above it and preheat the oven to broil. If your oven doesn't have a broiler setting (if the broiler is under the oven, which won't fit the roast), preheat the oven to 450°F.

4. Place the roast, bones sticking up, on a baking sheet and season the meat with the salt and pepper. Cover the ends of the bones with foil to prevent them from burning. Put the roast under the broiler until the meat is seared to deep brown, about 10 minutes. Remove from the oven and discard the foil. Reduce the oven temperature to 350°F. Season the meat side of the racks with the rosemary and pat the rosemary into the meat to adhere.

5. Spoon the stuffing into the center of the roast and sprinkle the breadcrumbs on top. Return the roast to the oven to cook until a meat thermometer inserted into the rack (but not touching a bone) registers 135° to 140°F for medium-rare, 35 to 45 minutes if you cooked the meat under a broiler, about 20 minutes if you browned it in a 450°F oven. Remove the roast from the oven and let it rest for about 15 minutes.

6. Remove and discard the butcher's rope. Cut between the bones to cut the racks into individual chops. Serve one or two chops plus a big spoonful of the stuffing per person.

PLUM AND SESAME GLAZED LAMB DENVER RIBS

LAMB

¼ cup plus 2 tablespoons hoisin sauce

¼ cup plus 2 tablespoons plum wine

¼ cup plus 2 tablespoons rice vinegar

⅓ cup packed light brown sugar

2 tablespoons white miso paste

2 tablespoons soy sauce

½ teaspoon finely chopped garlic (about 1 large clove)

4 racks lamb Denver ribs, about 1½ pounds each

SALAD

¼ cup rice vinegar

2 tablespoons honey

1 small cucumber, very thinly sliced

1 small fresh red chile (such as jalapeño or Fresno), seeded and cut into thin strips

GLAZE

1 cup mirin

1 cup soy sauce

1 cup rice vinegar

¼ cup honey

2 cloves garlic, minced

1 teaspoon chopped fresh ginger

Pinch of crushed red pepper flakes

2 tablespoons toasted mixed black and white sesame seeds (optional)

I love spareribs in general, but I love lamb spareribs the most. This preparation is from China Grill and they are the best ribs I've ever tasted. For a long time, whenever I was in that part of town, I'd sneak in, sit at the bar, and order these. I got addicted to them so I'm glad they agreed to share their recipe with me. You could also make this recipe using pork St. Louis ribs instead of lamb. When figuring out how much pork to buy, go by the weight, not the number of racks, as a rack of pork ribs weighs almost twice as much as a rack of lamb spareribs.

MAKES 6 TO 8 APPETIZER SERVINGS

1. For the lamb: In a nonreactive baking dish or another container large enough to contain the ribs, combine the hoisin, wine, vinegar, brown sugar, miso, soy sauce, and garlic. Put the rib racks in the marinade and turn to cover the ribs all over with the marinade. Cover the dish with plastic wrap and put the ribs in the refrigerator to marinate for at least several hours or overnight.

2. For the salad: In a medium bowl, stir together the vinegar and honey. Add the cucumber and chile and toss to combine. Cover the bowl with plastic wrap and refrigerate for 2 to 5 hours before serving.

3. When ready to cook the lamb, preheat the oven to 350°F.

4. Remove the ribs from the marinade and lay them bone side down in a baking dish. Cover the ribs with a sheet of parchment paper and then cover the pan tightly with foil. (The parchment keeps the foil from eroding from the vinegar in the marinade.) Put the ribs in the oven to roast until the meat is fall-off-the-bone tender, about 3 hours. To check for doneness, pull on one bone; it should pull away easily from the rack.

5. For the glaze: In a medium skillet, combine the mirin, soy sauce, vinegar, honey, garlic, ginger, and red pepper flakes. Stir over medium heat to combine the ingredients. Reduce the heat to medium-low and cook the sauce until it thickens to a glaze, about 3 minutes. Remove from the heat and set aside.

6. Remove the ribs from the oven and brush them with the glaze. Sprinkle with the sesame seeds, if using. Serve the spareribs warm, with the salad on the side.

ROASTED LEG OF LAMB WITH GARLIC

1 boneless lamb leg (about 8 pounds)

10 to 15 cloves garlic, thinly sliced

2 tablespoons kosher salt

1 teaspoon freshly ground black pepper

Maldon or another flaky sea salt

BUTCHER'S NOTE:
Ask your butcher to remove the silverskin and the glands, which can give off a bitter flavor.

This was the first expensive cut of meat I tried to cut. I was about fifteen years old and my dad didn't want me to cut it. But I gave it a try. I ended up cutting right through the top round and completely missed the femur bone. I destroyed the roast to the point that we couldn't send it to the customer. I bought it with my work money and took it home to my mom. We didn't have money to lose. I learned a lesson. For this recipe, I use a boneless leg, so when it's done, all you have to do is slice it, put it on a plate, spoon some Mint Chimichurri (page 63) over it—or whatever condiments you like. To make a smaller version of this, for two or three people, use a boneless top round and cook it until a meat thermometer registers 135°F for medium-rare.

To make a lamb jus, make a lamb stock using the femur bone removed from this roast in place of the bones in the recipe for Brown Veal Stock (page 31). Use that stock to make the Port Wine Reduction (page 214).

SERVES 8 TO 10

1. Preheat the oven to 425°F.

2. Using a boning knife, make slits about 1 inch deep over the outside surface of the lamb. Slip a garlic slice into each slit, making sure the garlic is fully submerged so it doesn't burn when cooked. Season the lamb all over with the salt and pepper, including the open pocket where the bone was removed. Tuck the ends under the roast to create a football-like shape. Using butcher's rope, tie the leg into a roast, making six knots about 1 inch apart (see "Tying a Roast," page 145).

3. Put the lamb on a roasting rack set in a roasting pan and roast until a meat thermometer inserted into the deepest portion of the lamb registers 130°F, 1 to 1½ hours. Remove the lamb from the oven and let it rest on a cutting board for about 10 minutes.

4. Discard the butcher's rope and slice the lamb against the grain into ¾-inch-thick slices.

LAMB LOIN CROSSCUT WITH GARLIC CONFIT

In conceptualizing his restaurant, City Hall, the chef-owner Henry Meer asked me to help him come up with unusual, lesser-known cuts, and the lamb loin crosscut was one that I showed him. To prepare them the way he does, start with 4 crosscut lamb loin chops (1¼ inches thick, about 18 ounces each), roll the belly flap meat around the loin, tucking 3 cloves of Garlic Confit (page 64) between the loin and the belly flap of each chop. Tie butcher's rope around each chop to hold it together. Salt and pepper the loins on both sides, cover, and refrigerate, ideally overnight. When you're ready to cook them, preheat the broiler. Rub the lamb with olive oil and season with flaky salt and fresh thyme leaves. Broil the chops for about 3 minutes per side for medium-rare (it will register 130°F with a meat thermometer inserted close to but not touching the bone). Serve with Honey Mustard (page 64) or your choice of condiment (see Pat's Favorite Lamb Condiments, page 63).

Mint Chimichurri

Spice Red Pepper
Walnut Pesto

Tangy
Yogurt Sauce

Garlic Confit

Honey Mustard

Salsa Verde

PAT'S FAVORITE LAMB CONDIMENTS

As much as I love lamb, I love it even more with different sauces.

Below are some of my favorite condiments for lamb.

MINT CHIMICHURRI

2 cups fresh mint leaves (about 2 bunches)

1 cup fresh flat-leaf parsley leaves (about 1 bunch)

2 cloves garlic

1 small serrano chile, halved and seeded

¼ cup rice vinegar

¼ cup extra-virgin olive oil plus more as needed

1 teaspoon kosher salt

MAKES ABOUT ½ CUP

In a blender or food processor, combine half of the mint, the parsley, garlic, and chile and pulse to begin to chop the ingredients. Add the vinegar, oil, and the remaining mint and pulse until the herbs are finely chopped; don't pulse so much that you form a paste. Transfer the chimichurri to a bowl and stir in the salt and more oil if necessary to have a loose, spoonable consistency.

TANGY YOGURT SAUCE

7 ounces whole-milk Greek yogurt

¼ cup fresh lemon juice

2 tablespoons extra-virgin olive oil

2 large cloves garlic, grated or minced (about 1 teaspoon)

2 teaspoons kosher salt

MAKES ABOUT 1 CUP

In a small bowl, stir together the yogurt, lemon juice, oil, garlic, and salt.

SALSA VERDE

1 cup loosely packed arugula

⅓ cup pitted green olives, such as picholine

¼ cup fresh oregano (or marjoram) leaves

¼ cup fresh mint leaves

1 tablespoon capers, rinsed

3 anchovy fillets

2 cloves garlic

½ teaspoon crushed red pepper flakes

1 cup extra-virgin olive oil

2 tablespoons fresh lemon juice

1 teaspoon freshly ground black pepper

½ teaspoon kosher salt

MAKES ABOUT 2 CUPS

In a blender or food processor, combine the arugula, olives, oregano, mint, capers, anchovies, garlic, and red pepper flakes and pulse to puree the ingredients to a paste. Add the oil in a thin steady stream while the machine is running. Transfer the salsa to a bowl and stir in the lemon juice, pepper, and salt.

SPICY RED PEPPER WALNUT PESTO

3 large red bell peppers

1 small yellow onion, peeled and quartered

5 cloves garlic

2 tablespoons pomegranate molasses

1 teaspoon Aleppo pepper or paprika

1 teaspoon ground cumin

2 teaspoons kosher salt plus more to taste

4 tablespoons extra-virgin olive oil

¼ cup walnut halves, lightly toasted and roughly chopped

1 teaspoon fresh lemon juice plus more to taste

MAKES ABOUT 1 CUP

1. Roast the red peppers on a grill or under a broiler until they are blackened all over. Put the peppers in a bowl and cover it with plastic wrap to steam them for at least 10 minutes. Peel and discard the skins (don't rinse the peppers under water) and pull out and discard the cores and seeds.

2. In a food processor, combine the peppers, onion, garlic, pomegranate molasses, Aleppo pepper, cumin, salt, and 2 tablespoons of the oil and pulse until the mixture is just pureed. Add the walnuts and the remaining 2 tablespoons oil and puree until the nuts are very finely chopped but not pureed. Stir in the lemon juice. Add more lemon juice or salt to taste.

HONEY MUSTARD

¼ cup plus 2 tablespoons honey

¼ cup Dijon mustard

¼ cup whole-grain Dijon mustard

1 tablespoon fresh thyme leaves

MAKES ¾ CUP

In a medium bowl, stir together the honey, mustards, and thyme. Cover and refrigerate until you're ready to serve, or for up to 1 week.

GARLIC CONFIT

½ cup whole peeled cloves garlic

1 cup olive oil, or as needed

1 sprig fresh rosemary

MAKES ½ CUP

In a small saucepan, combine the garlic with enough oil to cover (the amount will vary depending on the size of the pan you are using). Heat the oil over medium-low heat until the first bubble rises to the surface. Reduce the heat to low, add the rosemary, and cook the garlic until it is golden, 20 to 30 minutes. Remove from the heat and let the garlic cool in the oil. Remove and discard the rosemary sprig. Use the garlic or refrigerate it in an airtight container, submerged in oil (add more oil to the container if necessary to cover the garlic).

BRAISED LAMB NECK MOROCCAN STYLE

3 lamb necks (about 1½ pounds total), each split in half by your butcher

½ teaspoon kosher salt plus more for seasoning

½ teaspoon freshly ground black pepper plus more to taste

All-purpose flour for dusting

2 tablespoons extra-virgin olive oil

1 stalk celery, finely chopped

1 carrot, finely chopped

3 medium shallots, finely chopped

5 cloves garlic, minced

½ teaspoon ground cloves

½ teaspoon ground allspice

½ teaspoon crushed red pepper flakes

1 cup dry red wine

½ cup canned crushed tomatoes

2 cups beef stock (see Brown Veal Stock, page 31; or low-sodium store-bought), or as needed

1 orange

¼ cup pitted oil-cured olives

Tangy Yogurt Sauce (page 63)

I love lamb neck but I feel like I was the only one eating it until recently. Now it's been discovered. One of the first chefs who asked me for lamb neck was Lidia Bastianich; she wanted me to cut a little off the top and the bottom, to square it off, and then she used it to make a lamb neck version of osso buco, which is the perfect thing to do with it because it is so tender and meaty when braised. For this dish I braise it with Moroccan-style seasonings and serve it with yogurt sauce.

SERVES 6

1. Preheat the oven to 350°F.

2. Season the lamb with the salt and pepper and dust it lightly with flour.

3. In a Dutch oven, or other overproof pan large enough to hold the necks in a single layer, heat the oil over high heat until it slides easily in the pan, about 2 minutes. Add the lamb and sear it until it's golden all over, 10 to 12 minutes. Remove the lamb from the pan but do not wipe out the pan. Add the celery and carrot, season with salt, and cook until softened, about 10 minutes. Add the shallots, garlic, ground cloves, allspice, and red pepper flakes and cook until the shallots are a rich brown color, about 5 minutes. Add the wine and cook until it reduces by half, about 5 minutes. Stir in the tomatoes. Return the lamb necks to the pot and add as much stock as needed; the liquid should come just to the top of the meat. Cover the pot with the lid (or cover it with foil if you are using a pan without a lid). Put the lamb in the oven and cook until the meat is fork-tender and falling off the bone (it will separate easily when you stick a fork in it), 2½ to 3 hours. Check to make sure the liquid isn't boiling, just gently simmering. If it's boiling, reduce the oven temperature by 25°F. Remove the lamb from the oven, uncover, and let cool in the liquid for at least 15 minutes and up to 1 hour. (To prepare the necks a day in advance, let them cool to room temperature and refrigerate them in the liquid for up to 24 hours. Reheat the necks with the liquid over medium heat.)

4. Use a citrus zester to pull off the zest from half the orange in very thin curls and set aside for garnish. Finely grate the zest from the rest of the orange. Squeeze the orange.

5. Remove the lamb from the sauce to a plate. Skim the fat off the sauce, stir in the orange juice, and bring the liquid to a boil over high heat. Reduce the heat and simmer the sauce over medium heat until it's thick enough to coat the back of a spoon, 10 to 20 minutes. Turn off the heat and stir in the olives and grated orange zest.

6. To serve, put one portion of the neck on each plate, spoon the reduced sauce over the meat, and top with the orange zest strips. Serve with the yogurt sauce on the side.

CHOPPED MEAT

BRANDING OUR MEAT

In the late 1990s a new kind of middleman showed up in the meat industry: purchasing agents, or brokers. These brokers would go to restaurants and say, "Pay us a fee and we'll buy all your meat for you." Once the purchasing company got an order from a restaurant, they would have someone, usually in another state, sitting behind a desk calling different meat suppliers who would bid on an order. Whoever came in the cheapest, sometimes even by only a penny, would win that order. But for that system to have been truly beneficial to the restaurants who were buying the meat, or for it to be fair to the companies bidding on the order, the purchasing company would had to have been comparing the very same meats against one another. But they weren't even trying to do that. They were just trying to deliver the cuts that restaurants wanted at the lowest price. And there was no personal relationship there. It was not a good thing for a family-run, specialized company like ours. It quickly became apparent to me that we needed to set ourselves apart. We needed to create a brand, and the way I set out to do that was with our chopped beef.

By chopped beef, I'm referring to what most people know as "ground beef." The difference is a matter of terminology, but my dad feels strongly about not calling it ground beef, which conjures up an image of meat that has been ground poorly or that is mushy or emulsified, like something you would use to make bratwurst or hot dogs.

Chopped beef is traditionally made from trimmings. We don't do that. We start with whole muscle. This is something my grandfather, the original Pat LaFrieda, pioneered in the 1930s. Using whole muscle instead of scraps was unique in itself. On top of that, he developed a custom blend, a combination of equal parts clod, chuck, brisket, and short ribs, to get the exact meat-to-fat ratio and flavor profile he wanted. Then he tempered, or chilled, the meat before grinding it, which helped the meat maintain its integrity when it passed through the plate and blade of the grinder, so it came out in long, noodle-like strands, not pasty or beat up in any way. The way chopped beef was originally made, way back when, was with knives. The butcher would put the meat on a cutting board and hit it with two cleavers, one in each hand—right left right left—until it was chopped fine. The way our meat is chopped, it comes out clean and defined, as if it were chopped a thousand times by knives. My grandfather took great pride in our chopped beef, and with good reason. He was way ahead of his time.

We were known for our chopped beef for many years and we sold a lot of it to chefs all over town, but I don't think the chefs who were buying from us even knew what kinds of cuts were in the blend. They just knew that they liked it, and that their customers liked it. But I knew that what we were doing with chopped beef was unique, and that I had to get that message out. One day, I took a label with our logo on it and instead of printing it to say "chopped beef," I put "LaFrieda's Original Chopped Beef Blend." I also specified that the chopped beef wasn't made out of trimmings and I called out the cuts themselves, and the breed and grade of the meat we were using. This might sound basic now, but back then nobody had ever done this. Chopped beef was chopped beef and the most detail you might see on a label was the fat content.

Now, if a restaurant asked a broker for a price on chopped beef, I couldn't be included in that bidding process. By giving our chopped beef a name and being so specific, I was telling our restaurant customers that this was a different product. To make a comparison, it wouldn't be just looking at one price against another. A restaurant would have to taste our product against the others. Once they could see and taste a difference in the product, they wanted the one they wanted. They wanted ours. They didn't care about saving pennies.

Not long after my branding campaign with the chopped meat, in 1998, Henry Meer, who at the time owned a popular restaurant in SoHo, came to me and asked if I could develop a custom blend just for him. He was opening a second restaurant, City Hall, in Tribeca. It was a classic steakhouse concept and he wanted to serve a really great burger. Henry liked our Original Blend, but he wanted his to have a bit more fat and to be a little sweeter. I think he also just wanted something that nobody else had, and I was happy to give it to him. It was the first custom blend I made. Henry put our name on his menu; under the word "burger" it read, "Pat LaFrieda's custom blend of short rib and brisket." That was the first time anyone had ever put our name on a menu, and it was truly a pivotal moment for us. After that, more and more restaurants began asking for their own custom blends. Today, our burger blends represent as much as 15 percent of our business. We do over fifty custom blends, each one a little different. I consider it my responsibility to be able to offer two competing restaurants on the same New York City block two distinct chopped beef blends, so that they can offer their customers two different burger experiences.

Now it seems almost obvious for a chef to choose what kind of meat to put in his burgers; pretty much all of the good restaurants are doing it. I don't think it's a trend. It's more like an evolution. American chefs and the people they are feeding have discovered something reasonably simple that makes their favorite comfort food that much better. They'll never go back. Why would they?

Whatever efforts I may have made about branding, without a doubt our best tool as a business has been the restaurants who buy from us. People in the restaurant business, chefs especially, talk to each other. They ask each other, "Hey, where do you get this?" Or, "Do you know who can do that for me?" Through a mutual friend, I had become friendly with the chef Floyd Cardoz, who was working uptown at the St. Regis hotel's fine dining restaurant, Lespinasse. We supplied them with all their meat, including about four hundred lamb racks a week. Eventually Floyd quit the St. Regis to work for Danny Meyer, who at the time owned Union Square Cafe, Gramercy Tavern, Eleven Madison Park, and an upscale Indian restaurant, Tabla, where Floyd was going to work. Floyd put me together with Danny, and I started selling chopped beef to Union Square Cafe for their burgers. Not long after that, Danny's group started talking about opening a little burger stand in Madison Square Park and they asked me to come up with some blends for them. We went back and forth a few times until we got to the blend they wanted. The stand, Shake Shack, was a home run. They had a line wrapped around Madison Square Park waiting for a burger from the day they opened.

At the original Shake Shack in Madison Square Park in Manhattan, the wait for a burger is often up to an hour long.

to make over 1,200 four-ounce burgers a day, so I wasn't going to refuse. But I also had no idea how I was going to make it happen. Twelve hundred is a lot of burgers no matter how you look at it. When I got off the phone, I went outside. There was a guy who had been hanging around for weeks begging for a job at LaFrieda Meats. He'd been laid off at one of the companies in the now fast-disappearing 14th Street Meat Market; he was almost homeless and definitely jobless. I offered him a job forming burger patties. He's from Ecuador, so to this day (he still works for us), we call him "Ecua." I went down to the Bowery where the restaurant supply stores are located and bought biscuit cutters. And when I got back, our cleaning lady, Lorena, had assembled a team of five people to put down the biscuit cutters, fill them with four ounces of Shake Shack burger blend, and then put them in a box. We did this round the clock every day for weeks, if not months. My dad was not happy. "What are we gonna do next, go there and cook it for them?"

Besides gaining this huge account, Shake Shack changed our business in another way. Before Shake Shack, we had never formed a burger patty, and, in fact, my father was vehemently opposed to it. He'd been asked before and refused. "We're butchers!" he always said. We would make the chopped beef. They could form the burgers. Besides, he told them, "The best burger you can make is made by hand."

But with Shake Shack, it was a different story. They were doing such volume that about six months after they opened they came to us and told us they wanted what they call "pucks," which are formed patties, but formed extra tall, so the guy cooking them can push down on them on the flattop, which caramelizes the outside. We were selling them the meat

Eventually I had a custom machine built for the job. I designed it myself and it made only one thing: Shake Shack pucks. I've since upgraded to several machines. We didn't have any kind of agreement with Shake Shack; they could have pulled out at any moment and I would have been stuck with the machine. But when you're building a business, you have to have faith. Faith that if you have a good product, that if you give people what they want and you're honest, your customers will keep coming back to you. I had faith that Shake Shack would like what we were doing for them and that this investment would pay off, and it did. Despite how much our business has grown and changed, they are still our biggest customer. Today, they are a worldwide boutique chain.

MARKETING LaFRIEDA MEATS

One thing I had to do when I started working for my father was to look carefully at the instances when I wanted to follow what he did, and those when I would have to do things my own way. My father has always been my greatest role model, so at times the choice wasn't easy. One of the first things I had to change was the marketing and branding of LaFrieda Meats.

Our "slogan," which my dad came up with in the 1970s and had printed on T-shirts, was "Eat My Meat!" Back then, the Village was very gay. My dad supplied a lot of the gay restaurants and bars around the neighborhood. They loved him and he loved them. For a long time, he was known as "the gay butcher." Our T-shirts, with "Eat My Meat!" emblazoned on the back, became a cult item. Everyone in the West Village wanted one. Other than my mother handing out business cards to chefs in the neighborhood, the gay community walking around with those T-shirts represented our entire marketing strategy.

My dad eventually had "Eat My Meat!" painted on our vans as well. Back then, he had all our trucks painted by hand by a homeless guy who was also an artist. Any time we got a new truck, my dad would walk up to the Meat Market and wander around the streets until he found the painter. Then my dad would buy the guy a bottle of blackberry brandy—that was his thing—and bring him down to Leroy Street, where the painter would stand there and hand-letter LaFrieda Meats on both sides of the van and "Eat My Meat!" on the back. Each truck was different from the next one.

I knew this wasn't smart. I wanted everything to look the same, and I wanted our trucks to look like no other meat company trucks in the city. "Dad, we need a logo," I said. And he said, "What's that?"

Customers and people in the neighborhood often asked my father for an "Eat My Meat!" T-shirt, and my father was happy to give them away.

On a piece of cardboard I drew what I thought would look nice, and would project the image of who we are and what we did: a steer's head with grass from left to right. It's the logo we still have to this day. From that point on, as one truck would break down, I'd get a new one rather than fix it, so that I could start to build a nice fleet. My father said, "What are you doing spending money on trucks? What does it matter if they're dirty on the outside?" But it mattered. It all mattered.

Today, we have thirty trucks. Ironically, my dad is in charge of them. He buys them. He arranges for them to be painted with our logo and outfits them in the way we need. And he arranges for them to be cleaned daily. Those trucks are a huge part of our public image; I get texts often and pictures sent to me every day from friends and customers who see our trucks on the street. Besides our restaurant customers, they are our single biggest means of advertising.

ALL ABOUT CHOPPED MEAT

Chopped meat, also known as "ground meat" and, in the case of ground beef, "hamburger," is meat that has been passed through a grinder. Traditionally it is made with scraps, but as I've said, what makes ours special is that we grind whole muscle. A lot of iconic American dishes start with ground meat, including hamburgers, meatballs, meatloaf, sloppy Joes, and sausages of all kinds. In Hispanic cuisine, ground beef or pork is combined with spices and other ingredients, such as nuts and dried fruit, to make picadillo, which is used to make tacos and also as stuffing. In England, ground beef, or what they call "mincemeat," is topped with mashed potatoes and baked to make shepherd's pie. And French steak tartare is nothing but fresh minced meat combined with other ingredients.

BUYING CHOPPED MEAT

When buying chopped meat, you basically have three options. You can order from a butcher, the advantage here being that you can specify the cuts you want, and that will make all the difference in terms of the flavor of your chopped meat. You'll also know it's been freshly ground. I equate freshly chopped meat to freshly baked bread. The aroma, flavor, and texture that you get from meat straight from the grinder, just like bread fresh from the oven, doesn't compare to that of commercial chopped beef. The downside to using a butcher for your chopped meat is that you don't always know how clean their grinder is. The grinders are usually in the back of the shop so you can't see them. They've got to be cleaned every day, otherwise meat gets caught inside and who knows how long it stays there. You don't *see* horror stories. But if you know and trust your butcher, it's definitely a great way to go.

The second option is to buy your chopped meat from a grocery store, preground and packaged. The advantage to this is that you know it was ground in a large commercial facility, which, like ours, undergoes USDA inspections on a daily basis. The downside to prepackaged meat is that you don't have control over the cuts that make up the blend, and in fact you can be pretty certain you're getting scrap meat. You'll be safe eating it, but it won't be as flavorful as a meat ground with quality cuts. It's also not freshly ground. If you do buy packaged chopped meat, look for one with a 20-percent fat content.

The third and what I believe is the best option is to grind your own chopped meat. This way, you know what cuts and the quality of the meat that's going into your chopped meat. Grinding your own also means you also have control over the cleanliness of the grinder. And it means you're getting the freshest possible product.

CHOPPED MEAT SAFETY

Note that if you are grinding your own chopped meat, you need to be aware of the risk of E. coli. The bacteria live on the outside of meat, but in the case of a whole muscle, such as a steak, the bacteria are killed when it's cooked. (E. coli is killed if a temperature of 165°F is maintained for 1 minute.) But when whole muscle is passed through a grinder, what was once the exterior is now distributed throughout the meat, and the interior of the meat will not get to that temperature unless you are cooking a burger to very well-done. To protect from the threat of E. coli, the USDA recommends cooking hamburgers to an internal temperature of 160°F, but if you buy your chopped meat from a butcher you trust or you grind it safely yourself in a grinder with clean parts, don't be afraid of a rare burger. The amount of exposure you would get to E. coli from a hamburger ground under clean conditions is not dangerous to the majority of individuals, but to be on the safe side, to retard the growth of pathogens, combine water and vinegar in equal parts and spray this on the exterior of the meat before grinding it. You especially want to do this if you are feeding children under five years old, the elderly, or anyone with a compromised immune system.

TYPES OF CHOPPED MEAT

We aim for an 80:20 ratio of lean to fat for all of our chopped meats. After a lot of experimenting, we think that's the perfect place to be. To make chopped meat for burgers and other applications besides sausage, you will pass the meat through the grinder twice, first through the ³⁄₁₆-inch die and then through the ⁵⁄₃₂-inch die. If your grinder has dies in only two sizes, use the larger die followed by the smaller one. For LaFrieda Signature Sausages (page 80), each sausage recipe specifies die sizes.

Almost any part of the animal can be turned into chopped **beef** and if you're looking at prepackaged chopped meat, you have no idea what you're getting other than the lean percentage specified on the package. For specific blends, see "Pat's Favorite Blends" (page 74). Chill beef to 28° to 30°F before grinding it.

Chopped **veal** is often used in combination with pork or beef to make meatballs, meatloaf (see Four-Meat Meatloaf, page 93), and ragù Bolognese. When buying chopped veal or the meat to chop yourself, specify equal parts shoulder, belly, and flank, which will give you the 80:20 meat-to-fat ratio. Chill the meat to 28° to 30°F before grinding it.

Chopped **duck** is delicious as a ravioli or spring roll filling. To make it, start with a whole, boned duck and breasts together. Chill the duck to 26° to 28°F before grinding it.

Pork is so tender and flavorful that every muscle but the shank is suitable for making chopped pork. That said, pork butt is hands down the best option. It has the ideal 80:20 meat-to-fat ratio, and it's also economical. Chopped pork is most often used to make sausages (see Grandpa's Italian-Style Pork Sausages, page 82) and, along with veal (and sometimes beef), it's traditionally used to make Italian meatballs and ragù Bolognese. Pork tends to be stickier than other meats so it needs to be even colder (26° to 28°F) before passing it through the grinder.

Chopped **lamb** is used to make Merguez sausage (page 88), meatballs, and burgers; it is the key component of shepherd's pie (a casserole of seasoned lamb under a blanket of mashed potatoes) and in the classic Greek moussaka. When buying chopped lamb or the meat to chop yourself, specify a combination of two-thirds shoulder to one-third belly for an 80:20 meat-to-fat ratio, and chill the lamb to 28° to 30°F before grinding it.

The issue to overcome with chopped **turkey** is its low fat content, which translates into a lack of flavor. Dark meat has a lot more flavor, and ground dark meat represents 90 percent of what we sell to restaurants. At the retail level, people buy almost exclusively white meat chopped turkey, because at home people try to eat low fat, where the priority of restaurant chefs is flavor. When buying chopped turkey or the meat to chop yourself, specify a 50-50 combination of light (breast) and dark (thigh) meat for a 90:10 ratio; if you want more fat, increase the proportion of dark meat. In addition to chopped turkey, we make a turkey burger blend with cheese and herbs added to enhance the flavor (see Chophouse Turkey Provolone Burgers with Fennel-Shallot Marmalade, page 101). Turkey needs to be chilled to 26° to 28°F before grinding it.

Chopped **chicken** is popular with chefs who use it to make sausage, meatballs, chili, burgers, or in any dish calling for ground beef. Like turkey, chicken tends to be extremely lean, and dark meat definitely has more flavor than light. When buying chopped chicken or the meat to chop yourself, specify a 50-50 combination of light (breast) and dark (thigh) meat. Chicken needs to be chilled to 26° to 28°F before grinding it.

Beef

Veal

Lamb

Duck

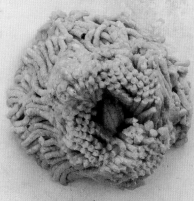

Turkey

Pork

Chicken

THE BLACK LABEL BURGER

Years ago, when we first started aging steaks at LaFrieda Meats, Riad Nasr, who was then the chef at Minetta Tavern, asked me if I had any ideas for an ultimate burger. I had just started playing around with putting aged beef into chopped beef blends. Grinding aged beef had never been done before and we didn't know how it would go, because with dry-aging, you have a crust on the outside that naturally has pathogens on it (see "Dry-Aged Steaks," page 184). But you cut the crust off dry-aged meat before you do anything with it, including grinding it, so by being very conscientious, I was able to create dry-aged blends that were safe for the consumer.

After experimenting with a few blends, I finally created one for Riad to try. It contained 30 percent aged New York strip so good you could slice it and eat it raw. (The rest of the blend is a secret.) This was meat that nobody else would ever grind. But it made for what I knew was a sublime burger.

It was my cousin and partner Mark Pastore's idea to invite a bunch of chefs to try it, including Riad and his partner, the chef Lee Hanson. We put together a dinner at a restaurant where we made these burgers. A couple of them loved it. A couple of them hated it. Riad and Lee went bonkers over it. After the tasting, Riad said he not only wanted the aged-burger blend, but he wanted it to be exclusive. I told him we could be exclusive, and he said, "Do we need legal documentation?" I shook his hand and I said, "There's your documentation: You have the exclusive."

Mark, the food writer Josh Ozersky, and I always fight about who named it "Black Label." Josh says he named it. Mark thinks he did. I don't know who did. But regardless, that burger was a success beyond all of our successes. I got more attention over the Black Label burger at Minetta Tavern than over any other item that I've ever made. Minetta also offers a second burger, a short rib blend, which is half the price of the Black Label, but still, Riad told me that in the first year, he sold 13,500 Black Label burgers, twice as many as they sold of the short rib burgers. Almost every party that sits down orders the Black Label burger as an appetizer. The restaurant splits it four ways, so everyone gets a few bites and still has room for dinner. I kept my word with Riad. I don't know how many restaurants have asked for the Black Label blend, but I've turned down every one. I've made other aged-beef blends, but nothing even close to what I made for Riad.

For those who want to play with making your own aged-burger blends, using the instructions in "Grind Your Own" (opposite page), grind a combination of 50 percent dry-aged rib-eye or New York strip steak (ideally aged at least forty days) with 50 percent fresh chuck. Cook it up as you would any other burger and serve it on the best brioche bun you can find. This burger deserves it.

PAT'S FAVORITE BLENDS

I have created more than fifty burger blends, all of which combine different whole muscles in order to create distinct flavor profiles. These are the three that I reach for when I am cooking burgers at home.

ORIGINAL BLEND

Equal parts: clod + chuck + trimmed brisket + short rib

This is my grandfather's blend, and it's still my favorite. It incorporates the most flavorful cuts on the animal, and it's juicy without having any lingering fat that coats your mouth.

SHORT RIB BLEND

Two-thirds short rib + one-third trimmed brisket

In this blend, you can really taste the clean, sweet flavor of the short rib meat. Both short rib and brisket are braising meats, meaning they're tough but flavorful. Ground, they stay firm, so there is some resistance when you bite into the cooked burger.

HANGER BLEND

Two-thirds hanger + one-third clod

This blend combines the very rich flavor of hanger steak with clod, which has a classic steak flavor similar to the New York strip. Biting into a burger made with this blend is like biting into a chopped steak.

GRIND YOUR OWN: A STEP-BY-STEP GUIDE TO GREAT CHOPPED MEAT

▪ Select and purchase the cuts you want to grind. I've given you specifics for each type of meat (see "Types of Chopped Meat," page 72), as well as beef blends in "Pat's Favorite Blends" (opposite page).

▪ Cut the meat into long strips that will fit into your meat grinder (1 inch wide does the trick for most home grinders). You never want to cut the meat into chunks. The long strips enable the meat to be pulled through the grinder by the auger, which is basically a big screw; it grabs the meat and drags it, so you don't have to constantly push it through.

▪ Lay the meat in a single layer on a baking sheet and put it in the freezer to chill until it is stiff but still pliable and reaches the desired temperature, which varies depending on the type of meat. Chilling the meat ensures that it won't get pasty when it passes through the grinder. Use a meat thermometer to test the temperature of the meat before you pass the meat through the grinder.

▪ Fit the correct die onto your grinder; the size will vary depending on the recipe you are using. Most of our recipes call for two different sizes of die. Have both handy and clean. Some grinders come with only two dies, small and large. That's fine; just pass the meat through the larger die first and then the smaller.

▪ If your grinder has a speed setting, adjust it to the slowest setting. Slowing down the grinder speed prevents the meat from getting overchopped.

▪ Put as much meat as comfortably fits in the hopper and pass it through the grinder into a large bowl, making sure to keep the meat moving steadily through, and adding more meat to the hopper as there is room. If the meat passes through too slowly, the knife and plate will heat up and as a result "cook" the meat as it passes through. When the meat is moving through the grinder, its protein and fat act like a lubricant, keeping the blade and knife cool. Do not put those parts in the refrigerator or freezer before grinding meat. Chilling the parts will make them brittle, and a piece could break off and end up in your food. Passed through at a steady pace, the meat will regulate the temperature perfectly.

▪ After you've passed the meat through the grinder the first time, take the head off the grinder. There will be a scrap of meat that didn't get pushed through because there was no meat behind to push it. We call this "push meat." Take the push meat out and set it aside so it's there when you need it. (We put it on top of the grinder.)

▪ Change the die if the recipe you're using calls for you to do so and put the head back on the grinder and tighten it up.

▪ If you are adding spices to make sausages or our custom turkey burger blend (page 101), add them now and gently toss them in with the meat. Even if you are not adding spices or other ingredients, give the meat a gentle toss with your hands before adding it to the grinder.

▪ Add the meat to the hopper. You will need to push it through using a long stick called a "bat," "plunger," "pusher," or "stomper." Begin passing the meat through and adding more meat to the hopper as there is room. After you've added all the meat to the hopper, add the "push meat" to help push the meat through. The push meat never gets ground; it is sacrificed, but the idea is that you are only sacrificing one piece of meat instead of two. Your meat is now ready to use.

PAT'S GUIDE TO THE PERFECT BURGER

People often ask me, "What's your favorite burger in the city?" Even if I had one, I couldn't say. But the truth is, I like a lot of burgers in the city. It's not so much what's my favorite burger, as what I am in the mood for in that moment. If it's for a classic 8-ounce burger, I might go to Market Table or City Hall. If I want a smash burger, maybe I'll grab a double burger at Shake Shack. The aged-beef burger at Minetta Tavern is in a category by itself, and if I have a craving, nothing else will satisfy it. I sometimes go to The Spotted Pig, where I know I can get a burger cooked rare with a nice char on the outside, and I often go to Burger & Barrel for a lamb burger. There are so many good ones. I always think the better question would be: What makes a great burger? For me, a burger is the sum of its parts, starting with the meat and then the bun, and ending with how the patty is shaped and cooked. When all of these come together, you have hamburger perfection.

1. THE MEAT

To make a good burger, you must use good meat. Plain and simple. See "Types of Chopped Meat" (page 72) and "Pat's Favorite Blends" (page 74) for specifics.

2. THE SIZE OF THE PATTY

The right size patty ensures that you will be able to cook the patty to the proper internal temperature without killing the outside, and there is only one way to make sure you have the right size: Weigh it. If you do not weigh the meat for burger patties, you will end up with patties that are slightly (and sometimes not so slightly) different in size, which means they are all going to cook differently. For lamb and beef burgers, I like an 8-ounce patty, formed 1 inch high, which will give you a 4-inch diameter. For turkey burgers, I make a 6-ounce patty. When forming burger patties, after weighing the meat, roll the portions into balls, and gently pat them into patties. You want the meat to be loose so that as the fats liquefy, they run through the patty. Overworking the meat will also cause the integrity of the chopped pieces to break down; maintaining that integrity is what makes a great hamburger patty taste like chopped steak.

3. THE WAY IT'S COOKED

People have strong opinions when it comes to cooking burgers. I prefer cooking them on an open grill. I grew up grilling burgers and eating burgers that someone else had grilled. I like the flavor of any food that comes off a grill. People who like panfried burgers argue that it cooks in its own juices. But I don't want my meat to cook in its juices. Whatever juices are going to fall out of my burger, I want them to fall out.

4. THE TEMPERATURE IT'S COOKED TO

Whether you're cooking your burger in a skillet or on a grill, it's important that you cook it over high heat. You want to get a nice, charred crust on the outside without overcooking the inside (unless you're talking about a turkey burger, see Chophouse Turkey Provolone Burgers with Fennel-Shallot Marmalade, page 101). I like both beef and lamb burgers rare. To help me achieve this, I always use a meat thermometer. Letting the burger rest after cooking is also key as it allows the internal meat to cook from the external heat. This gives you a burger with a more even doneness. If you're cooking a lot of burgers, keep track of how long you're cooking them and write down the results. With time, you'll start to see exactly what it takes, using your equipment, to get the burger you want.

The following are the temperatures to which I recommend you take beef and lamb burgers, steaks, and chops. Take the meat off the grill when you hit the first number, then let the meat rest for 5 or 10 minutes, during which time the temperatures will rise 5°F, to get them to the desired doneness.

Rare: 120° to 125°F

Medium-rare: 125° to 130°F

Medium: 130° to 135°F

Medium-well: 135° to 140°F

Well: 140° to 145°F

5. THE BUN

As much as I'm a meat guy, I am also a bread guy. The bun is just as important, or at least *almost* as important, to a great burger. Here are my favorites. No matter what kind of buns I use, I like to toast them before I split them, so the outside is brown and crunchy and the inside is soft.

English muffin: A great, crispy burger bun. One thing I love about English muffins is how accessible they are. You are probably never more than a mile away from an English muffin.

Supermarket White: Many burger enthusiasts prefer this type of bun to artisanal buns because they see the bun as nothing but a vessel to hold the meat. A bun like this is so light and insubstantial that your mouth goes right through it, as if you were biting into cotton candy, and straight to the meat. With or without seeds of some sort. That's your call.

Big Marty's Sesame: The classic old-school burger bun with sesame seeds. It gives you the perfect meat-to-bun ratio for an 8-ounce burger. My only issue with Big Marty's is that the seeds aren't toasted. I fix that by toasting the buns (and seeds) under a broiler or on the grill until they're deep golden.

Martin's Potato Rolls: The ultimate soft burger bun. I love these for regular-size burgers—and I like their smaller counterpart (not pictured) for sliders. They're bright yellow, doughy, and sweet, almost like challah bread. You could toast them, but I also like them straight from the bag.

Brioche: The ideal buns. They're packed with butter, and so delicious. This is what Minetta Tavern serves its Black Label burger on (page 74). If you can get your hands on homemade brioche rolls, you don't need to look any further.

6. THE WAY IT'S DRESSED

What you put on your burger is matter of taste. I eat a lot of burgers, and I like a lot of the combinations my chef customers put together. But when I make them at home, I always dress them the same way—with sliced grape tomatoes, arugula, and a dollop of mayo.

Supermarket White

Big Marty's Sesame

English muffin

Brioche

Martin's Potato

SMASH BURGER

A smash burger is a burger where the patty is formed tall, or even round, and then smashed down while it's on a griddle. The idea is that while you're smashing the patty, you're also helping to get a nice char on the outside. A smash burger is typically made with a 4-ounce patty. I am an 8-ounce meat guy, so I always order doubles.

To make one double smash burger, form two (4-ounce) balls of chopped (ground) beef and season them all over with kosher salt and freshly ground black pepper. Put the balls in a very hot skillet or on a griddle. While they're cooking, smash the balls down with a spatula to ¾ inch thick. Have a Martin's Potato Roll handy. Cook the patties for about 3 minutes per side for medium-rare. Stack the patties on the bun, dress it however you like, and eat.

LaFRIEDA SIGNATURE SAUSAGES

There are many types of sausages, from just about every type of meat, including chicken, turkey, duck, veal, lamb, and, of course, pork. The three original Italian-style sausages that my grandfather made—sweet, hot, and provolone—are by far the most popular. People always rave about how good our sausages are. The reason is that we use whole muscle, not scraps, to make them. We use lots of good-quality spices. We don't skimp on anything, and the result is juicy sausages redolent with spices.

One of the advantages to making your own sausages, besides ensuring good ingredients and a tasty product, is you can be sure there are no chemicals, such as MSG (monosodium glutamate), nitrates, or nitrites in them, which a lot of commercial sausages have. MSG is used as a flavor enhancer, and nitrates and nitrites are used to help maintain the red color of the meat; but they're all terrible for you—you definitely don't need them in your sausage.

When you cook sausages, you never want to prick them first. If you prick holes, the fat will seep out through the holes and the result will be dry sausages. The casings have natural pores so they aren't going to explode. When you don't prick them, the meat simmers in the fat inside the casing, making them juicy and flavorful. My favorite way to cook sausages is on a grill, but you can also cook them in a hot skillet.

For detailed instructions on grinding the meat for these sausages, refer to the instructions in "Grind Your Own" (page 75), using the die sizes given in the individual sausage recipes.

Sausage casings can be purchased at many butcher shops as well as online sausage-making sources. They are sold in larger quantities than you will need for these recipes, but you can store them, packed in salt (which is how they are sold), refrigerated, for up to a year.

STUFFING SAUSAGES

To stuff sausages, transfer the sausage meat to a sausage stuffer, or a stand mixer fitted with a sausage stuffing attachment and a plastic stuffing tube. Put a baking sheet below the stuffing tube to catch the sausages as they are stuffed. Carefully slide the casing onto the stuffing tube. Leave about 3 inches of casing hanging off the end of the tube. Begin cranking the sausage meat into the casing, guiding the stuffed sausage with one hand to keep the meat moving evenly; the idea is to keep the meat moving consistently through the casing so the sausages are neither overstuffed nor understuffed. As the casing is stuffed, curl the sausage into a coil. When all the sausage has been stuffed, slide the remaining casing off the tube and tie a knot at both ends as close to the meat as possible. Twist the sausages several times to create links as specified in the individual recipes, alternating the direction you twist. Store the sausages in a resealable bag and cook them within 1 week of making them or freeze them for up to 3 months.

Sweet Italian Sausage

Hot Italian Sausage

Chicken Apple Sausage

Chorizo

Chorizo with Jalapeño

Provolone and Parsley Sausage

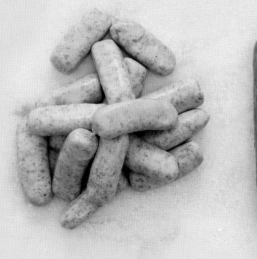

Breakfast Sausage

Cotechino

Merguez

GRANDPA'S ITALIAN-STYLE PORK SAUSAGE

2 tablespoons fennel seeds

3 tablespoons ground fennel

1 tablespoon fine sea salt

1 tablespoon freshly ground black pepper

1 tablespoon sugar

¼ teaspoon ground nutmeg

2 teaspoons crushed red pepper flakes (optional for hot sausages)

¼ teaspoon cayenne pepper (optional for hot sausages)

3 pounds pork butt, cut into 1-inch-wide strips and chilled to 26° to 28°F, or ground pork butt

Enough hog casings for 3 pounds of sausage, rinsed and patted dry

We have a lot of family pride in our sausages. Anytime we are gathered together to eat, there are sausages involved in the feast, and very often my father will tell a story about his sausages and his mother-in-law's sausage lasagna. My dad thought my mother's parents were always picking on him, and whatever he did was never good enough: He was just a butcher. "My mother-in-law, Marie, made a great lasagna with sausage," he says. "One Sunday we were going to my in-laws to eat and she was making this lasagna. I was really looking forward to having a big slice. But then, when I was eating the lasagna, I started feeling sicker by the minute. And I realized it was the sausage that was making me sick." My dad didn't say anything during dinner, but on the way home he told my mother about the sausage. My mom told my dad, "Now I gotcha!" She thought my dad was always picking on her parents unfairly. She revealed to my dad that the sausages were in fact *his* sausages. "I knew my mother was going to make lasagna for you," she said, "so I brought her five pounds of your sausages." My dad was really upset by this. "I kept my mouth shut," he said "but I worried about it the whole way home." Two weeks later we were at my grandparents' house again and my dad said to my grandmother, "Marie, that lasagna you made the last time was delicious. And those sausages! Where did you get those sausages?" My grandmother said, "Ha! I got you! Those weren't your sausages. I wouldn't cook those things! I went up to the avenue instead and bought some from the butcher!" My dad just looked at my mom and said, "See?" It goes to show that no matter what else they might have thought of him, my father knows his meat!

MAKES ABOUT 3 POUNDS/16 (4-INCH) LINKS

1. In a small skillet, toast the fennel seeds over high heat, shaking the pan to keep the seeds from burning, until they're fragrant, about 1 minute. Transfer the seeds to a bowl. Add the ground fennel, salt, pepper, sugar, and nutmeg, and stir to combine. If you are making hot sausages, add the red pepper flakes and cayenne to the mix.

2. If you are grinding your own, fit your meat grinder with a ½-inch die (or the larger of the two dies if you're using a grinder with only two sizes). Pass the meat through the grinder into a large bowl. Sprinkle the seasonings over the meat and toss the meat gently with your hands to distribute the seasonings. Pass the meat through the grinder a second time using the same die. If you're using preground meat, gently toss the meat with the seasonings. Cover the bowl and refrigerate the meat until you're ready to stuff the sausages. Stuff using instructions for "Stuffing Sausages" (page 80), twisting the links off every 4 inches.

CHICKEN APPLE SAUSAGE

2 pounds chicken thighs, cut into 1-inch-wide strips and chilled to 26° to 28°F, or ground dark meat chicken

2 small onions, minced

2 sweet apples (such as Golden Delicious), peeled and minced

2 tablespoons finely chopped fresh sage

2 tablespoons light or dark brown sugar

1½ teaspoons fine sea salt

1 teaspoon ground fennel

½ teaspoon freshly ground black pepper

Enough hog casings for 2½ pounds of sausage, rinsed and patted dry

Chicken apple is one of our biggest selling sausages. It's slightly sweet, it's great in a sausage sandwich, and it also makes a delicious breakfast sausage.

MAKES ABOUT 2½ POUNDS/10 (4-INCH) LINKS

If you are grinding your own, fit your meat grinder with a ½-inch die (or the larger of the two dies if using a grinder with only two sizes). Pass the meat through the grinder into a large bowl. Add the onions, apples, sage, brown sugar, salt, fennel, and pepper to the bowl with the chicken and toss gently with your hands to distribute the ingredients. Pass the meat through the grinder a second time using the same die. If you're using preground meat, gently toss the chicken with the onions, apples, and seasonings. Cover the bowl and refrigerate the meat until you're ready to stuff the sausages. Stuff using instructions for "Stuffing Sausages" (page 80), twisting the links off every 4 inches.

CHORIZO

3 pounds pork butt, cut into 1-inch-wide strips and chilled to 26° to 28°F, or ground pork butt

2 medium yellow onions, minced

½ cup plus 2 tablespoons white wine

¼ cup plus 1 tablespoon crushed red pepper flakes

1 tablespoon plus 2 teaspoons paprika

1 tablespoon plus 1 teaspoon fine sea salt

2½ teaspoons cayenne pepper

2 teaspoons garlic powder

1½ teaspoons dried oregano

1¼ teaspoons ground cinnamon

1 teaspoon ground cumin

Enough hog casings for 3½ pounds of sausage, rinsed and patted dry

Fresh chorizo is a very spicy, very flavorful Mexican sausage often cooked with potatoes as a taco filling, or scrambled with eggs; it's not to be confused with Spanish chorizo, which is a hard, cured sausage, similar to hard salami.

MAKES ABOUT 3½ POUNDS/14 (4-INCH) LINKS

If you are grinding your own, fit your meat grinder with a ½-inch die (or the larger of the two dies if you're using a grinder with only two sizes). Pass the meat through the grinder into a large bowl. Add the onions, wine, red pepper flakes, paprika, salt, cayenne, garlic powder, oregano, cinnamon, and cumin. Toss the meat gently with your hands to distribute the ingredients. Pass the meat through the grinder a second time using the same die. If you're using preground pork, gently toss the meat with the onions, wine, and seasonings. Cover the bowl and refrigerate the meat until you're ready to stuff the sausages. Stuff using instructions for "Stuffing Sausages" (page 80), twisting the links off every 4 inches.

CHORIZO WITH JALAPEÑO

Follow the recipe for regular chorizo but add 10 jalapeño peppers, seeded and minced (about 3 ounces) when you add the onions, wine, and spices.

PROVOLONE AND PARSLEY SAUSAGE

4 pounds pork butt, cut into 1-inch-wide strips and chilled to 26° to 28°F

1 cup grated aged provolone cheese (about 3 ounces)

½ cup grated Pecorino Romano cheese (about 2 ounces)

¼ cup plus 2 tablespoons finely chopped fresh flat-leaf parsley leaves

1 tablespoon plus 1 teaspoon garlic powder

1 tablespoon plus 1 teaspoon fine sea salt

1 tablespoon freshly ground black pepper

Enough sheep casings for 4 pounds of sausage, rinsed and patted dry

We make our cheese sausages in the Luganega style; they're about half the width of other pork sausages, and instead of being twisted into individual links, the sausage is made into a single two-pound length that coils up like a garden hose. We grind the meat finer than for other pork sausages because it is stuffed in a sheep casing, which is more delicate than hog casings. I cook a lot of different things with the sweet and hot pork sausages, but with this sausage, I always cook it the same way: on the grill. I like to put the whole coil on the grill because it looks nice and it's also convenient to cook it all as one. It's not difficult to flip as long as you have a long spatula to get under it; it's like flipping a big pancake.

MAKES ABOUT 4 POUNDS/2 (2-POUND) COILS

Fit your meat grinder with a ¼-inch die (or the larger of the two dies if you're using a grinder with only two sizes). Pass the meat through the grinder into a large bowl. Sprinkle the provolone, pecorino, parsley, garlic powder, salt, and pepper over the meat. Toss the meat gently with your hands to distribute the ingredients. Pass it through the grinder a second time using a ⁵⁄₃₂-inch die (or the smaller die if you're using a grinder with only two sizes). Cover the bowl and refrigerate the meat until you're ready to stuff the sausages. Stuff using instructions for "Stuffing Sausages" (page 80). When one coil weighs 2 pounds, tie it off and start a fresh coil.

BREAKFAST SAUSAGE

2 pounds pork butt, cut into 1-inch-wide strips and chilled to 26° to 28°F, or ground pork butt

2½ teaspoons ground sage

2 teaspoons fine sea salt

½ teaspoon freshly ground black pepper

½ teaspoon Aleppo pepper or ancho chile powder

¼ teaspoon dark brown sugar

⅛ teaspoon ground cloves

Enough hog or sheep casings for 2 pounds of sausage, rinsed and patted dry (if you are stuffing the sausages, not making patties)

Breakfast sausages should be ground more finely than Italian-style pork sausages because we want the sausages to feel lighter and more delicate. This recipe is for patties, but if you prefer to make them into links, stuff them into either hog or sheep casings using the method in Grandpa's Italian-Style Pork Sausages (page 82), twisting them off every three or four inches.

MAKES 2 POUNDS/8 PATTIES, 16 LARGE (4-INCH) LINKS, OR 24 SMALL (3-INCH) LINKS

1. To chill the meat most efficiently, place the meat in a single layer on a tray and in the freezer.

2. In a small bowl, combine the sage, salt, black pepper, Aleppo pepper, brown sugar, and cloves.

3. If you are grinding your own, fit your meat grinder with a ¼-inch die (or the larger of the two dies if you're using a grinder with only two sizes). Pass the meat through the grinder into a medium bowl. Sprinkle the seasonings over the meat and toss the meat gently with your hands to distribute the ingredients. Pass the meat through the grinder a second time using a 5/32-inch die (or the smaller die if you are using a grinder with only two sizes). If you're using preground pork, sprinkle the seasonings over the meat and toss gently to combine. Cover and refrigerate for at least 1 hour or until you're ready to shape the patties or make the links. (The patties will hold their shape better if you chill the meat first.)

4. For patties, divide the meat into eight (4-ounce) portions. Roll each portion into a ball and gently pat it into a patty about ¾ inch thick. For links, stuff the sausage into sheep casings, twisting them off to make either 3- or 4-inch links.

COTECHINO

2½ pounds pork butt, cut into
    1-inch-wide strips and chilled
    to 26° to 28°F, or ground pork
    butt

2 ounces grated Parmigiano-
    Reggiano cheese (about ½ cup)

2 cloves garlic, minced

1½ tablespoons fine sea salt

1 tablespoon freshly ground black
    pepper

2 teaspoons cayenne pepper

1 teaspoon ground nutmeg

1 teaspoon ground cinnamon

1 teaspoon ground cloves

Enough hog casings for 2½ pounds
    of sausage, rinsed and patted dry

Cotechino is a pork sausage from the north of Italy made with an unusual combination of Parmesan and spices, including cinnamon, nutmeg, and cloves. It is an Italian tradition to eat lentils with cotechino on New Year's Eve to bring prosperity in the year ahead. I'm not superstitious, but it couldn't hurt, and it sounds delicious.

MAKES 2 ½ POUNDS/10 (4-INCH) LINKS

If you are grinding your own, fit your meat grinder with a ½-inch die (or the larger of the two dies if you're using a grinder with only two sizes). Pass the meat through the grinder into a large bowl. Add the Parmesan, garlic, salt, black pepper, cayenne, nutmeg, cinnamon, and cloves. Toss the meat gently with your hands to distribute the ingredients. Pass the meat through the grinder a second time using the same die. If you're using preground pork, sprinkle with the Parmesan, garlic, and seasonings and toss gently to mix. Cover the bowl and refrigerate the meat until you're ready to stuff the sausages. Stuff using instructions for "Stuffing Sausages" (page 80), twisting the links off every 4 inches.

MERGUEZ

1½ teaspoons crushed red pepper flakes

1½ teaspoons cayenne pepper

1½ teaspoons fine sea salt

¾ teaspoon freshly ground black pepper

2 cloves garlic, smashed

½ teaspoon paprika

¼ teaspoon ground cumin

¼ teaspoon ground coriander

¼ teaspoon fennel seeds

¼ teaspoon ground fennel

2½ pounds lamb (two-thirds shoulder meat to one-third belly), cut into 1-inch-wide strips and chilled to 28° to 30°F, or ground lamb

¼ cup red wine

Enough sheep casings for 2½ pounds of sausage, rinsed and patted dry

Merguez is a spicy lamb sausage that is traditional in North Africa. I originally started making it for Alex Guarnaschelli, the chef and television personality and a close friend. What I love about merguez is that it has so much flavor on its own, you can use it to make a quick meal. Alex tosses the loose meat with fresh tomatoes and other ingredients to make a delicious pasta dish. If you're going to use it to make pasta or as a component to another dish, don't bother stuffing it.

MAKES 2½ POUNDS OR 1 LARGE COIL

1. In a small bowl, combine the red pepper flakes, cayenne, salt, black pepper, garlic, paprika, cumin, coriander, fennel seeds, and ground fennel and mix thoroughly.

2. If you are grinding your own, fit your meat grinder with a ½-inch die (or the larger of the two dies if you're using a grinder with only two sizes). Pass the meat through the grinder into a large bowl. Sprinkle the wine and seasonings over the meat and toss the meat gently with your hands to distribute the seasonings and incorporate the wine. Remove the die and replace it with a 5⁄32-inch die. Pass the meat through the grinder a second time. If you're using preground lamb, sprinkle it with the wine and seasonings and toss gently to mix. Cover the bowl and refrigerate the meat until you're ready to stuff the sausages. Stuff using instructions for "Stuffing Sausages" (page 80), making it into one coil rather than twisting off individual links.

SAUSAGE AND PEPPER HEROES

¼ cup extra-virgin olive oil

4 yellow, orange, or red bell peppers, thinly sliced

1 large yellow onion, thinly sliced

1½ teaspoons kosher salt

1 teaspoon light brown sugar

6 cloves garlic, thinly sliced

2 teaspoons dried oregano

2 pounds Grandpa's Italian-Style Pork Sausages (sweet or hot; page 82)

6 long crusty sandwich rolls, preferably semolina

If you grew up in New York City, you definitely have memories of eating sausage and pepper sandwiches at a street fair, the most famous being the Feast of San Gennaro, which takes place in Little Italy for eleven days every September. Not only did we go to San Gennaro, but my father had a cafe on Mulberry Street called Dixie Rose, so we also had a stand at the Feast. Sausage and pepper heroes were one of the things we looked forward to at the Feast, but we didn't have them only at San Gennaro. That's what we, and all the neighbors, grilled up in our backyards all summer long. A few times a year in Bensonhurst, Brooklyn, where I grew up, the city would shut down the street where we lived for block parties. One of our neighbors had a sprinkler attachment with holes drilled in it, so we would open up a hydrant, put that on, wait fifteen minutes until the water was no longer rusty, and then run through the sprinkler. This is not just in movies. This is what we did in Brooklyn, and what we ate was a sausage and pepper hero. It's an inexpensive Italian American comfort food that I serve on a regular basis in my backyard today.

MAKES 6 SANDWICHES

1. In a large skillet, heat the oil over medium heat until it slides easily in the pan, about 2 minutes. Add the bell peppers and onion, and season with the salt and brown sugar. Cook until the peppers and onion begin to soften and caramelize, but not so long that the onion becomes soft and mushy, about 10 minutes. Add the garlic and cook until it is light golden, about 5 minutes. Stir in the oregano and remove from the heat.

2. Preheat a grill to high heat. Put the sausages on the grill and cook, turning often, until they are cooked through, about 10 minutes. While the sausages are grilling, toast the bread so the outsides are crunchy and the insides soft. Put the sausage inside the rolls and pile the peppers and onion on top.

CRESCENT BREAKFAST SAUSAGE WITH PANETTONE FRENCH TOAST

1½ pounds Breakfast Sausage (page 86), formed into crescents

1 large (1½ pounds) loaf panettone (or pandoro), preferably star-shaped

12 large eggs

¾ cup heavy cream or whole milk

1 tablespoon vanilla extract

2 teaspoons ground cinnamon

½ teaspoon kosher salt

3 tablespoons unsalted butter, or as needed

Maple syrup for serving

My mother used panettone to make the most delicious French toast for us, and now I do the same for my kids. Panettone is a bread people give at Christmastime. It's slightly sweet and always stale so it makes the perfect French toast. Sometimes you can find panettone baked in a star-shaped loaf; when you cut it crosswise it gives you slices in the shape of stars (or look for pandoro, a similar Italian Christmas bread that always comes as a star). That, with our breakfast sausages and everything covered in maple syrup, is the best breakfast you'll ever eat. Note that if you're using a star-shaped loaf, the slices will be different sizes, as the cylinder is smaller at the top. Having different sizes is part of the fun of the presentation. Kids love the small stars. The sausage meat can be shaped any way you want. Here I made them into crescent-shaped moons to complement the stars.

SERVES 6

1. Preheat the oven to 200°F.

2. In a large skillet, cook the breakfast sausages over medium heat until they're browned and cooked through, about 3 minutes per side.

3. Lay the panettone loaf on its side and use a serrated knife to cut it into six 1-inch cross sections.

4. In a shallow baking dish, whisk the eggs, cream, vanilla, cinnamon, and salt. Heat 3 tablespoons of butter on a griddle or 2 tablespoons of butter in a large skillet over medium-high heat until it's bubbling and hot but not brown, about 2 minutes. One at a time, put the panettone slice in the egg mixture and let it sit for about 1 minute per side to absorb the egg. Lift the panettone out of the egg and into the skillet, being careful not to break it, and cook it until it's golden brown on each side, 2 to 3 minutes per side. (If you're using a griddle, you'll be able to cook more than one star at a time, but in a skillet, you'll need to cook one at a time.)

5. Transfer the French toast to a baking sheet and put it in the oven while you cook the remaining French toast, adding more butter to the griddle or skillet as necessary; add the French toast to the baking sheet as it's done.

6. Serve the French toast with a sausage crescent on top and maple syrup poured all over both.

FOUR-MEAT MEATLOAF

2 tablespoons extra-virgin olive oil

2 cups finely chopped yellow onion
(about 2 medium)

4 cloves garlic, minced

1½ cups shredded mozzarella
cheese (about 6 ounces; not
fresh mozzarella)

1 cup grated Pecorino Romano
cheese (about 4 ounces)

2 tablespoons finely chopped fresh
flat-leaf parsley leaves

1 pound chopped (ground) beef

1 pound chopped (ground) pork

1 pound chopped (ground) lamb

1 pound chopped (ground) veal

½ cup Italian-Style Breadcrumbs
(page 94; or store-bought)

4 teaspoons kosher salt

2 teaspoons freshly ground black
pepper

4 large eggs

2 teaspoons paprika

¾ cup Tomato Sauce (page 95; or
store-bought)

I t was with this meatloaf that I got my son, Patrick, to eat something other
than chicken tenders. My mother used to make it for me when I was his age.
The four different meats—veal, lamb, beef, and pork—are kept separate and
layered in the pan so when the meatloaf is cooked, it's like the meat version of
an Italian rainbow cookie. For years I struggled with what to do with the grease
that rendered from the meat as it cooked and that ended up in the bottom of my
meatloaf pan. When I asked my mother about this, she told me about something
called a perforated meatloaf pan. She bought one thirty years ago and has been
using the same one ever since. The perforated part rests inside the pan, leaving
space between it and the pan so the grease has a place to drip into when the
meatloaf is done, and you just lift out the perforated part and the grease stays
in the pan. It's brilliant. Use a 9 by 5-inch loaf pan, preferably perforated, to
make this.

MAKES 8 SERVINGS

1. Preheat the oven to 375°F.

2. In a skillet, heat the oil over medium heat until it slides easily in the pan, about
2 minutes. Add the onion and garlic and cook until the onion is tender and light
golden brown, about 15 minutes. Remove from the heat and set aside to cool to room
temperature.

3. In a medium bowl, combine the mozzarella, pecorino, and parsley.

4. Put each meat—the beef, pork, lamb, and veal—in a separate bowl. To each
bowl, add 2 tablespoons of the breadcrumbs, 1 teaspoon of the salt, ½ teaspoon
of the pepper, and 1 egg. Divide the onion and garlic evenly among the bowls. Add
1 teaspoon of paprika each to the bowls with the beef and lamb. Use your hands
to gently combine each meat with the other ingredients, working it just enough
to combine.

5. Put the beef into the loaf pan and pat it down with a rubber spatula to create
a flat, even surface. Sprinkle one-third of the parsley-cheese mixture over the
beef. Put the pork on top of the beef. Smooth it out in the same way you did the
beef and top it with another one-third of the parsley-cheese mixture. Repeat with
the lamb, topping it with the remaining parsley-cheese mixture, and finish with a
layer of the veal.

(continued)

6. Put the loaf pan on a baking sheet and bake the meatloaf for 1 hour. Remove the meatloaf from the oven and spoon the tomato sauce over the top, spreading it over the surface of the meatloaf. Return the meatloaf to the oven and bake until a meat thermometer inserted into the center registers 145°F, about 30 minutes.

7. Take the meatloaf out of the oven. If you are not using a perforated pan, using oven mitts, tilt the pan to drain off the excess fat. Let the meatloaf rest in the pan for at least 15 minutes. If you are using a perforated pan, remove the meatloaf to a cutting board and slice it. Otherwise, slice it in the pan.

ITALIAN-STYLE BREADCRUMBS

I know that many of my chef friends wouldn't approve, but I love packaged Italian-style breadcrumbs. They're just so easy and they taste great. If you take the time to make your own, they're definitely worth it. These are so delicious I can just eat them by themselves straight out of my hand.

To make 1 cup of Italian-style breadcrumbs, start with 1 cup finely ground fresh white breadcrumbs. Spread them out on a baking sheet and lightly toast in a 325°F oven until they are golden. Let them cool to room temperature, then mix the toasted breadcrumbs with 1 teaspoon kosher salt, 1 teaspoon finely chopped fresh flat-leaf parsley leaves, ½ teaspoon garlic powder, ½ teaspoon sugar, and ¼ teaspoon dried oregano.

TOMATO SAUCE

2 tablespoons extra-virgin olive oil

2 cups finely chopped yellow onion
(about 2 medium)

2 teaspoons kosher salt plus more
to taste

3 cloves garlic, minced

2 (28-ounce) cans of peeled
tomatoes (crushed or whole;
if whole, chop the tomatoes
and reserve the liquid)

1 medium carrot, peeled

2 tablespoons tomato paste

1 teaspoon dried oregano

½ teaspoon freshly ground
black pepper

Tomato sauce—also called "red sauce" or "gravy"—is a key building block to many of my family's recipes. It is to Italian Americans what veal stock is to the French. Although the sauces are very similar in Italian American households, every family's red sauce is a little bit different. To make tomato sauce, we start with canned peeled Roma tomatoes. That part everyone agrees on. But as to which tomatoes, that's where things get complicated, and everyone has an opinion. I've always been told by chefs to look for tomatoes labeled "San Marzano," which refers to a superior variety of tomato and also to the region in Italy where this tomato is grown. But things have gotten confusing lately because there is now a brand of tomatoes called San Marzano, which aren't San Marzano tomatoes at all; they come from San Marzano seeds, but they are actually grown on U.S. soil. The best way to decide what brand of tomatoes you want to use is to buy a few different brands and taste the tomatoes cold, straight from the can. Find the one you like best, buy a whole case, and you won't have to think about it again for awhile. I like to use crushed tomatoes. This recipe makes a big batch of sauce because you always want to have some left over. It tastes better the next day and the day after that. You'll notice we add a whole carrot and then take it out and toss it when the sauce is done. The carrot helps to take away any bitterness the tomatoes might have. I usually forget the carrot, but my mother is adamant about including it.

MAKES ABOUT 6 CUPS

In a large pot, heat the oil over medium heat until it slides easily in the pan, about 2 minutes. Add the onions, season with 2 teaspoons of salt, and cook, stirring often, until soft and caramelized, about 25 minutes. Add the garlic and cook until it is golden and fragrant, 3 to 4 minutes. Add the tomatoes (including their juice) and the carrot, reduce the heat, and cook the sauce over low heat, stirring occasionally, until you get your first bubble indicating a simmer; you're cooking over very low heat so this will be awhile—1½ to 2 hours; if it starts to bubble much sooner than that, the heat is too high. Stir in the tomato paste, oregano, and pepper, and cook the sauce for another 30 minutes. Remove the carrot and discard it. Add more salt to taste.

BILL'S BURGERS' DOUBLE BEEF SLIDERS

ONIONS

2 tablespoons extra-virgin olive oil

4 medium red onions, halved and thinly sliced into half-moons

½ teaspoon kosher salt

¼ teaspoon freshly ground black pepper

SLIDERS

2¼ pounds chopped (ground) beef

1½ teaspoons kosher salt

¼ teaspoon freshly ground black pepper

1 tablespoon canola or another neutral-flavored oil

12 slices American cheese

12 slider-size hamburger buns, such as Martin's Potato Rolls

4 tablespoons (½ stick) butter, melted

Ketchup

Mustard

48 dill pickle slices

T he most common mistake when making sliders is the ratio of meat to bread: the bun is too big and the patty is too small. Because the patties are so small, they are often overcooked. For me, a perfect slider has a three-ounce patty, where most sliders are made with about two ounces of meat. Bill's Bar & Burger serves great sliders. What Bill's does differently is that they make one long rectangular patty. They serve the sliders with three buns in a row, right next to each other, with one long patty lying on top. It looks like three separate sliders but you soon find out that you have to cut between each bun to divide the patty into separate sliders. This way you can cook them on the grill without them falling through the grates, and if you're cooking a bunch of sliders, you have fewer to flip. Their rectangular patty makes three 1½-ounce sliders—too small for me—so I always order mine double, with two patties (I'm going to get my three-ounce slider one way or another).

MAKES 12 DOUBLE SLIDERS/4 SERVINGS

1. For the onions: In a large skillet, heat the olive oil over medium-low heat until the oil slides easily in the pan, about 2 minutes. Add the onions and cook, stirring occasionally, until they are very soft, about 20 minutes. Season with the salt and pepper and continue cooking until they are deeply browned and caramelized but not burned, about 10 minutes. Remove the pan from the heat.

2. Preheat the broiler or preheat a grill for toasting the buns.

3. To make the sliders, divide the meat into eight (4½-ounce) portions. Form each portion into a rectangular patty about 5 x 2 inches and ½ inch thick. Season the patties on both sides with the salt and pepper.

4. On a griddle or in a large skillet, heat the canola oil over medium heat, about 2 minutes. Place the patties in the pan, making sure not to overcrowd it (you can fit 4 in a large skillet; more on a griddle), and cook for 1 minute without moving them so they crisp up on the outside. Flip the patties, lay 3 cheese slices across 4 of the patties, and cook the other side until crisp, about 1 minute more for a medium-rare slider.

5. While the sliders are cooking, break the buns into rows of three and lay them out so they're open. Brush the cut sides of the buns lightly with the melted butter and broil or grill to toast them lightly, 1 to 2 minutes. Keep an eye on them so that they don't burn. Spread the buns with ketchup and mustard and lay 3 or 4 pickle slices across the buns.

6. Take the plain (no cheese) slider patties out of the pan or off the grill and lay them on the buns and lay one cheese-topped slider patty on top of each plain patty. Top each set of sliders with about 3 tablespoons of the caramelized onions, put the tops of the buns on, and serve.

MACARONI PIE

1 pound sweet Grandpa's Italian-Style Pork Sausages (page 82; or store-bought)

Kosher salt, for the pasta water

1 pound spaghetti

6 large eggs

1 cup grated Pecorino Romano cheese (about 4 ounces)

½ teaspoon freshly ground black pepper

6 ounces sliced Genoa salami (about 24 slices), julienned

½ cup extra-virgin olive oil, or as needed

In my family we always say that you can get further with a few steaks and a kind word than with just a kind word. This is a philosophy that I definitely put to the test. When I was younger, I used my access to meat—the fact that I was known as the guy who could get you whatever kind of meat you wanted—as a bargaining commodity. I used it to get access to nightclubs in Manhattan when I was underage, to get out of speeding tickets, and to get permission from fathers to date their daughters. And at home, after school, sometimes I'd say, "Hey, Dad, can you give me some steaks? I'm going over to Norma Jean's to trade for a macaroni pie." Norma Jean was my best friend during high school. The pie is a mix of sautéed meats and spaghetti with just enough egg to bind it; it's panfried in olive oil so it gets golden and crispy on the outside. Norma Jean's mother, who was from Abruzzi, Italy, made hers with Genoa salami and pepperoni, but I substitute Italian sausage for the pepperoni. I've never seen anything like this dish except coming out of Norma Jean's mother's kitchen or my own, which is something, considering all the restaurants I've eaten in. If you are making your own sausage for this, note that you don't need to stuff it, as you'll be cooking the sausage meat loose.

SERVES 6 TO 8

1. Take the sausage out of the casings if it is stuffed and put the meat in a large skillet. Cook it over medium-high heat, breaking it up while it cooks, until it's cooked through, about 5 minutes. Remove the sausage from the heat, drain off the fat, and set the sausage aside to cool to room temperature.

2. Bring a large pot of water to a boil. Add salt (about 1 tablespoon per quart), then add the pasta and cook until it's not quite al dente, about 2 minutes less than the time given on the package. Drain and set the pasta aside to cool to room temperature.

3. In a large bowl, beat together the eggs, pecorino, and pepper. Stir in the salami. Add the cooled pasta and sausage and stir to combine. (If the pasta or sausage is still warm, the heat will cook the eggs in the bowl, which you don't want to do.)

4. In a large high-sided skillet, heat half of the oil over medium heat until it slides easily in the pan, about 2 minutes. Add the pasta mixture and spread it out evenly. Push down on the pasta with a dinner plate to encourage it to brown, and cook until the bottom is browned and crispy in places, about 6 minutes. To flip the pie, place the plate on top of the pasta and invert the pie out of the pan onto the plate. Add the remaining ¼ cup oil to the pan and slide the pie off the plate into the pan with the uncooked side down. Cook until the second side is browned, about 6 minutes. Slide the pie onto a plate and serve warm or at room temperature.

CARNE CRUDO

When I do cooking classes at Eataly, I always make *carne crudo,* or "raw meat." It's the most bare-bones version of steak tartare you can imagine, with only three ingredients: beef, olive oil, and salt. This is not so much a recipe as a technique, and a lesson in what ingredients to buy, given to us by Alex Pilas, the executive chef at Eataly. You can make the chopped beef by passing it through a grinder or you can chop it by hand. Make sure it is chilled. I prefer to use the less fatty "select" or "choice" grades when making crudo.

To make 4 servings of carne crudo, chill 14 ounces beef top round to 28° to 30°F and pass it twice through a ¼-inch die, or use a large chef's knife to chop the chilled meat into ⅛- to ¼-inch pieces. Drizzle the meat with ¼ cup high-quality olive oil and sprinkle it with 1 teaspoon Maldon or another flaky sea salt. Gently fold the meat over itself using a large spoon, until the oil and salt are mixed throughout, taking care not to mash the meat in the process. Serve immediately with crostini or crackers.

Chophouse Turkey Provolone Burgers with Fennel-Shallot Marmalade

PICKLED CUCUMBER STRIPS

¼ cup sugar

2 tablespoons sherry vinegar

1 teaspoon kosher salt

1 English cucumber, thinly sliced lengthwise on a mandoline

FENNEL-SHALLOT MARMALADE

½ cup sugar

½ cup champagne vinegar

2 medium shallots, finely chopped

1 small bulb fennel, minced (about 1 cup)

1 teaspoon kosher salt plus more to taste

TURKEY PROVOLONE BURGER BLEND (SEE NOTE)

2 pounds chopped (ground) turkey (half light meat, half dark meat)

6 ounces aged provolone cheese, grated (if you're grinding your own turkey blend, cut the cheese into 1-inch cubes)

1 tablespoon plus 1 teaspoon finely chopped fresh flat-leaf parsley leaves

1 teaspoon freshly ground black pepper

1 teaspoon garlic powder

1 teaspoon ground sage

6 burger buns, lightly toasted

The secret to this turkey burger is our custom turkey blend. We always sold straight-up ground turkey, but when we started to be known for our custom burger blends, I put this together, as restaurants known for great burgers wanted an alternative for customers who didn't eat red meat. Turkey doesn't have a lot of flavor, therefore, I grind the turkey with aged provolone and seasonings so it's more like a seasoned turkey sausage patty. Because poultry has to be cooked through, I make turkey burgers six ounces instead of my usual eight; any bigger and by the time you've got the inside to the right temperature, the outside would be burned.

MAKES 6 BURGERS

1. For the cucumbers: In a small saucepan, combine the sugar, vinegar, and salt and bring the liquid to a boil. Turn off the heat and let cool to room temperature. In a bowl, combine the cucumber strips and cooled liquid. Cover and refrigerate for at least several hours and up to a week.

2. For the marmalade: In a medium saucepan, combine the sugar and vinegar and heat over medium heat until the sugar dissolves, 2 to 3 minutes. Add the shallots and cook, stirring occasionally, until they are translucent, 10 to 12 minutes. Stir in the fennel and salt and cook, stirring occasionally, until the fennel and shallots are tender, about 20 minutes. Turn off the heat and let cool to room temperature. Add more salt to taste.

3. For the turkey burger blend: In a large bowl, combine the turkey, provolone, parsley, pepper, garlic powder, and sage. Gently mix the ingredients together with your fingertips, being careful not to smash the meat. Divide the meat into equal portions (about 6 ounces each) and refrigerate until you're ready to cook them.

4. To cook the burgers, preheat a grill, grill pan, or skillet over high heat. Place the patties on the grill, or two at a time in the grill pan or skillet, and cook them over medium-high heat until a meat thermometer registers 155°F, about 5 minutes per side.

5. To assemble the burgers, put the turkey patty on each bun. Spoon 1 heaping tablespoon of the marmalade on each burger and top with 2 cucumber strips.

NOTE: If you want to make the turkey provolone blend the way we do, first grind the meat (see "Types of Chopped Meat" page 72) using a ¼-inch die into a large bowl using the instructions in "Grind Your Own," page 75. Add the seasonings and cubes of provolone to the bowl with the ground turkey and toss gently to distribute the ingredients. Then pass the turkey through the grinder a second time using the same die size.

PORK MEATBALLS WITH TOASTED PIGNOLI AND GOLDEN RAISINS

⅔ cup pine nuts

2 pounds chopped (ground) pork

1⅓ cups golden raisins

1 cup Italian-Style Breadcrumbs
(page 94; or store-bought)

6 ounces grated Pecorino Romano
cheese (about 1¾ cups) or half
pecorino, half Parmigiano-
Reggiano cheese

3 ounces aged provolone cheese,
cut into ¼-inch cubes

⅔ cup finely chopped fresh flat-leaf
parsley leaves

3 large eggs, lightly beaten

4 cloves garlic, minced

2 teaspoons kosher salt

½ teaspoon freshly ground black
pepper

For these meatballs, I borrowed the idea of adding pignoli (pine nuts) and golden raisins from my grandfather's Pork Braciole (page 148). They're the best meatballs in the world. Traditionally, Italian meatballs are cooked in red sauce. If I happen to be making both these and red sauce at the same time, I might throw the meatballs into the sauce, but they don't need it. They're so flavorful that I like to bake them and eat them straight from the oven. They're always the first thing done when I'm cooking a big meal, so I snack on them. With leftovers, I make a sandwich with nothing but crusty bread, meatballs, and additional provolone.

MAKES ABOUT 3 DOZEN MEATBALLS

1. Preheat the oven to 350ºF. Line a baking sheet with parchment paper or foil.

2. In a medium skillet, toast the pine nuts over medium heat, shaking the pan often, until golden brown all over, 4 to 5 minutes. Transfer the pine nuts to a plate so they don't continue cooking, and set them aside to cool to room temperature.

3. Put the pork in a large bowl. Add the pine nuts, raisins, breadcrumbs, pecorino, provolone, parsley, eggs, garlic, salt, and pepper. Gently work the ingredients together with your fingertips. Don't overwork the meat or press it together, or your meatballs will be tough and heavy. Roll the meat into 36 balls (about 2½ ounces each, a little bigger than golf balls).

4. Lay the meatballs in a single layer on a baking sheet and bake them until they are cooked through, about 20 minutes. Let the meatballs cool slightly before removing them from the pan.

POULTRY

BUYING MY COUSIN MARK

My dad had a longstanding policy of not soliciting sales and not having sales-people. When I first came to work with him and suggested hiring a salesman, he said, "The problem with salesmen is that at the end of the week, you have to pay them." When I did need to go out and get new business, I put on a suit and tie and went around to restaurants to meet with chefs. Then I'd come back to the shop and cut the meat for their orders and pack it up, and in the morning, I'd hop in the van to make deliveries, pulling my hat down over my eyes, hoping nobody would recognize me as the guy who'd been there in a suit the day before. But as we began to get busier, I couldn't be everywhere at once. I needed help. I knew I wanted someone who would be not just an employee, but more like a partner. I wanted my cousin Mark.

Mark isn't my cousin by blood. The story with Mark is that his father worked in the meat industry until his untimely death, when Mark was four-teen years old. Mark was this young kid, hanging around the 14th Street Meat Market, who everyone tried to help. My family kind of adopted him, and my siblings and I all think of Mark as our cousin. To me, he's even closer than that—he is my brother. Mark and his mother, Helga, share all our holiday dinners. They're family. It's that simple.

Left to right: Pat Jr., Pat Sr., and Mark Pastore at Wyebrook Farms.

The reason I wanted Mark to come work with me is that he was and is my best friend. Also, like me, he'd been working in the business all his life, so he knew it inside and out. But the main reason I wanted Mark is that he is the best people-person I have ever met. He's funny. He's entertaining. And he gets along with everyone. He can walk into a room with twenty chefs—twenty personalities, all of them different, all of them creative types, some of them maybe a little difficult—and he'll walk out an hour later and all twenty want to hang out with him. He's a master with people. And the thing is, it's genuine. It's just who Mark is.

Mark had worked at a couple of meat establishments before coming to work with me, but at the time I got him he was working at a place that was heavily controlled by the mob. The meat business in New York has always had strong ties to the mob through its control of labor unions. Big Paul Castellano—onetime head of the Gambino family

who went down in the famous shoot-out in front of Sparks Steak House—owned Dial Poultry, a distribution center that supplied poultry to three hundred butchers in New York City. At one time the FBI asked Frank Perdue why he was meeting with the biggest mob guy in the country, Castellano, and Perdue said, "Because I need to get my chickens in supermarkets in New York and I can't do it without him." Mark didn't know that the company he was working for was mob-controlled until one day the FBI and the SEC raided the place. "Where there's smoke, there's fire," he said. So he left and came to work for me.

One day after Mark came to work with me, I got a visit from a few of the guys affiliated with Mark's old company. My dad was always very clear that our family would never be associated with the mob in any way. But being Italian American, and being located in the Village, we crossed paths with some of these guys, and became friendly with them, and occasionally they stopped by to say "hello," and kill some time. When we were located on Leroy Street, we were open through the night and our doors were always open, so we received all kinds of visitors. We were always very vulnerable; it's not like we were behind a buzzer and a camera. Anyone could come by, and on this particular night, a few of these mob-related guys came in. They made small talk with me, asked me how I was, and then one of them said as if he had just thought of it, "Hey, Pat. By the way. We're gonna need Mark back." Now that Mark knew the place was mob run, he didn't want to go back. I said, "Mark can't go back. Tell your guys we need him." And the guy said, "You know I can't tell them that." So I asked him, "What would it take for you to leave us alone?" The guy proposed a trade. "Why don't you just promise to buy a certain amount of meat from us every week?" I had already been having problems with poultry.

The company we had been working with for a long time, and that we were very happy with, Cooking Good, was bought by Perdue. Now that they were part of this big corporation, they'd changed their minimum order from eight pallets a day to sixteen pallets a day with each pallet containing two thousand pounds of poultry. That was far more than we could move in a day. I made a deal. I would buy three pallets of poultry a day from his pals in exchange for them leaving Mark alone. The company was obviously in trouble. I knew they wouldn't be around long and it would be a short-lived arrangement, and I was right. I got them off Mark's back, and I got Mark. The company closed three months later.

Mark has been with us for over ten years. He's now a partner in the business. He does an amazing job. Our customers absolutely love him. I can honestly say there is no way we would be where we are today without him.

THE GUY IN THE BLUE COAT

Right around the time the mobsters disappeared, we started getting bigger and bigger, and a few "jobbers" stopped by the Leroy Street location to pay me a visit. Jobbers are small-time guys in the meat business. They don't have brick-and-mortar operations. They work off the backs of their trucks. They go to meat companies such as mine, pick up product, mark it up a little bit, and deliver it. There were always jobbers, but now that the mob was gone, they started to get more territorial. One night some of these jobbers came to LaFrieda Meats. I was out front. My men were loading the trucks, and one of them came up to me and said, "Pat, you're taking too much of our business. One night there's gonna be an accident. The only reason it hasn't happened already is that there are too many guys in white coats walking around here. We'd have to shoot five or six of 'em before we got to the right guy." I'd recently lost my Aunt Lisa, who was like a second mother to me, to cancer. I'd just "bought" my cousin from some of the biggest mob guys this country has ever known. I was in the midst of transforming my grandfather's company in a huge way. I wasn't about to let some small-time wannabes in beat-up vans intimidate me. I said, "That's fine. You're not gonna have that problem. When the shooters come, tell them to look for the guy in the blue coat. That's the color I'll be wearing." The next day I ordered a stack of blue coats with "Pat Jr." embroidered on the front, just for me. To this day I'm the only butcher in my plant who wears a blue coat. In fact I'm the only butcher I know who wears a blue coat.

ALL ABOUT POULTRY

In recent years, heritage breeds of turkey and chicken have begun to appear at farmers' markets and specialty food stores. Unlike with pigs, with these birds, the heritage breeds do not translate into better flavor. Heritage birds contain very little breast meat, and the dark meat of the legs and thighs is often stringy and chewy. We occasionally get a chef who requests heritage breeds of chicken and turkey, but they go back to our all-natural, conventional breeds pretty quickly. When it comes to other forms of poultry, which includes everything from Cornish game hens to ducks to quail, very little has changed in the industry: The demand remains steady and so does the product.

BUYING POULTRY

When buying poultry, look only for USDA Grade A, which denotes birds that are plump, with clean skin that is free of blemishes, tears, and feathers. Poultry spoils faster than other meats, so use it within one or two days. I don't like freezing any meats, but I especially don't like freezing poultry because it has even more purge than other meats (see "Fresh vs. Frozen," page xviii).

COOKING POULTRY

The most difficult part of cooking poultry—especially larger birds such as turkey, chicken, and duck—is that the leg meat and breast meat cook so differently. More often than not, the breast becomes overcooked and dry before the legs are done. The obvious remedy for this is to cook the parts separately, as they are for Tuscan Fried Chicken with Lemon (page 122). A lot of people believe chicken should be rinsed under cold water before cooking to get rid of any salmonella or other bacteria that the bird might carry, but don't do this. The bacteria will be killed when you cook the bird.

ABOUT CHICKEN

Chickens are available in different sizes and ages; each has its own name, and is traditionally used differently. For specifics, see "Chicken and Other Birds" (page 110). In addition to knowing the size you want, look for Grade A, all-natural birds, raised free of cages, antibiotics, and hormones. The main difference when it comes to buying chicken does not have to do with flavor. I have done blind taste tests where I put inexpensive, supermarket birds against those with fancy claims about what they were fed. They all taste exactly the same; nobody could tell the difference. Make your decision instead based on how the birds were raised. You also want to smell chicken before buying it; it should not have any odor.

ABOUT TURKEY

Turkeys are native to North America: The Mayans and the Aztecs domesticated them. Although turkey is eaten in other countries, such as England, Israel, and China, turkey is not a part of those cuisines the way it is part of America's and Mexico's. Although the demand for turkey spikes in late November, it is steady all year long, as whole birds, boneless breasts, parts, chopped turkey, and our seasoned grind, which our customers use for burgers (see Chophouse Turkey Provolone Burger with Fennel-Shallot Marmalade, page 101). Seek out Grade A turkey and look for one that is all-natural. The ones we prefer are from a "never-ever" program, which means that neither those birds nor any in their lineage have ever had antibiotics or growth hormones, and they eat a vegetarian diet and roam free of cages. Most important, only buy those labeled "fresh," not "frozen." Fresh turkey guarantees that the bird has never been held at a temperature below 26°F, which the industry considers to be the safest temperature at which turkeys can be stored for extended periods of time. This confuses people because the freezing temperature of water is 32°F, but the definition of freezing when it comes to meat is minus 10°F. To add to the confusion, at 26°F, fresh turkeys feel almost rock solid, as if frozen. I often get calls from a chef after delivery, saying, "Pat, I ordered a fresh turkey; this is frozen." And I have to explain it to them. Turkeys that are considered "frozen" are kept at below 0°F. Turkeys are kept at a colder temperature than chicken because of shelf life; they don't move out of retail stores as fast as chickens. The industry wants the turkeys at the colder temperature to ensure they

don't spoil. "Self-basting" turkeys are injected with fluids (generally including broth, salt, sugar, and spices, which should all be identified on the label) to keep them moist during roasting. The maximum amount of solution allowed is about 3 percent and is included in the net weight of the turkey. If you want to go that route, look at the ingredients the basting fluids contain before purchasing such a turkey and avoid any that include chemicals or preservatives.

ABOUT DUCK

Duck farming began in the United States in the 1870s, when the Pekin duck was first introduced from Asia, where the Chinese had been domesticating ducks for as long as four thousand years. My favorite two breeds of ducks are: Pekin (sometimes labeled "Long Island duckling") and Muscovy, which come from two farms, one on Long Island, the other in Pennsylvania. The Muscovy are slightly leaner than Pekin ducks; both are delicious, with a lot of meat on them. Long Island ducks are the most common; you'll find them even at regular grocery stores. You will have to seek out Muscovy ducks at specialty food stores or online sources.

Duck meat is darker than that of the other poultry. Because of this, and because ducks can store a lot of fat (they were originally migratory and needed fat for fuel), duck meat has a rich, meaty taste and texture. While ducks have a reputation for being fatty, almost all of the fat is located under the skin rather than in the muscles, which are actually fairly lean. With a little patience and skill, duck fat can be rendered out during cooking, which allows the skin to get extremely crispy. As with all animals, the younger the bird, the more tender the meat. Ducks younger than six weeks of age, called broiler or fryer ducklings, weigh three to six pounds and have very tender meat. Roaster ducks are under sixteen weeks old, with meat that is still tender; they weigh five to eight pounds. Mature or old ducks are at least sixteen weeks old but typically older than six months; these birds, which are generally used for breeding, weigh six to ten pounds.

CHICKEN AND OTHER BIRDS

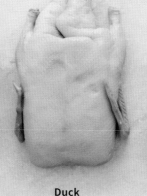
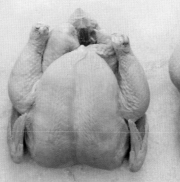

Turkey   Duck   Capon   Roaster   Stewing Hen

A whole **turkey** is synonymous with Thanksgiving, and it seems that every year people all over America are trying to figure out the best way to cook it. Deep-frying (see Christopher's Deep-Fried Turkey with Giblet Gravy, page 124) is without a doubt the best way I've found to cook turkey. Another key to moist turkey is that you don't buy anything over 14 pounds, otherwise the white meat will dry out before the legs are done.

If you're not up for cooking a whole bird, a boneless turkey breast, rolled and tied, makes a great roast. Brine it first, and leave the skin on while you cook it, as the skin prevents the breast from drying out in the oven.

A whole **duck** makes a magnificent roast. The most common variety, Pekin duck, weighs 5 to 6 pounds. Roasting a duck is a bit trickier than roasting a chicken because you have to render the fat from the skin, which is done by piercing the skin before it's cooked. Mom's Duck à l'Orange (page 126) is the most foolproof recipe I know for whole duck, and probably my favorite duck preparation.

The most desirable product made of duck or goose liver is foie gras. Sterile Moulard ducks, which are a cross between a female Pekin and a male Muscovy, are pasture-raised for about four months. Then for the next few weeks they are force-fed corn, or a mixture of corn and soy meal. This process results in an engorged liver that is extremely rich, silky, and slightly sweet when cooked. The full foie gras lobe is graded by letter: "A" denotes the firmest and most desirable foie gras, while Grade B is of lesser quality, with more veins and bruising, and Grade C is most often relegated to commercial mousse and sausages.

Capons are castrated male chickens between 2½ and 8 months old; they weigh 8 to 10 pounds and have very light-colored meat. They are castrated at a young age and fed a rich diet of milk and grains, which makes them fattier and more flavorful than chicken. Capons can be used in any recipe that calls for chicken.

Roasters, so named because they are the chicken used for roasting, are between 6 and 8 months old and weigh 4 to 9 pounds. They yield more meat per pound than broiler chickens so they're a good value, but they are not as tender. They're often used to make stock.

Stewing hens are hens that lay eggs. They are between 10 months and 1½ years old, and weigh from 4 to 7 pounds. Because of the animal's age, the meat is tough and stringy, so they are generally used for stewing, or to make stock or soup. While these are still sold to restaurants, they are uncommon these days on the retail level except in butcher shops and poultry shops. Today, home cooks more often use capons and broiler chickens to make stock and soup.

Broiler Chicken   **Pheasant**   **Guinea Hen**   **Cornish Hen**   **Poussin**   **Quail**

A **broiler chicken**, also called a fryer, is 6 to 10 weeks old and weighs 2½ to 4½ pounds. This is an all-purpose bird with a lot of white meat that can be used for frying (see Tuscan Fried Chicken with Lemon, page 122), barbecue, or basically any chicken dish.

A **pheasant**, a bird native to China, weighs about 2½ pounds. It has a gamey flavor and is very low in fat so it is important not to overcook it or it will dry out. Although people think of pheasants as game birds, those you see at retail are farm-raised. They are typically roasted, though they can also be braised. One bird feeds two people.

The **guinea hen** or guinea fowl weighs 2½ to 3 pounds, and is a relative of the chicken. Because they are not domesticated and therefore use all of their muscles, guinea hen is composed of dark meat. The meat is very lean, so guinea hen is often braised to keep the meat from getting stringy. It can also be roasted just like a chicken.

Although they're often called Cornish game hens, **Cornish hens**— 4 to 6 weeks old and weighing 1 to 2 pounds—are not game birds. And though they are called *hens,* they can be male or female. Sometimes called "Rock Cornish," they are a cross between the Cornish Game and Plymouth breeds of chicken, a hybrid that was developed in Connecticut in the 1950s to be a single-serving bird. Recently, some restaurants have begun using Cornish hen for fried chicken; that way they can serve the bird, in parts, which is a pretty cool idea.

A **poussin** is less than 28 days old and weighs between 14 and 16 ounces. It's also called a spring chicken.

After chicken and turkey, **quail**, which weigh about 6 ounces, are the most common bird Americans cook and eat. Quail are usually sold semi-boneless, meaning the wing and leg bones are intact, so they maintain the shape of a whole bird, but the breast and backbones have been removed so you can more easily pull apart the meat and eat the quail. You usually see quail grilled, often complemented with balsamic, served two on the plate as an entrée or one as an appetizer.

Butterflied Chicken

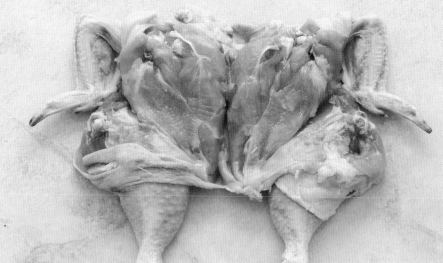

Frenched Breast

Boneless, Skin-on Breast

Boneless, Skinless Breast

Tender

Bone-in, Skin-on Thigh

Leg

Liver

Boneless, Skinless Thigh

Drumstick

Wing

Drumette

Wingette

Wing Tip

Lollipops

CHICKEN CUTS

A **butterflied chicken** is one in which the backbone and breastbone have been removed, so you can lay the chicken flat. It's a great way to prepare a chicken if you want to cook it on a grill.

A **frenched breast**, more commonly called an "airline breast," is a skin-on, boneless breast half with the drumette attached, though the meat has been cleaned off the drumette bone. It got its name because it was served by airlines back when they offered full in-flight meals. You rarely see them at retail. It's a restaurant cut, done purely for presentation.

The **boneless, skin-on breast** is made by removing the rib bones from a whole breast and cutting the breast in half. The skin, which is mostly fat, protects the meat while it cooks, so if you're going for flavor, this is the way to go. If you don't want to eat the skin, cook your chicken with the skin on and remove it before eating the chicken.

A **boneless, skinless breast**, made by removing the skin from half of a boneless breast, accounts for 90 percent of all chicken breasts sold. It is one of the least expensive proteins in the world. Where the demand for legs has steadily increased and the price of wings has tripled, the price of breasts has not changed, not even accounting for inflation, since I started working for my father in 1994. Because skinless breasts are so low in fat, they don't have much flavor, which means you have to bring flavor to them by marinating them or breading them.

Chicken **tenders**, which you may know as "chicken fingers," refer to strips of meat found under the breast. Prepared in the same manner as the cutlets, chicken tenders are both my son's and daughter's favorite meat.

The chicken **leg** includes both the drumstick and the thigh, the only dark meat on a chicken. Legs are sold with both pieces attached as well as separated.

The **bone-in, skin-on thigh** is my favorite piece of chicken, and it's also the favorite of chefs. It has a lot of flavor and is so moist that even cooked without the skin it's still moist and flavorful. Thighs are more forgiving than chicken breasts, which dry out if they're overcooked even by a little bit. Thighs used to be economical, but as demand has gone up, so has price.

Drumsticks consist of delicious dark meat, but there is not a lot of it; it's mostly tendons and bone.

Remove the femur bone and skin from a chicken thigh, and you've got a **boneless, skinless thigh**, which can be used in any recipe that calls for boneless breasts. You'll want to go by the weight of the meat not the number of pieces; the average boneless, skinless breast weighs 8 ounces where a boneless, skinless thigh weighs 3 ounces.

Chicken **liver** can dry out easily if it's overcooked, but otherwise, it has a rich, slightly sweet flavor. Chopped chicken liver is a mainstay at New York delicatessens, and chicken liver pâté, served on toast, has become a popular appetizer in recent years; I'm addicted to it. I'll take those toasts over tomato-topped bruschetta any day.

A lot of authorities say that chicken **wings** are technically white meat because they lack myoglobin (a protein found in animals that causes red pigmentation in its meat). But they cook and eat like dark meat, and that's all I care about. There are three sections to the wing: the drumette, wingette, and wing tip. When wings are offered segmented at the joint into wingettes and drumettes, they are often sold as "Buffalo wings" or "party wings."

The **drumette** is the section that attaches to the breast and looks like a miniature drumstick.

The **wingette** is shaped like a safety pin of bone with meat around it.

The **wing tip** is often trimmed from retail chicken wings. If you trim them from your wings or a whole chicken that you plan to roast, reserve them for making stock. There's no part of the chicken you should throw out.

Chicken **lollipops** are frenched chicken wingettes and drumettes with the meat pushed up to one end so that the end has a round cap of meat and the bare bone functions as the handle (see "Making Chicken Lollipops," page 116, and Josh Capon's Chicken Lollipops with Ancho Chile BBQ Sauce, page 120).

BUTCHERING TECHNIQUES
How to Cut a Chicken into six (or eight) Pieces

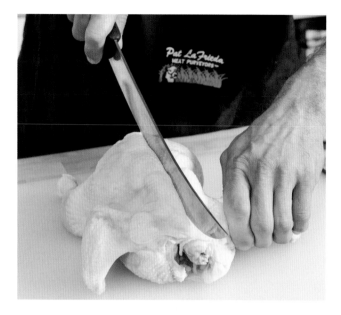

1. To cut a bird into serving pieces, first split your bird in half: Lay the chicken on its breast.

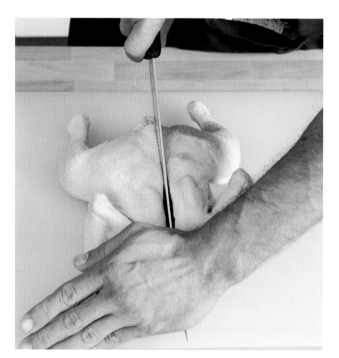

2. Using a large knife, rest your hand on the blade toward the front and push evenly on the front of the blade while you push down on the handle to break through the backbone.

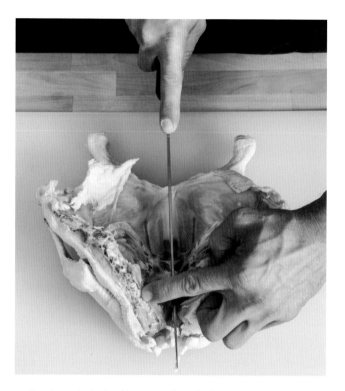

3. Cut through the backbone until you find the septum, which is in the center of the chicken and separates the two breasts.

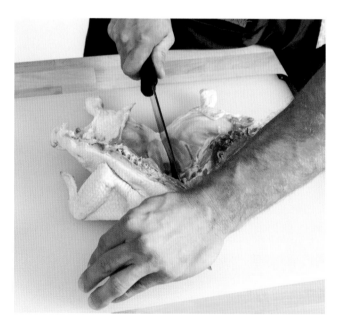

4. Once you have identified the septum, center the blade directly over it and split the septum in two. Put pressure on the front of the knife and cut right through the septum, then pull the knife back toward you to cut through any points that may still be intact.

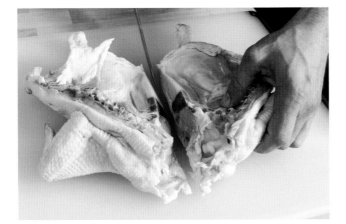

5. Now you have two half chickens.

7. To remove the wing from the breast, lay the breast down on the cutting board and pull the wing back to loosen the joint. Use your knife to cut right through the bone to remove the wing. At this point, you have butchered a chicken into six pieces.

6. To cut the chicken into six pieces, pick up one half and position it so the leg bone is pointing toward your body. Identify where the breast meets the leg and use a large knife to cut gently through the skin to reveal the joint. Make sure to cut the skin closer to the leg side so that the white meat is protected with more skin.

8. To cut the bird into eight pieces, with your large knife, press down on the "V" where the drumstick attaches to the thigh; you'll feel the cartilage—continue to push down and cut right through that.

9. Final Product

Making Chicken Lollipops

Chicken lollipops are chicken wing drumettes and wingettes with the bones frenched, and all the meat pushed to one end of the bone, so they look like lollipops. They are a fun presentation; kids and grown-ups love them. What I like about this technique is that you take two different pieces of chicken and make them into something that looks just the same. Nobody besides you and a butcher would ever know they were two different joints.

1. The whole wing.

3. Cut the wings into drumettes and wingettes by cutting them at the joint.

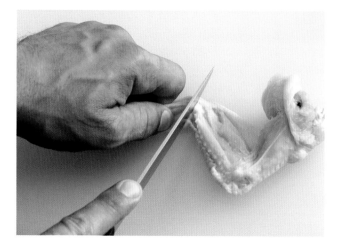

2. Use a boning knife to cut off the wing tip and discard it. If you're starting with wingettes and drumettes, skip ahead to photo 3.

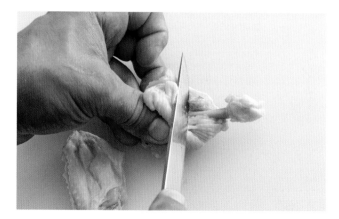

4. Start with the drumettes (the part that was attached to the bird): Put a drumette on your cutting board and, with the boning knife perpendicular to the bone, starting at the end that was attached to the wingette, cut through the meat and connective tissue until you reach the bone, turning the drumette as you cut it in order to release the meat and tissue all around the bone.

5. Use the knife to push the meat from one end of the bone to the other so the meat is all bunched up like a lollipop.

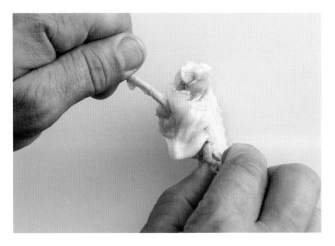

7. Pull one of the bones (it makes no difference which of the two bones) out of the wingette.

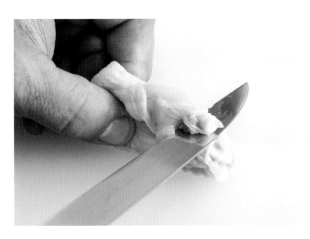

6. Next, do the wingettes (the part that was attached to the wing tip): Each wingette has two bones fused together by cartilage at the end of the wingette. First, with the knife parallel to the bones, start cutting through the cartilage at both ends to separate the bones.

8. Use the knife to push the meat to the end of the remaining bone.

8. The lollipopped wingete, drumette, and the wing tip.

CARVING A TURKEY

The most important part about serving a whole turkey is carving it correctly. The reason people get in trouble with this is that they use the wrong knife. They tend to reach for their chef's knife, because it's big. You want to use an 8½-inch boning knife for everything I'm showing you here, except slicing the breast once it's removed from the carcass. For that, you can use your chef's knife. Serve the turkey on a big platter, with one whole breast, the other breast sliced and fanned out, and the parts all around it.

1. Lay the turkey breast side up. Pull one wing away from the body and cut it off the turkey where it meets the breast. Do the same on the other side.

3. Find the sternum with your knife and, starting at the leg end, run the knife along the breastbone from one end of the bird to the other.

2. Put your knife between the femur and hip joints (where the thigh meets the body) and cut the joint but not all the way through; you don't want to remove the leg. Repeat with the second leg.

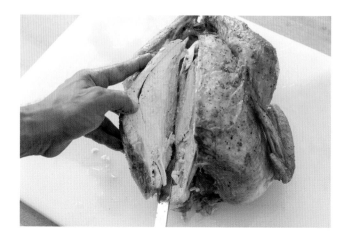

4. Slide the knife down the side of the rib cage to free the breast from the rib bones.

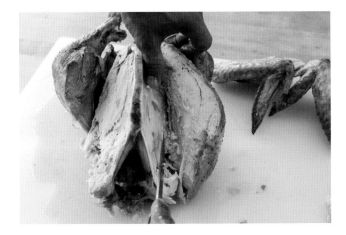

5. Remove the breast in one whole lobe and set it aside. Repeat, removing the other breast in the same way.

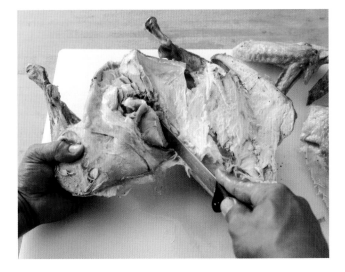

6. Now all you have left on the carcass are legs. (You leave them on until now because they keep the turkey balanced while you carve off the breasts.) Pull down on one leg, put your knife between the femur and hip, and cut right through the joint to remove the leg. Remove the other leg in the same way.

7. Find the "oysters" on the carcass; the oyster is a delicious dark meat muscle on the back. There are two of them on each bird, located on the back, on each side of the spine between the spine and the femur socket. Carefully carve underneath the oysters and gently scoop each one out with your knife.

8. The turkey deconstructed.

JOSH CAPON'S CHICKEN LOLLIPOPS WITH ANCHO CHILE BBQ SAUCE

BBQ SAUCE

5 dried chipotle chiles

1 dried ancho chile

⅓ cup sugar

4 cloves garlic, coarsely chopped

⅓ cup fresh lemon juice

⅓ cup fresh orange juice

¼ cup fresh lime juice (about 5 limes)

1 tablespoon *nam pla* (Asian fish sauce)

DIPPING SAUCE

1 cup buttermilk

8 ounces blue cheese

4 ounces cream cheese

1½ teaspoons fresh lemon juice

1½ teaspoons malt vinegar

1 teaspoon kosher salt

¼ teaspoon freshly ground black pepper

A dash of hot sauce

1 medium shallot, minced

1 clove garlic, minced

Finely chopped fresh parsley leaves

CHICKEN

1 quart vegetable oil for deep-frying

24 chicken lollipops, about 4½ pounds

1½ tablespoons kosher salt

½ teaspoon freshly ground black pepper

¾ cup all-purpose flour for dusting

Black and white sesame seeds (optional)

I am always trying unusual cuts to present to chefs. Josh Capon was the first to use these chicken lollipops. At his restaurant, Burger & Barrel, he makes wings two ways—with a classic Buffalo wing sauce and with this sweet and spicy barbecue sauce.

MAKES 24 LOLLIPOPS/6 OR MORE SERVINGS

1. For the BBQ sauce: Wipe the chipotle and ancho chiles clean with a paper towel. Tear the chiles open and remove and discard the seeds and stems. Toast the chiles in a skillet over medium heat, turning them once, for about 1 minute per side until they are fragrant. Take the chiles out of the pan so they don't keep cooking; if you overtoast them, they will get bitter.

2. In a medium heavy-bottomed skillet, combine the sugar and just enough water (about 1 teaspoon) so it's the consistency of wet sand. Cook the sugar over medium heat without stirring it, until it is light golden brown, about 8 minutes. Stir in the garlic and cook until the sugar is deep golden brown, 3 to 4 minutes more. Add the ancho and chipotle chiles, the lemon juice, orange juice, and lime juice and stir to combine. Increase the heat to high and bring the liquid to a boil. Reduce the heat and simmer until the liquid has reduced by half, about 12 minutes. Remove from the heat and stir in the *nam pla*. Set the sauce aside to cool to room temperature, then transfer to a blender or food processor and puree until smooth, about 30 seconds.

3. For the dipping sauce: In a blender, combine the buttermilk, blue cheese, cream cheese (at room temperature), lemon juice, vinegar, salt, pepper, and hot sauce and puree until smooth. Add the shallot and garlic and pulse just to combine. Turn the sauce out into a bowl and refrigerate until you're ready to serve it. Sprinkle with parsley before serving.

4. For the chicken: Fill a large saucepan 4 inches deep with oil, fasten a deep-fry thermometer to the side of the pan, and heat the oil over high heat to 350°F.

5. Preheat the oven to 200°F. Line a baking sheet or ovenproof plate with paper towels.

6. Season the chicken lollipops with the salt and pepper and dust them lightly with flour. Carefully drop half of the chicken wings into the oil and fry until they are golden brown and cooked through, 8 to 10 minutes (longer if the wings are very large). Remove the lollipops from the oil, transfer to the lined baking sheet, and place them in the oven to stay warm while you cook the remaining lollipops. When all the wings are done, put them in a large bowl, pour ¾ cup of the sauce over them, and toss to coat the wings with the sauce. Sprinkle sesame seeds over the wings if you are using them. Serve the wings with the dipping sauce, carrot sticks, and celery sticks on the side.

TUSCAN FRIED CHICKEN WITH LEMON

2 whole broiler chickens (about 3 pounds each), cut into 8 pieces each; see "How to Cut a Chicken into Six (or Eight) Pieces," page 114

2 tablespoons kosher salt plus more for seasoning

½ teaspoon freshly ground black pepper plus more for seasoning

¼ cup plus 2 tablespoons fresh lemon juice plus more for seasoning

2 quarts vegetable oil, or as needed

1 cup all-purpose flour

4 large eggs

6 sprigs fresh thyme

6 sprigs fresh sage

6 sprigs fresh rosemary

6 cloves garlic, crushed

I first ate this fried chicken at Cesare Casella's now-closed restaurant, Beppe. Cesare is a wonderful Italian chef who now has Salumeria Rosi on the Upper West Side and Upper East Side of Manhattan. His signature is a bunch of fresh rosemary sprigs that he always has in his left pocket. When he had Beppe, all of New York was talking about how great his beans were. Those beans were delicious, but this fried chicken with lemon and rosemary is my favorite Cesare dish; it's the best I've eaten in all my restaurant travels. What makes it unusual is that where American fried chicken is dredged in flour, then egg, then flour again (or breadcrumbs), this version does not have an outer coating of flour or breadcrumbs. The crunchy exterior is simply the fried chicken skin coated in an egg wash. The result is fried chicken perfection.

MAKES 4 SERVINGS

1. Lay the chicken pieces out on a baking sheet and season with the salt and pepper and the lemon juice. Cover the chicken with plastic wrap and set aside to marinate at room temperature for 1 hour.

2. Preheat the oven to 200°F. Put a wire cooling rack inside a rimmed baking sheet.

3. Pour enough oil into a large pot or Dutch oven to come up 2 inches. Fasten a deep-fry thermometer to the side of the pan and heat the oil over high heat to 375°F.

4. Place the flour in a medium bowl. Beat the eggs in another medium bowl. Dredge the chicken in the flour, dip it into the beaten eggs, and carefully slide it into the hot oil, starting with the larger pieces, and making sure not to crowd the pot. Fry the chicken until it is golden brown and crunchy, 15 to 20 minutes, flipping the chicken halfway through the cooking time using tongs; keep the temperature of the oil between 325° and 350°F (the oil temperature will drop when you add the chicken). Remove the chicken as it is done to the rack in the baking sheet to drain. Season the chicken liberally with salt and pepper, squeeze the lemon juice over it, and put it in the oven to keep warm. Add more chicken to the pot as there is room and fry it and season it in the same way.

5. After you've fried all the chicken, add the thyme, sage, rosemary, and garlic to the oil and fry them until they're crisp, about 10 seconds. Remove the chicken from the oven, scatter the garlic and herbs over the chicken and serve.

CHRISTOPHER'S DEEP-FRIED TURKEY WITH GIBLET GRAVY

1 gallon boiling water

1 cup packed light or dark brown
    sugar

1 cup kosher salt

1 whole turkey (12 to 14 pounds)

3 gallons vegetable oil, or as needed

SAFETY TIPS
FROM CHRIS

1. Use an electric fryer. It is much safer than a propane fryer, because there's no chance of the flame from the fryer igniting the oil, since there is no flame.

2. Always take care with hot oil. Don't overfill the fryer with oil, and use gloves.

3. Never put a frozen (or partially frozen) turkey in a fryer.

For the last several years, we have been deep frying our turkeys for Thanksgiving. Deep-frying turkey can be messy, but it makes for the best whole turkey I've ever tasted—the white meat is moist, the dark meat is flavorful and the skin is crisp and beautifully browned. The other reason I like deep-fried turkey is that I send my brother Christopher outside to do the frying, and I just get to eat it without doing any of the work.

SERVES 8 TO 10

1. In a large container, combine the boiling water, brown sugar, and salt and stir to dissolve the sugar and salt. Add 1 gallon of cold water and let the brine cool to room temperature.

2. Remove the neck and giblets (the liver, heart, and gizzard); use poultry shears to snip off the wing tips at the outermost joint and reserve them for making giblet gravy. Immerse the turkey in the brine and refrigerate it for 24 hours or overnight. Remove the bird from the brine, rinse it off, and pat it dry.

3. Fill a turkey fryer halfway with oil and heat the oil until it reaches 350°F. Gently lower the turkey into the oil and fry it for about 45 minutes, until it reaches an internal temperature of 155°F (the temperature will rise to the USDA-recommended 165°F while the turkey rests); do not let the oil get above 350°F. Remove the turkey from the oil, tent it with foil, and let it rest for 20 to 30 minutes before carving it.

4. Carve the turkey using the instructions in "Carving a Turkey" (page 118). Serve with giblet gravy.

GIBLET GRAVY

1 tablespoon canola oil

Turkey neck, gizzard, heart, and
    wing tips

3 tablespoons all-purpose flour

4 cups low-sodium chicken stock,
    or as needed

3 sprigs fresh thyme

¾ teaspoon kosher salt plus more
    to taste

MAKES ABOUT 2 CUPS

In a medium saucepan, heat the oil over medium heat, about 2 minutes. Add the neck, gizzard, heart, and wing tips and cook until they're browned, 5 to 6 minutes per side. Sprinkle with the flour and stir to coat the pieces. Add the stock and thyme and bring the liquid to a boil. Reduce the heat and simmer, uncovered, until the stock has reduced by half and is thick enough to coat the back of a spoon, about 45 minutes. Pour the gravy through a fine-mesh strainer and discard the solids. Return the gravy to the saucepan and stir in the salt. Serve warm.

FOIE GRAS MOUSSE

1 pound foie gras, cleaned of veins
if necessary

2 tablespoons plus 2 teaspoons
cognac

2 tablespoons plus 2 teaspoons
heavy cream

¾ teaspoon kosher salt

¼ teaspoon freshly ground black
pepper

¾ ounce black truffles, finely
chopped (optional)

Toast points for serving

This recipe is from Il Mulino; they use it to stuff the Veal Rib Chops Valdostana (page 23). You can also serve it on its own with toast points.

MAKES 4 CUPS

In a food processor, combine the foie gras and cognac and puree it until the foie gras is smooth, about 2 minutes. Add the cream, salt, and pepper and puree until the mixture has a smooth mousse-like consistency, about 1 minute. Scrape the mousse into a bowl, and gently fold in the truffles, if using. Serve at room temperature.

MOM'S DUCK À L'ORANGE

3 cans (12 ounces each) frozen orange juice concentrate

1 whole duck (5 to 6 pounds)

2 teaspoons kosher salt

½ teaspoon freshly ground black pepper

½ teaspoon ground ginger

2 tablespoons sugar

2 tablespoons apple cider vinegar

2 tablespoons cornstarch

Grated zest of 2 oranges (about 2 tablespoons)

1 orange, peeled and separated into segments

My mother made this duck, which is an adaptation of a recipe from her grandmother, my French great-grandmother, Marie Louise Villien. My great-grandmother met and married my great-grandfather, Carlo Galvagni, in Italy and immigrated to the United States by way of Canada. For their three children this duck was considered a delicacy, reserved for special occasions. But since my mother married a butcher, she made it whenever my dad had ducks at the shop that were going to go bad if they weren't cooked very soon. I think sometimes my dad brought them home, even when they were salable, because he loved this dish.

SERVES 4

1. Pour 2½ cans of the orange juice concentrate into a saucepan just big enough to hold the duck, reserving the remaining ½ can to make the glaze. Add 6 orange juice cans of water to the pan and bring it to a boil over high heat. Immerse the duck in the liquid and reduce the heat to low. Simmer the duck for 45 minutes, turning it a few times so it cooks evenly.

2. Preheat the oven to 350°F.

3. Take the duck out of the liquid. Measure 2½ cups of the broth and skim the fat off the top (discard the remaining broth). Pat the duck dry and rub it with the salt, pepper, and ginger. Place the duck breast side up in a roasting pan with a rack and put it in the oven to roast until a meat thermometer inserted into the thickest part of the leg registers 155°F and the leg easily pulls away from the body, 1 to 1¼ hours. If it is already deeply browned before it is done, reduce the oven temperature to 325°F.

4. In a small saucepan, combine the sugar and vinegar and cook over medium heat until the sugar is caramel colored, about 2 minutes. Stir in the reserved duck broth. In a small bowl, whisk the remaining ½ can orange juice concentrate and the cornstarch. Add the mixture to the pan and bring the sauce to a boil over high heat. Reduce to a simmer and cook, stirring constantly, until it is just thick enough to coat the back of a spoon, 1 to 2 minutes. Turn off the heat and stir in the orange zest and segments.

5. Remove the duck from the oven and let it rest for 10 minutes before carving it.

6. To carve the duck, lay it breast side down on a cutting board. Using a boning knife, cut along both sides of the backbone and pull the backbone out. Turn the duck so it is breast side up, and with your knife parallel to the breastbone, cut the breasts (with legs attached) off the rib cage and put them on the cutting board. Cut through the hip joint to remove the leg from each breast. Cut through the joint to separate the drumstick and thigh. Thinly slice the breast meat. Lay the duck slices on a platter with the drumsticks and thighs around it. Spoon about ½ cup of the sauce over the duck and serve the rest of the sauce on the side.

PORK

THE PLIGHT OF PIGS

LaFrieda Meats has always supported small farms. Our family business started out very small so we can understand many of their struggles and challenges. Therefore, when we can, we give them our business. Small farms are also very important to us because they are willing to raise animals in a way that brings better quality—not just lower cost—to the market. Sometimes these family farms are the only source of something we want, and nowhere is that more evident than when it comes to heritage breeds of pigs.

Heritage breeds are traditional livestock breeds. Although there is no official certification for "heritage," the widely accepted understanding is that in order for an animal to be labeled as "heritage," it needs to have a unique genetic makeup (not crossed with other breeds), and to be raised on organic or sustainable farms. There are many different varieties of heritage pigs, such as Berkshire (also called Kurobuta), Duroc, Yorkshire, Hampshire, Choctaw, Large Black, Mangalitsa, Tamworth, Ossabaw Island, and Red Wattle. Each of these has different qualities, but the one thing they have in common is that they contain a lot of fat, in the form of both a fat cap and marbling, which translates into tender, moist, and flavorful meat.

The demand for these breeds is something that sprang up fairly recently. When I was a kid working with my dad, nobody talked about how pigs were raised, what they ate, or the breed. What they talked about, if anything, was pork's fat content. Pork had a reputation as being a fatty, decadent choice. Then, in 1987, the National Pork Board started a campaign, "The Other White Meat," to combat this reputation and position pork as a tasty low-fat alternative to chicken and other healthy proteins; it became one of the most successful campaign slogans of all time. The meat business, I always say, is a perfect example of capitalism at work. If there's a demand, the industry meets it. Therefore during that time, pork growers began raising hogs that were low in fat. By breeding the leanest genetics together, they were able to reduce the fat content by as much as 30 percent, and in the end, a pork tenderloin, the kind you would purchase in any grocery store or butcher shop today, has less fat than a skinless chicken breast. Pork farmers began breeding species that mature quickly and have a high meat yield, or are able to gain weight within a confined facility. In the United States, three breeds of pigs account for 75 percent of the pigs raised. No matter how you looked at it, when it came to industrially raised pork, flavor was not the priority. But while the marbling was being bred out of this "commodity" pork, heritage pigs were being left alone, and their meat, richly marbled, is among the most flavorful meat there is.

I'm in the business of giving chefs what it takes to make spectacular meals for their customers. For me, a hog that is bred to be low-fat is not a good thing. I needed to find another option. The customer who made the most noise about getting better pork was Jeff Butler; he was then the chef at Mario Batali's trattoria, Lupa, in Greenwich Village. Jeff was really trying to do something special at Lupa, to get noticed, and one of the things he insisted on was juicy, flavorful pork, which he was using to make one of Lupa's specialties, pork saltimbocca. To give Jeff what he wanted, we first had to find a farmer who raised heritage breeds. Once we did that, we had to find someone who was able to supply us in the quantities we needed on a regular basis. It was very challenging.

Meanwhile, Patrick Martins, through his company Heritage Foods, had started to supply Lupa and some other restaurants in the city with breed-specific heritage pork. But Patrick was having his own challenges. Doing business on the island of Manhattan, and in particular making deliveries in Manhattan, was and still is an enormous, almost insurmountable, challenge. Patrick was renting trucks and driving around town making deliveries by himself. It took him all day, and by the end of the day, he had seven or eight parking tickets lined up on his windshield. Each one of those costs $125—minimum. We typically spend $100,000 a year on parking tickets. And there are companies that spend five times that. At that time for Patrick, $1,000 a day in parking tickets was enough to put him out of business pretty quickly. And then there was the question of the trucks. Since he didn't have a truck, he was delivering in a U-Haul and risked delivering meat to restaurants that was above the temperature that the health department requires. Meat has to be below 42°F to pass health inspections (we keep it below 40°F to be on the safe side), which means that if Patrick made a delivery to a restaurant and the health department happened to be there before the meat got down to an acceptable temperature, that restaurant, not Patrick, would be penalized. Restaurants at the level Patrick was working with could not afford to take this kind of risk. A few years after Jeff Butler had started making those first requests at Lupa, Mario called me and said, "Pat, maybe you can help this guy out . . ." I met with Patrick, he told me about what he was doing and the problems he was having, and we decided to work together. Today, LaFrieda Meats provides the infrastructure that Patrick needed. And he now does what he's always done and is great at it: He finds the pigs and sells the pigs to restaurants. The heritage pork is delivered to LaFrieda Meats. We separate, pack, and deliver it.

Because of this effort, the farms that Patrick supports are able to get their product to the consumer, and in some instances, stay in business. But the big winner is the consumer. People in New York have access to a really special product they might otherwise never have had the opportunity to try.

ALL ABOUT PORK

Pork is the most widely eaten meat in the world, especially in America. It is thought to be the first animal that was domesticated, around 5000 BC. This probably has to do with the fact that pigs can eat anything. Bacon, which is made from pork belly, is a predictable staple on America's breakfast table. Before refrigeration, salt pork was a regular part of America's larder, and you still see it in traditional American recipes, especially in the South. Although pork became less popular for a while because of its reputation as a fatty, unhealthy meat, that is changing. The demand for flavorful, higher fat pork started with chefs, but it has since trickled down to the consumer.

BUYING PORK

While the USDA has eight grades for beef, there are only two for pork: "acceptable," which is sold as raw meat to consumers, and "utility," which is reserved for prepackaged products such as commercial sausages, canned hams, and other canned meats.

There are two basic types of fresh pork on the market. The first is "commodity pork," which you'd find in a grocery store. To meet consumer demand, the fat has been bred out of this pork, which tends to be dry and not particularly flavorful. Many stores sell all-natural pork, which is commodity pork with those claims. It might be healthier than one that is not all natural, but it won't be any moister or more flavorful. The second type of pork is from heritage breed pigs. Unless you are shopping at farmers' markets where you might find some of the more exotic breeds mentioned above, you will probably find only Berkshire (Kurobuta). Heritage pork costs about four times what commodity pork costs, but for those who put a premium on flavor, it's worth it.

When shopping for pork, look for meat that is light pink, almost white in color. Some heritage breeds have a bit more of a reddish hue, but the rule of thumb is that the lighter the meat, the more tender it is. You also want to smell the pork; if it is fresh, it will have virtually no scent. Last, with tender, quality pork, if you were to press into it with your finger, which you can often do through the plastic, your finger would leave an indentation in the meat the way it would if you were to press into butter. If it springs right back, you're looking at tough, rubbery meat. Don't buy it.

COOKING PORK

Several years ago I took my dad to a restaurant in the city; he ordered a pork chop and when he cut into it and the center was pink, he wanted to send it back. He thought it was undercooked. That's the mentality of my dad's generation: People thought pork had to be cooked to well-done because of the fear of trichinosis, a parasitic infection caused by eating pork that was infected with the larvae of a species of roundworm and had not been cooked through. But today, trichinosis is almost unseen—only about a dozen cases a year are reported in the United States, and those are from eating wild, not commercial pigs. In 2011, even the USDA changed their recommendations for cooking pork from 160°F to 145°F plus a three-minute rest time, and the USDA tends to be over-cautious. I recommend cooking pork from 130° to 135°F; the temperature of the meat will jump up to closer to 140°F after the meat rests, which will give you meat that is cooked to medium, which I think is ideal. My father still won't eat pork unless it's cooked at least to medium-well.

COOKING A WHOLE HOG

A whole hog is a great way to feed a large group. It provides a lot of food and the spectacle of cooking it also provides entertainment. Cooking a whole hog is a tradition in Asian and Pacific cultures and it's getting increasingly popular here. When ordering a whole hog, you can specify any size from a suckling pig, which weighs about 8 pounds and is 2 to 4 weeks old, to a full-grown hog, which can weigh upward of 400 pounds. The younger hog will be more tender, but a more mature animal will have more flavor.

The easiest way to cook a whole hog is in a Caja China, which is an outdoor cooking box made of wood and lined with metal. The meat is put between racks, then the Caja China is closed, and hot coals are placed on top. The pig cooks from the radiant heat of those coals. The finished product is moist and delicious. It's also a safe way to cook. Just be sure to have a metal trashcan to dispose of the charcoal when you're done cooking.

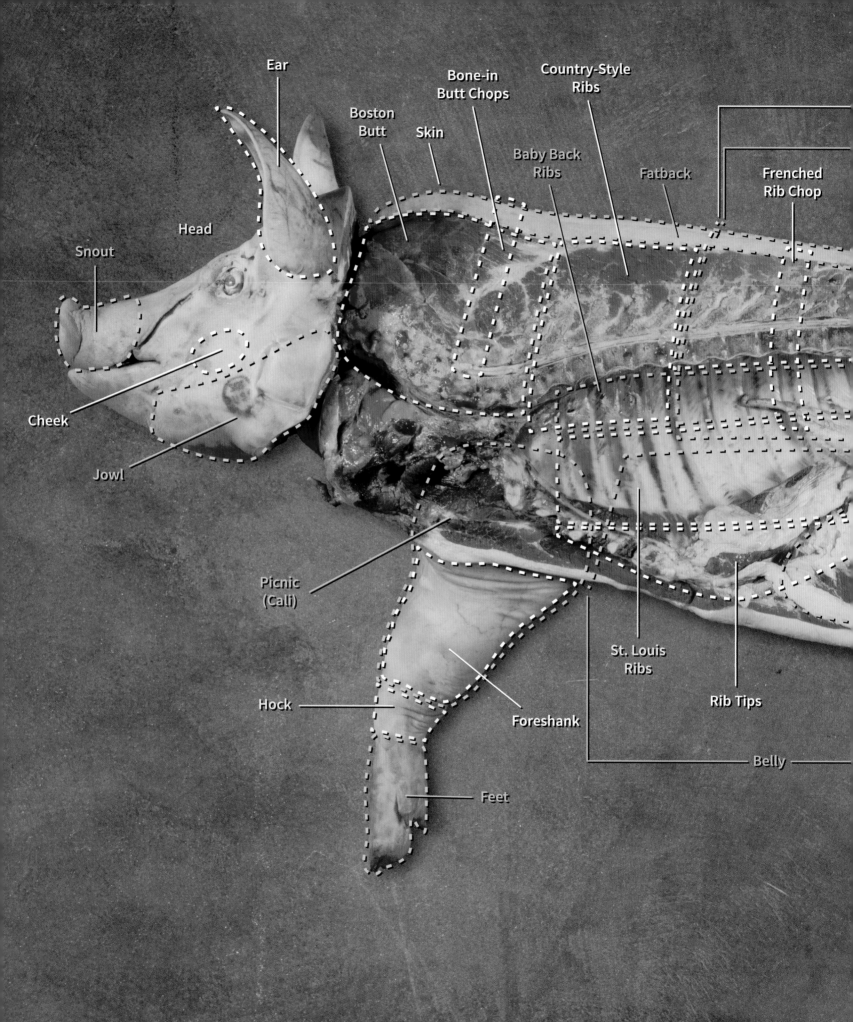

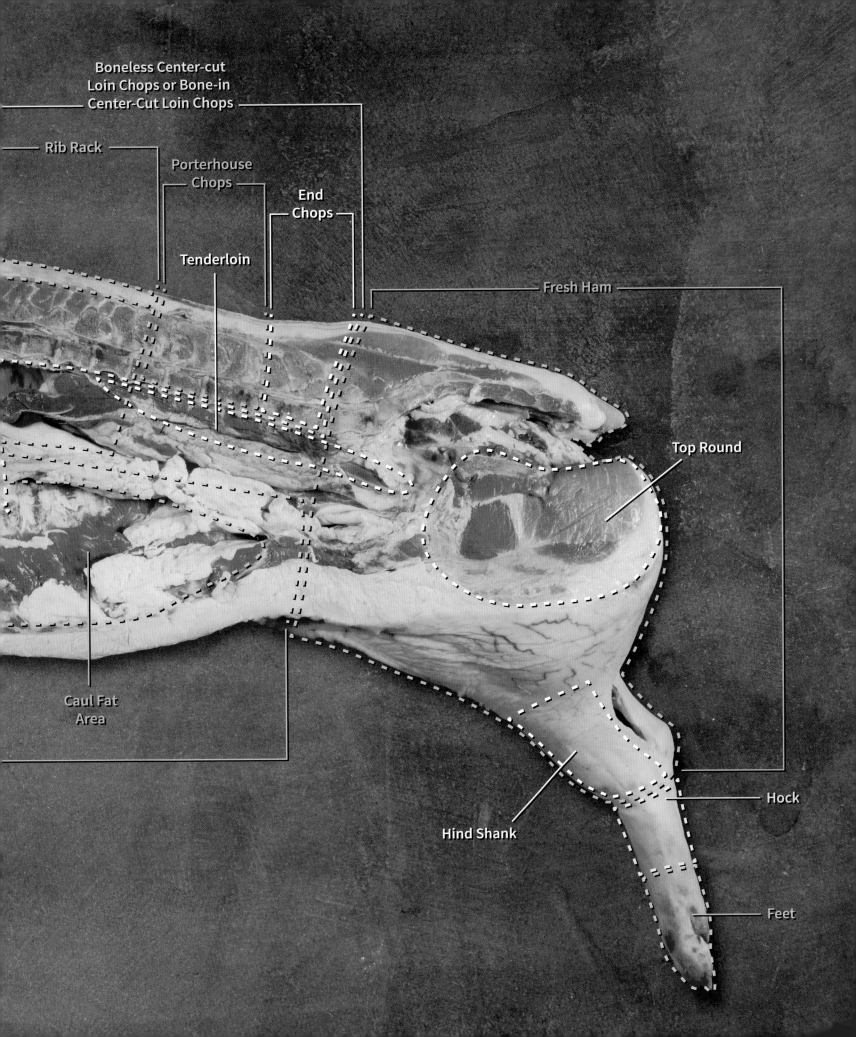

Boneless Center-cut
Loin Chops or Bone-in
Center-Cut Loin Chops

Rib Rack

Porterhouse
Chops

End
Chops

Tenderloin

Fresh Ham

Top Round

Caul Fat
Area

Hind Shank

Hock

Feet

PORK CUTS

"High on the hog" is a southern expression that refers to living large. It came from the fact that a cut higher on the hog, closer to its spine, is the more expensive meat on the animal, as opposed to the shanks, trotters, and belly. I don't know that I agree, since some of my favorite cuts come from lower on the hog, such as the belly, which could hardly be any lower, and St. Louis ribs, which I prefer to baby back ribs, which are as high as the hog gets. And cooked correctly, I love shanks too. The loin, the juiciest, most flavorful cut on the animal is the source of porterhouse and rib chops, which are luxurious cuts on any animal. The nice thing about pig, however, is that there isn't a cut that isn't tender, juicy, and flavorful.

ODDS AND ENDS

Although you might see a pig's **head** displayed at a whole hog cookout because it looks cool, the truth is there isn't much meat on it; it's mostly fat. Once the cheeks and jowls are removed, what's left of the head is usually boiled down to make headcheese.

Pig's **ears**, composed solely of cartilage and fat, are very tough; there's a reason why they are used as dog chew toys. Braised, they can become tender and flavorful. They have become more popular recently with the nose-to-tail movement. At her gastropub, The Spotted Pig, chef April Bloomfield braises and then fries pig's ears, and serves them as part of a salad.

Fatback is a layer of fat that is found between the skin and the loin. Rendered, it makes a flavorful fat for deep-fat frying and sautéing; it is sometimes rubbed on a baking dish in place of butter to keep food from sticking, or added to sausage blends to up the fat content. In Italian cuisine, fatback is cured to make *lardo,* which is served thinly sliced, like prosciutto, or sometimes whipped to spread on

toasted bread. Salted, fatback becomes salt pork, which is often used as a flavoring for stews and braises.

A mix of lamb and pork **kidneys** is used to make British steak and kidney pie. Pork kidneys are thought to be milder in flavor than other kidneys; still I get only a handful of requests for them, mostly from British chefs.

Pigs are omnivores whose powerful jaws allow them to root around even in the hardest earth for food. Their **jowls**, or jaw muscles, are big and strong, and the meat as fibrous and tough as any you'll find. The cheeks, which are about the size of a silver dollar, are also tough and fibrous. Both are often braised to make a rich filling for ravioli, or used to make *guanciale,* an Italian cured meat that is considered an essential ingredient in spaghetti alla carbonara. For a long time fast-food restaurants smoked the jowl to make bacon that was similar to the shape of the bun for their breakfast sandwiches. When Americans started making guanciale, the price of jowls went up, and fast-food places went back to regular bacon.

Pig's **blood** is used in many cultures to make traditional sausages, including *boudin noir* in France, black pudding in England, Irish pudding, and *biroldo* in Italy. It's also used in some cuisines as a thickener for soups and sauces. Blood is not widely consumed in the United States, and it's difficult to get on the retail level because of our strict food safety laws; most of it is used in large-scale manufacturing facilities where the conditions are carefully monitored.

Shanks are the toughest cut on any animal and must be braised to tenderize the meat and break down the sinew and cartilage. Pork **hind shanks**, crosscut into 1½- to 2-inch rounds, make a delicious and less expensive alternative to osso buco (see Pat's Whole Shank Osso Buco, page 26). The meat from either the hog's hind or **foreshanks** makes the best stew meat on the animal. Save the shank bones to make stock.

Pork **hocks**, also known as ham hocks, are the hog's ankles; the majority of hocks are smoked and used to add smoky flavor and a smooth, gelatinous

Head

Ear

Hind Shank

Foreshank

Hock

Foot

Fatback

quality to soups, stews, sauces, and greens. They're especially prominent in southern-style cooking.

Pigs' **feet**, also called trotters, are rich in gelatin. Although they are most often used to make stock and headcheese, in classical French cuisine they are stuffed and roasted; in recent years, New York chefs have begun to revive this tradition. Pickled pigs' feet are a snack food in Korean and Mexican cuisines and in the American South.

Pork **caul fat** is a thin, lacy membrane of fat that surrounds the hog's intestines. It is used to wrap foods, such as a chicken breast or fish cakes; the caul fat melts away when it's cooked and nobody ever knows it was there; it leaves whatever it is wrapped around moist and flavorful.

Pig skin, when roasted or fried until it's crispy, makes a great snack food. In the South, the fried skin is called "crackling"; in Latin America, they call it *chicharrones*. When making porchetta (see Eataly's Porchetta, page 163), the skin is left on the belly, which is wrapped around the loin, so the entire outside of the roast is like a crisp, flavorful shell.

Kidneys

Caul Fat

Jowl

Blood

Pig Skin

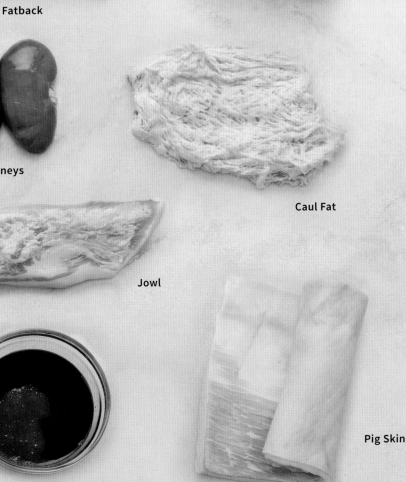

RACK AND LOIN

A **boneless loin** roast has had the rib bones removed. It is a juicy, luxurious roast with a cylindrical shape that makes it ideal for stuffing, rolling, and tying (see Biscotti-Stuffed Boneless Loin, page 159). It can also be cut into **boneless center-cut loin chops**. On any loin cut, I like to leave a ¼- to ½-inch-thick fat cap; the fat protects the meat from the heat and also bastes the meat while it cooks.

The **tenderloin** is the most tender cut on the pig and also the most expensive. It can be roasted whole or portioned into medallions. Because of its low fat content it doesn't have a lot of flavor, so it's often accompanied by a flavorful sauce or condiment.

Country-style ribs are the first four ribs on the hog. They contain a portion of the loin, and often even a little of the prized "lip" or "cap." They are about half the price of the loin because of their irregular size and shape; also, instead of pure loin muscle, they contain several muscles and therefore various levels of tenderness.

When you're breaking down the animal, after the porterhouses start to run out, there are a few more chops called **end chops** that you can cut; they have the same meat but not the appealing look of the porterhouse, so as a butcher, you get less money for them. For the consumer, they are a good economical chop.

Pork **porterhouse chops**, cut from the bone-in loin, consist of loin and tenderloin, divided by the iconic T-shaped bone.

Bone-in loin chop consist of only the loin side of the porterhouse chop; it's the pork equivalent of a strip steak. It's a great choice for people (like me) who don't love the tenderloin.

A **frenched 9-rib rack** is unusual on a retail level, and would more likely be cut into individual chops. If you have two frenched racks, you can make a pork crown roast (see Crown Roast of Pork with Pineapple Bread Stuffing, page 154).

A **frenched rib chop** makes a grand presentation. For a long time, no distinction was made between rib chops and porterhouse chops. Today, to meet market demand, rib chops and porterhouse chops are both labeled as such. (For more on that story, see Jimmy Bradley's Frenched Chop with Red Onion Soubise, page 156.)

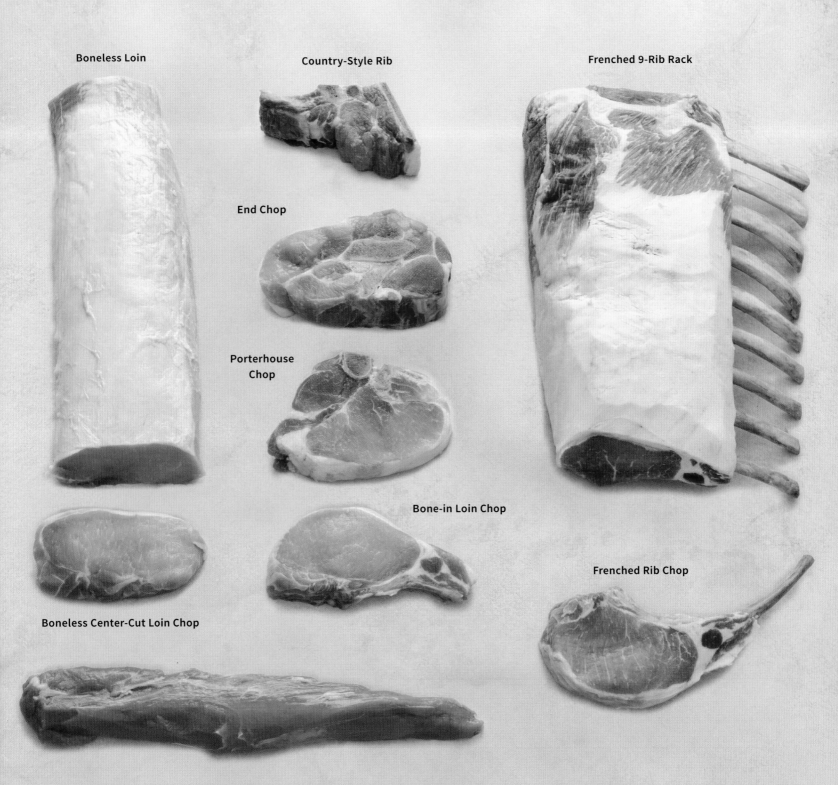

Boneless Loin

Country-Style Rib

Frenched 9-Rib Rack

End Chop

Porterhouse Chop

Bone-in Loin Chop

Frenched Rib Chop

Boneless Center-Cut Loin Chop

Tenderloin

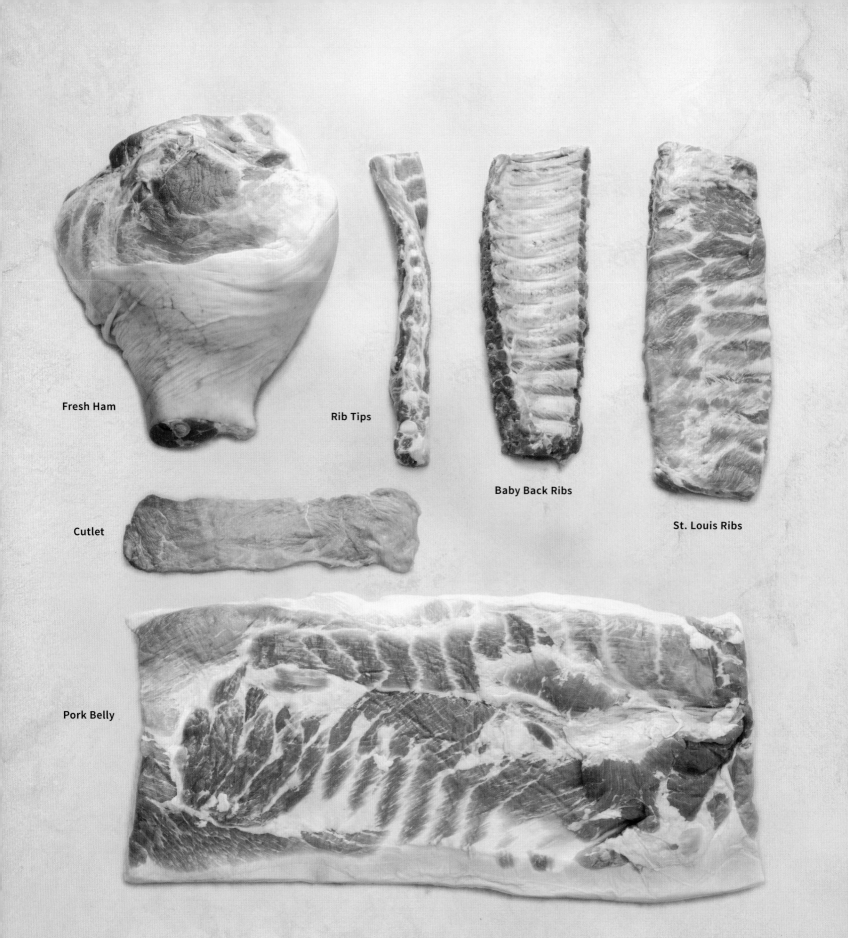

Fresh Ham

Rib Tips

Baby Back Ribs

St. Louis Ribs

Cutlet

Pork Belly

BELLY, RIBS, AND HAM

When people think of ham, they think of cured or smoked ham, but it can also refer to the cut of meat used to make those products: the upper thigh portion of the animal's hind leg. To distinguish between the two, I refer to the cut of meat as **fresh ham**. When I was a kid and first started cutting meat, there were only a few things my dad would let me touch, and fresh ham was one of them. If I miscut it a little bit, it wouldn't matter, because once I tied it, the mistake wouldn't be noticeable. Fresh ham can be roasted bone-in as you typically see in a spiral-cut ham, or boned and tied as it is for the Fresh Holiday Ham with Tangerine and Cloves (page 152).

Rib tips, which you most often see in Chinese restaurants, are from the skirt that is trimmed from spareribs in order to make St. Louis ribs. The skirt contains a lot of cartilage, which can make them difficult to eat because you have to navigate around that. They're really inexpensive and have a lot of meat on them, so they make a very economical alternative to spareribs.

Baby back ribs are cut from where the rib cage meets the spine at the very top of the animal. They are generally served as a full rack, which consists of between ten and thirteen bones. Baby backs have loin meat on the bones and intercostal meat between them, but they don't have a lot of either.

St. Louis ribs are spareribs that have been trimmed of cartilage and skirt. They come from below the back ribs and contain a lot of intercostal or "finger" meat between the bones, as well as belly and brisket meat on the bones. Many people think of and refer to St. Louis ribs as spareribs (and they are often sold as such), but if they were spareribs, you wouldn't be able to cut the rack between the bones into individual ribs with only a knife; you would be unlikely to see a rack of true spareribs at retail.

Pork **cutlets** can be sliced (¼ inch thick, against the grain) from the shoulder, loin, or leg, including the outside round, inside round, eye round, knuckle, and hip. All of these cuts are free of sinew and are tender so they don't require long cooking. Pork cutlets are often used in place of veal in dishes such as schnitzel and saltimbocca. Although this is done as an economical alternative, I think of it as an upgrade, because pork is so much more flavorful than veal. In my family, we use pork cutlets in place of beef to make Pork Braciole (page 148), which is traditionally made with beef. The Japanese love pork cutlets, called *tonkatsu,* which are coated in panko breadcrumbs and panfried.

Pork belly, a flavorful and very fatty cut, has historically been used almost exclusively to make bacon, but in recent years chefs have also begun roasting or braising it and serving it as an appetizer. A large, rectangular-cut pork belly weighs 12 to 18 pounds and has many striations, alternating layers of fat and muscle that give bacon its characteristic streaks.

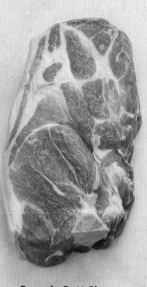

Bone-in Butt Chop

Pork Shoulder

Picnic (aka Cali)

SHOULDER

Bone-in butt chops, also called "Boston butt steaks," have a bone in the middle. On another animal, shoulder meat would have to be braised to tenderize it, but because pork is so tender, it can be seared just like a steak.

Pork shoulder is often referred to and sold as pork butt, but it's a misleading term because the cut comes from high on the pig's shoulder. Pork butt got its name from the wooden barrels, called butts, in which it was shipped and packed; this packing tradition originated in Boston, so the cut is also referred to as a "Boston butt." Because of its high fat content, pork butt is often roasted and shredded; it's the cut of choice for southern-style barbecue pulled pork; or roasted or braised to make Mexican carnitas.

The **picnic** is a bone-in roast found immediately below the butt on the front leg. It is less expensive than butt, and can be used in any recipe calling for butt; it is used to make stew meat or chopped meat. The cut is sometimes referred to as the "Cali" (for California style), and the Spanish-speaking butchers at LaFrieda Meats call it a *pernil*; they eat a lot of it.

Shank meat makes the very best stew meat because of its high collagen content. After braising for hours, the collagen breaks down and becomes gelatinous, giving the stew great flavor and texture.

Shank Meat

In recent years the demand for pork in America has increased more than for any other meat. I've seen a complete shift from an emphasis on low-fat to high in flavor, which means high in fat. The demand for flavorful, higher fat pork started with chefs, but it has since trickled down to the consumer.

Two racks of frenched rib chops (see "Frenching a Rib Bone," page 186) are tied together to make a crown roast (see Crown Roast of Pork with Pineapple Bread Stuffing, page 154).

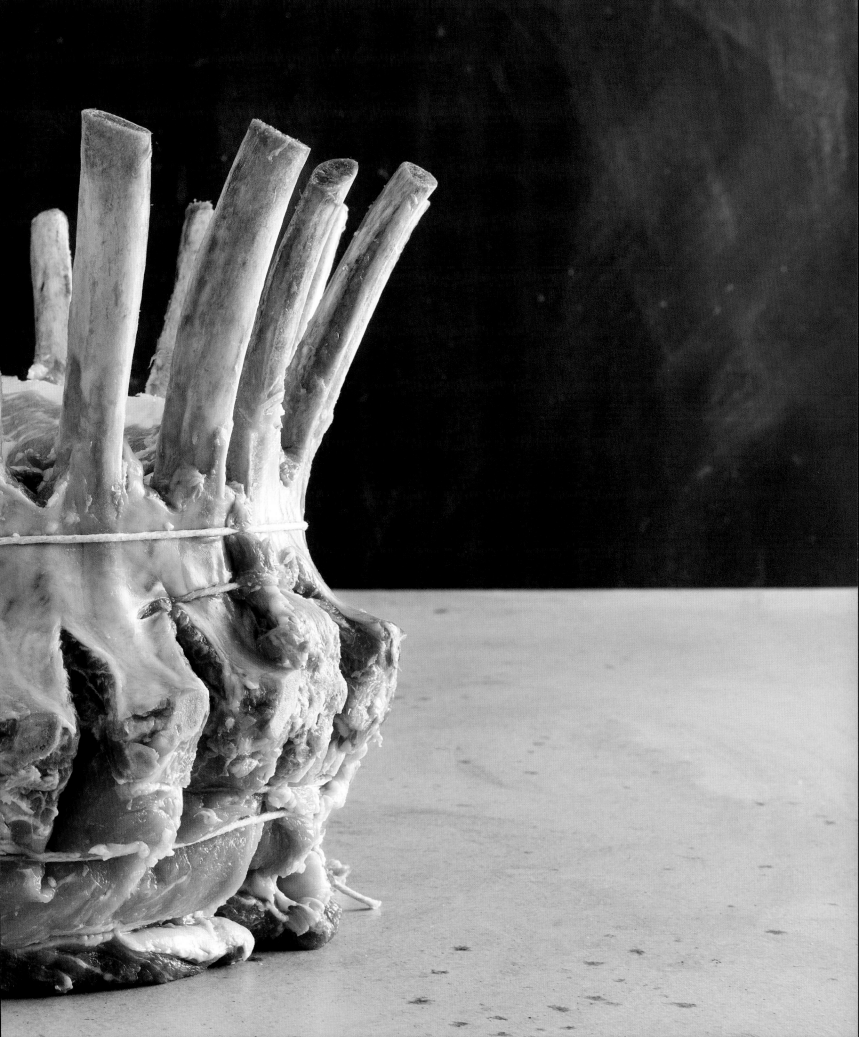

BUTCHERING TECHNIQUES
BUTTERFLYING A LOIN

1. Lay the pork loin on a cutting board with a short end facing you. Using a boning knife, start at the far end of the loin and cut two-thirds of the way up the side of the loin, pulling the knife toward you as you make a lengthwise cut into the loin.

2. Stop about ¾ inch from the left edge of the meat.

3. Rotate the loin so the cut is on the left and open the meat like a book, then make a second lengthwise cut halfway through the thicker portion of the loin.

4. Make sure not to cut all the way through. Open that section so it is like a three-panel brochure.

5. Orient the butterflied loin with one short end facing you and cover with the stuffing. Begin rolling up the loin away from you. Tie the roast with butcher's rope (see "Tying a Roast," opposite page).

TYING A ROAST

Tying a roast is something a lot of home cooks have the butcher do, but it's a good thing to learn to do yourself. If you tie your own roast, you can season the meat on the inside before you tie it; you can only season the exterior of the roast if it is tied by a butcher. One reason you tie a roast is to give it a uniform shape, which keeps the muscles tight and helps the roast cook evenly. The other time you tie a roast is if you are rolling a roast with filling inside, as we do in a number of recipes (including Grandma LaFrieda's Braised Stuffed Veal Breast, page 20; and Biscotti-Stuffed Boneless Loin, page 159). The instructions below will also help you tie smaller items that don't classify as an actual roast, such as Chipotle-Braised Tomahawk Short Ribs (page 207) and Skirt Steak Pinwheels (page 203).

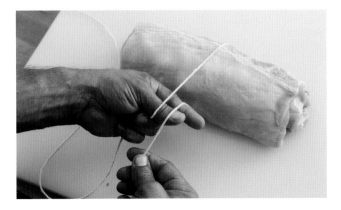

1. Start at the center of your roast (or whatever you are tying), lay the butcher's rope under the meat. (Starting at the center helps to hold the meat together while you tie the remaining knots. From there, you'll make your next ties at either end and then work inward; this ensures your knots are evenly spaced.) Put your thumb and forefinger together, parallel to the meat you're tying.

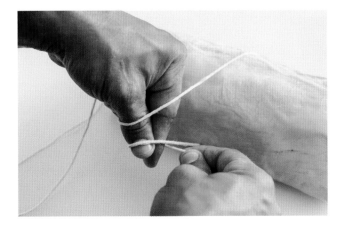

2. Pull the rope over your thumb and forefinger and then under them in the opposite direction; it's important that the source rope be in your left hand.

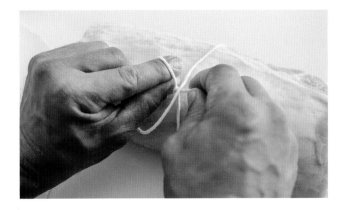

3. Take the cut end of the rope and wrap it around your thumb and forefinger of your left hand while at the same time rotating those fingers out and around the rope on the left.

4. Once your hand has completely come around the first (left) rope, grab the cut end of the rope with your left hand.

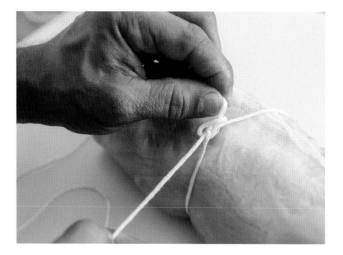

5. Pull the cut end of the rope through the hoop you've just created.

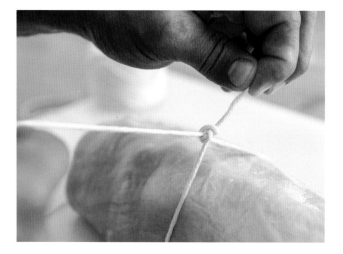

6. Grab the source rope with your right hand, and with forefinger and thumb of your left hand, grab the cut rope so it doesn't pull out of the loop; you will now have created a slip knot. if you don't tighten the knot, the whole knot will come apart when you tighten the rope around the meat in the next step.

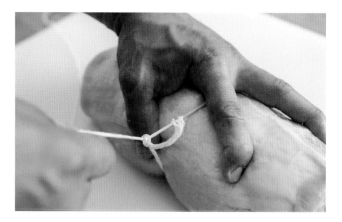

7. Hold the meat in place with your left hand and with your right hand, pull on the source rope; the tighter you pull the source rope, the tighter the knot will be and the tighter the rope will be around the roast.

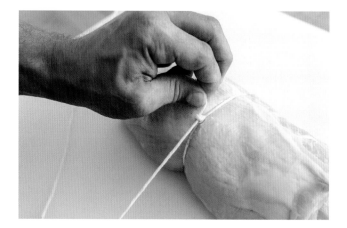

8. Pull evenly on both ends of the string to tighten the knot

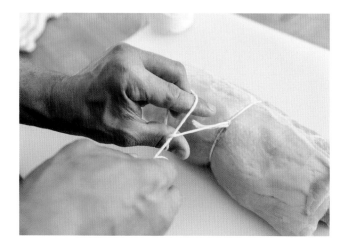

9. Tie the reinforcement knot.

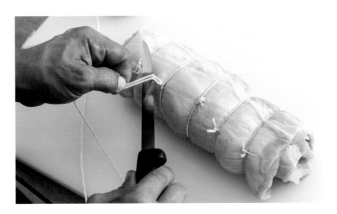

10. Continue making knots along the roast: After tying the first knot in the middle, make the second knot on the far right, then the far left, then work your way back toward the center.

11. As you finish each knot, but before cutting it, adjust it so that the knots are in a line, or close to it. After aligning each knot, use your knife to cut both sides of the rope, about ¼ inch from the knot.

PORK BRACIOLE

Tomato Sauce (page 95)

⅔ cup pine nuts

8 slices (¼ inch thick, cut against the grain; about 6 ounces each) pork butt

½ teaspoon freshly ground black pepper

1 cup grated Pecorino Romano cheese (about 4 ounces)

¾ cup golden raisins

3 tablespoons finely chopped fresh flat-leaf parsley leaves

Kosher salt

Pasta (see "Cooking Pasta for Sunday Sauce and Braciole," page 151)

BUTCHER'S NOTE:
Ask your butcher to cut consistent slices (¼ inch thick, against the grain), so that each braciole is more or less the same size.

Braciole is meat rolled and stuffed with ingredients and braised in red sauce. It is an integral part of Italian American cooking, and it is a Sunday tradition in my family. My grandfather started using pork instead of the usual beef to make braciole and that's the way we do it to this day. Pork is much more flavorful and tender than beef. I really love the pine nuts and raisins that are rolled (along with parsley and cheese) inside the meat. I like the combination so much that I adopted those ingredients for my meatballs (see Pork Meatballs with Toasted Pignoli and Golden Raisins, page 102). I burn pine nuts at least half the time that I toast them. The lesson is: Don't walk away from your pine nuts. They cook faster than you think.

We make this with spaghetti or linguine, but often my dad will drive all the way to Brooklyn to Pastosa Ravioli, a shop near where I grew up, that makes the best ravioli I have ever tasted. If I had a dying meal it would be my grandfather's pork braciole, cooked in my grandmother's red sauce, served over those ricotta cheese–filled ravioli on a Sunday afternoon.

In my family we leave the strings on the braciole so it stays together on the plate. Every time I serve them, I remind everyone at the table that there's string on their meat even though they already know.

MAKES 8 BRACIOLE AND ENOUGH SAUCE FOR 8 OR MORE

1. For the tomato sauce: Follow the recipe up to the point where you get the first bubble (about 1½ hours after you add the tomatoes). If you're using store-bought sauce, heat the sauce over medium heat, stirring often, until it begins to bubble.

2. In a small skillet, toast the pine nuts over medium heat, shaking the pan often, until the nuts are golden brown all over, 4 to 5 minutes. Transfer the pine nuts to a plate so they don't burn from the residual heat of the pan and set them aside to cool to room temperature.

3. Using the flat side of a meat mallet, gently pound the pork to thin it out slightly, being careful not to rip the meat. Lay the pork down on your work surface. Sprinkle the pepper over the pork slices. Scatter the cheese over the pork slices. Then scatter the pine nuts, raisins, and parsley over the cheese. Roll up each braciole and tie each shut with butcher's rope, using four knots per braciole, using instructions in "Tying a Roast" (page 145).

4. When the sauce has come up to a simmer, add the braciole to the sauce and simmer them until they're tender, about 1 hour. Season to taste. Serve with pasta.

SUNDAY SAUCE: PASTA WITH MEAT SAUCE

3 pounds beef short ribs, cut into individual 2-inch-long bones, or other meat (see note)

2 teaspoons kosher salt plus more to taste

1 teaspoon freshly ground black pepper

2 tablespoons extra-virgin olive oil

2 medium yellow onions, finely chopped

3 cloves garlic, minced

2 cans (28 ounces each) peeled tomatoes (crushed or whole; if whole, chop the tomatoes and reserve the liquid)

1 medium or large carrot, peeled and trimmed

2 tablespoons tomato paste

1 teaspoon dried oregano

Pasta (see "Cooking Pasta for Sunday Sauce and Braciole," opposite page)

In our family, Sunday is when everybody is home—or visiting the home of another family member. It's the day when nobody works, nobody has any outside activities going on, and everybody is just supposed to relax and be together. On the menu every week: "Sunday sauce," which is Tomato Sauce (page 95) with meat braised in it. Sunday sauce is our comfort food. You walk into a room and you smell that sauce cooking and it smells like a Sunday afternoon. You're happy. Everyone around you is happy. There are no problems in the world. Monday morning seems a long way off.

The meat that my mother or grandmother braised in the sauce changed from week to week. Deciding what meat went in the sauce was a matter of what my dad brought home, which was a matter of what he had too much of, or what would go bad by Monday when he reopened the shop. One week it might be spicy Italian sausages, another spareribs, the next short ribs, and so on.

SERVES 8 OR MORE

1. Season the meat all over with the salt and ½ teaspoon of the pepper. In a large pot, heat the oil over medium-high heat until it slides easily in the pan, about 2 minutes. Add the meat and cook to brown it on all sides, about 10 minutes. Remove the meat to a plate. Add the onions to the pot and cook them, stirring often so they don't burn, until they are tender and slightly caramelized, about 20 minutes; turn the heat down if the onions are burning. Add the garlic and cook until it is golden and fragrant, 3 to 4 minutes. Return the meat to the pot. Add the tomatoes (and their juices) and carrot, reduce the heat, and cook the sauce over low heat, stirring occasionally, until you get your first bubble indicating a simmer; you're cooking over very low heat so this will be awhile—1½ to 2 hours; if it starts to bubble sooner than that, you have the heat too high and you need to turn it down. Stir in the tomato paste, oregano, and the remaining ½ teaspoon pepper. Continue to cook the meat in the sauce for another hour (for a total of 2½ to 3 hours), until the meat is fork-tender. (If you're making sauce with sausage, you will not need to check it for doneness, but note that you will cook it for the same length of time: 2 to 3 hours total.) Remove the carrot and discard it. Add more salt to taste.

2. Serve with pasta.

NOTE: Other options for meat are beef chuck flap tail (cut into 2-inch cubes), pork butt (cut into 2-inch cubes), whole Italian sausage links, and pork spareribs (cut into 3-inch squares).

COOKING PASTA FOR SUNDAY SAUCE AND BRACIOLE

The preferred pasta shapes in our family are spaghetti and linguine, but you can use whatever shape of dried pasta you like, and you can also use my personal favorite: fresh ricotta ravioli. Below are my cooking methods for both dried pasta and fresh ravioli. As for how much to plan on serving, it depends on what else you're serving with it. We serve so many dishes on Sundays that each person eats only a small amount of pasta. One pound of pasta could serve as many as 8 people when they're also eating a portion of lamb crown roast, a few slices of skirt steak, and who knows what else. But if pasta with meat sauce is the main event, you'll want to count on serving closer to 1 pound of dried pasta for 4 people, or 1 pound of fresh ravioli for 3 people.

To cook dried pasta: Fill a large pot with water, salt it generously, and bring it to a boil over high heat. Cook the pasta until it's al dente, about 2 minutes shy of the time given on the package. Drain the pasta and transfer it back to the pot it was cooked in. Add enough sauce to coat the pasta (2 to 3 cups of sauce for every pound of pasta) and cook the pasta and sauce together over medium-high heat for about 2 minutes, to stain the noodle with the sauce and to make sure the pasta and sauce are nice and hot.

To cook fresh ravioli: Fill a large pot with water, salt it generously, and bring it to a boil over high heat. Cook the ravioli according to the package instructions until it's just al dente. Carefully remove the ravioli to a platter or individual serving dishes and spoon the sauce over and around the ravioli; you'll need 2 to 3 cups of sauce for every 2 pounds of ravioli. (Fresh ravioli is the one pasta I don't toss together with the sauce; if I did, the ravioli would fall apart and all the delicious filling would spill out.)

If you're serving pasta with meat sauce, serve the pasta with some meat on top, and another bowl of sauce and meat on the side. If you're serving braciole, put the pasta in individual serving bowls and put one braciole on each plate. Sprinkle the pasta with Parmesan and serve more cheese at the table.

CRISPY BREADED BONELESS CENTER-CUT LOIN CHOPS

On the rare occasions when my dad brought home a boneless loin, my mother always prepared it the same way: coated with mustard and breadcrumbs and then roasted. I love it, but I like it even better if the loin is first cut into individual chops; that way I get more surface area, which means more of the mustard-coated crispy exterior—my favorite part. Individual chops also don't take as long to cook, and I am not a patient person.

To serve 8, start with 8 (1-inch-thick) boneless loin chops. Beat 2 large eggs with 2 tablespoons milk and ¼ cup whole-grain mustard. Dredge each chop in flour, then in the mustard mixture, and then in 1 cup Italian-Style Breadcrumbs (page 94), pressing down to pack on the breadcrumbs. Heat ¼ inch of olive oil in a skillet over medium-high heat and fry the chops until they are crispy, 3 to 4 minutes per side. Put the chops on a baking sheet and put them in a 325°F oven until a meat thermometer registers 130°F. To make a whole 3- to 4-pound pork loin roast, dredge and coat the entire roast as you did the chops. Put it on a roasting rack or wire cooling rack set inside a roasting pan and roast at 325°F until a meat thermometer registers 130°F, about 1 hour.

FRESH HOLIDAY HAM WITH TANGERINE AND CLOVES

GLAZE

½ cup packed dark brown sugar

1 cup honey

1 teaspoon ground cinnamon

1 teaspoon ground cloves

½ teaspoon kosher salt

Grated zest of 12 to 16 tangerines (about ½ cup)

2 cups tangerine juice (about 10 tangerines)

HAM

1 boneless, skin-on fresh ham (16 to 18 pounds)

3 tablespoons kosher salt

½ cup whole cloves

2 tangerines, unpeeled, sliced into very thin rounds (about 10 rounds)

On holidays, at my Grandpa LaFrieda's house, we always had a fresh ham cooking. That ham was beautiful—it had a deep caramel-colored, sweet, sticky glaze on it that was covered in orange or tangerine slices—and cloves stuck all around it.

SERVES 12 TO 14

1. For the glaze: In a small saucepan, stir the brown sugar, honey, cinnamon, cloves, salt, and tangerine zest. Stir in 1 cup of the tangerine juice and bring to a boil over medium heat. Reduce the heat and simmer until the glaze has thickened and reduced to about 1 cup, about 6 minutes. Remove from the heat and set the glaze aside to cool for 20 to 30 minutes to thicken slightly.

2. For the ham: Position an oven rack in the lower third of the oven. Remove any racks above it and preheat the oven to 300°F.

3. Using a small paring knife, score the skin in straight lines on the diagonal and about 2 inches apart over the surface of the ham, making sure you cut just through the skin to the fat but not through the fat. Do the same thing in the other direction so you have diamond-shaped hash marks all over the ham.

4. Massage the salt all over the ham, including the cavity where the bone was removed. Tuck the ends of the ham under the ham so it is a uniform, football-like shape. Tie butcher's rope across the length of the ham (see "Tying a Roast," page 145), making each knot about 1½ inches apart. Stick the cloves into the ham.

5. Brush the glaze over the entire ham and inside the cavity; you will use about one-quarter of the glaze at this time. Put the ham skin side up on a roasting rack set inside a roasting pan. Roast the ham until a meat thermometer inserted into the thickest part of the ham registers 130° to 135°F, about 3½ hours, basting the ham with the glaze about once every hour during the cooking time (you will have to warm the glaze over low heat before basting, as it will become too thick to brush on).

6. Take the ham out of the oven and increase the oven temperature to 400°F.

7. Remove and discard the butcher's rope. Lay the tangerine rounds in a strip down the length of the ham. Put the ham back in the oven and roast until the skin is crisp and the tangerines are slightly caramelized, about 15 minutes. Let the ham rest for at least 20 minutes before carving it.

8. While the ham is resting, stir the remaining 1 cup tangerine juice into the remaining glaze and bring the glaze to a simmer over medium heat. Cook, stirring occasionally, until the glaze has thickened, 5 to 7 minutes.

9. Cut the ham into ¼-inch slices and serve with the glaze on the side.

CROWN ROAST OF PORK WITH PINEAPPLE BREAD STUFFING

1 crown roast of pork, from 2
  (8-rib) pork racks, frenched
  (see "Frenching a Rib Bone,"
  page 186), 12 to 14 pounds

¼ cup kosher salt

1 teaspoon freshly ground black
  pepper

1 tablespoon dried thyme

BUTCHER'S NOTE:
Ask your butcher to tie a crown roast
from two frenched 8-rib pork racks. Or
french the racks, sear them, and then
tie them yourself using the instructions
in "Making a Crown Roast" (page 54).
I've given instructions for both.

I knew I had to include my mother's Pineapple Bread Stuffing, and this crown roast was the perfect opportunity.

SERVES 12 TO 16

1. Position an oven rack in the lower third of the oven. Remove any racks above it and preheat the oven to broil (set it to high).

2. Season the crown roast all over with the salt and pepper. Place the roast, bones sticking up, on a baking sheet. Cover each bone with foil to prevent the bones from burning. Put the crown roast under the broiler until the meat is seared to deep brown, about 15 minutes. Remove the crown roast from the oven.

3. Reduce the oven temperature to 350°F.

4. Season the outside of the crown roast with the thyme. Spoon the stuffing into the center of the crown roast. Roast the crown roast until a meat thermometer inserted into the thickest part registers 135°F, about 1¾ hours, taking the foil off the bones about halfway throughout cooking time. Remove the roast from the oven and set it aside to rest for 20 minutes before cutting into it.

5. Slice in between each rib bone and serve each chop with the stuffing on the side.

PINEAPPLE BREAD STUFFING

½ pound (2 sticks) unsalted butter,
  at room temperature

2 cups sugar

1 tablespoon kosher salt

8 large eggs

2 cans (20 ounces each) crushed
  pineapple, drained

12 slices white sandwich bread
  (preferably stale), crusts
  removed, cut into ½-inch cubes

This stuffing is like a sweet bread pudding, served hot, and can be served as a side dish.

SERVES 16

1. If you are not baking this inside a crown roast, preheat the oven to 350°F. (If you are baking it in a crown roast, the oven will already be on.)

2. In a large bowl, cream the butter, sugar, and salt with a whisk for 1 to 2 minutes. Add the eggs one at a time, beating each one into the butter mixture before adding the next one. Add the pineapple and stir to combine. Add the bread and fold it in until it is evenly coated with the butter and pineapple.

3. Use the stuffing to stuff the Crown Roast of Pork or spoon it into a 9 x 13-inch baking pan (or two 8-inch square pans) and bake until the top is golden brown and crunchy, 45 to 55 minutes.

JIMMY BRADLEY'S FRENCHED CHOP WITH RED ONION SOUBISE

PORK CHOPS

4 bone-in pork rib chops (about ¾ pound each), frenched (see "Frenching a Rib Bone," page 186)

2 tablespoons extra-virgin olive oil

1 tablespoon kosher salt

1 teaspoon freshly ground black pepper

2 tablespoons finely chopped fresh thyme leaves

2 tablespoons finely chopped fresh rosemary

¼ cup pitted kalamata olives (about 20 olives), pureed but still slightly chunky

SOUBISE

4 small red onions, cut crosswise into ¼-inch-thick rings

¼ cup canola oil

½ teaspoon kosher salt plus more to taste

¼ teaspoon freshly ground black pepper plus more to taste

¼ cup sherry

1 cup low-sodium chicken stock

1 cup heavy cream

We changed how pork loin chops are sold industry-wide with this special cut. It happened with chef Jimmy Bradley, who was opening his first restaurant, The Red Cat, in 1999. Jimmy wanted the exact chop they serve at The Palm steakhouse, but The Palm's supplier had an exclusivity agreement; he couldn't sell to other restaurants. He told Jimmy to talk to us. At the time, pork loin chops were not sold separately as porterhouse chops and rib chops the way that beef is (rib chops are the equivalent to beef rib-eyes). If you ordered loin chops, you'd get some of each and you would have no control over what you got. Dividing the two chops and selling them as distinctly different products was unheard of. But Jimmy wanted uniformity; he wanted a frenched rib bone for a neat presentation, and he wanted everyone at the table to have the same experience. I told Jimmy we could do it. My dad thought I was crazy. "What are we going to do with all the porterhouse we're going to have left over?" he asked. And I told him, "We'll find someone that only wants those." Even though he resisted at first, my father ended up being the one who fulfilled Jimmy's order every week. My dad portioned the chops perfectly—each one weighed exactly twelve ounces and was trimmed to look exactly like the others—and that was the birth of The Red Cat's pork chop, which became known throughout New York. It was also the birth of us taking what historically was lumped together as one cut and separating it into two. We changed the entire industry. Today, we get orders for thousands of portions of both the rib chops and the porterhouses every week. This dish with a sauce made of grilled red onions and cream is one Jimmy Bradley serves at The Red Cat. It might be the most delicious pork chop preparation I have ever tasted. A veal chop would be great prepared in the same way.

SERVES 4

1. For the pork chops: Rub the chops with the olive oil and season them with the salt and pepper. Sprinkle the thyme and rosemary over the chops and press the herbs into the meat to make sure they adhere. Put the pork chops on a parchment-lined baking sheet in a single layer, cover them loosely with plastic wrap, and refrigerate them overnight or for at least several hours.

2. For the soubise: Preheat a grill or grill pan over medium-high heat. Toss the onion slices in a small bowl with the canola oil and season them with the salt and pepper. Place the onions on the grill or in the grill pan, reserving the oil in the bowl, and cook them until they are charred and softened slightly, about 5 minutes on each side. (If you are using a grill pan, you will need to cook them in two batches.) Remove the onions from the grill or grill pan and transfer them to a large skillet while you cook the second batch, if necessary.

(continued)

3. Add the oil reserved from the bowl to the skillet with the onions and cook the onions over medium heat for 10 minutes, stirring occasionally. Add the sherry, increase the heat to high, and cook until the sherry is thickened, about 1 minute. Add the stock and cook, stirring occasionally, until it is reduced and the onions are coated with stock, about 5 minutes. Add the cream and reduce the heat to low. Simmer lightly, stirring occasionally, until the sauce is thick enough to coat the back of a spoon, 6 to 8 minutes. Turn off the heat and add more salt and pepper to taste. This can be made up to several hours in advance. Warm it over low heat before serving.

4. Preheat a grill, grill pan, or skillet over medium-high heat.

5. Remove the pork chops from the refrigerator and place them on the grill or in the pan and cook until they are browned on both sides, 8 to 10 minutes per side, or until a meat thermometer registers 135°F. (They will continue to cook to 140°F once they're off the heat.)

6. To serve, spoon the onions and sauce on each plate. Place the chops on top and spoon the olives over the chops.

Chef-owner Jimmy Bradley at his New York City restaurant The Red Cat in Chelsea.

BISCOTTI-STUFFED BONELESS LOIN

STUFFING

¾ cup hazelnuts (unskinned)

¼ pound (1 stick) unsalted butter

2 cups finely chopped yellow onion (about 1 large)

1 teaspoon kosher salt

½ teaspoon freshly ground black pepper

6 ounces pitted prunes (about 24), finely chopped

2 cups (about 6 ounces) roughly chopped biscotti (page 160)

½ cup low-sodium chicken stock

2 teaspoons minced fresh sage leaves

2 teaspoons minced fresh thyme leaves

4 ounces Parmigiano-Reggiano cheese, cut into ¼-inch cubes

PORK ROAST

4-pound boneless pork loin roast, butterflied (see "Butterflying a Loin," page 144)

3 teaspoons kosher salt

½ teaspoon freshly ground black pepper

¼ cup canola or another neutral-flavored oil

SAUCE

2 tablespoons unsalted butter

1 large shallot, minced

1 teaspoon kosher salt plus more to taste

1 cup pitted prunes

1 cup Riesling

1⅓ cups low-sodium chicken stock

2 sprigs fresh thyme

I adapted this recipe with chef Giuseppe Fanelli, from Tre Dici restaurant, whom I have known for many years.

SERVES 8

1. For the stuffing: Preheat the oven to 325°F. Spread the hazelnuts in a single layer on a baking sheet and roast, shaking the pan from time to time for even cooking, until golden brown and fragrant, about 10 minutes. Remove the hazelnuts from the oven and set them aside until they are cool enough handle. Rub the hazelnuts in a dish towel to remove as much of the skins as possible. Roughly chop the nuts; reserve ¼ cup for the stuffing and set the rest aside for garnish.

2. Increase the oven temperature to 375°F for the pork roast.

3. In a large skillet, heat the butter over medium heat until the foam subsides, about 2 minutes. Add the onion, salt, and pepper and cook until the onion is tender and very light golden, about 10 minutes. Add the prunes and biscotti and cook, stirring occasionally, until the biscotti have softened and broken down slightly, about 5 minutes. Stir in the stock, ¼ cup of the hazelnuts, sage, and thyme. Turn off the heat and set the stuffing aside to cool to room temperature. Stir in the Parmesan.

4. For the pork roast: Lay the butterflied loin on your work surface with a short end facing you and season the side of the pork that is facing up with 2 teaspoons of the salt and the pepper. Turn the stuffing out onto the loin and use a rubber spatula or spoon to smooth it into an even layer. Roll from the side that was last cut. Using butcher's rope, tie one knot in the center of the roast. Make another knot at each end of the roast and working inward, make knots 1½ inches apart, along the length of the loin (see "Tying a Roast," page 145) until you reach the center. Season the outside of the roast with the remaining 1 teaspoon salt.

5. In a large skillet, heat the oil over medium-high heat until it slides easily in the pan, about 2 minutes. Put the pork loin in the pan to sear until it's golden brown, about 8 minutes. Transfer the pork loin to a roasting rack set in a roasting pan and roast until a meat thermometer registers 135°F, about 1 hour. Let the loin rest for 20 minutes before slicing.

6. For the sauce: While the pork is roasting, in a medium skillet, melt the butter over medium heat. Add the shallot, season with the salt, and cook, stirring often, until soft and translucent, about 4 minutes. Add the prunes, wine, stock, and thyme, increase the heat to high, and bring to a boil. Reduce the heat to low and simmer until the prunes are plump, about 10 minutes. Turn off the heat and let cool slightly. Remove and discard the thyme sprigs. With a slotted spoon, transfer the prunes to a blender. Puree the prunes, gradually adding as much of the liquid they were cooked in as needed to puree them. Return the pureed prunes to the skillet with the remaining liquid and cook over medium heat until the sauce is thick. Add more salt to taste.

7. Cut the roast crosswise into ½-inch-thick slices. Serve with the sauce poured over the meat or serve the sauce on the side.

ANISETTE BISCOTTI

3½ cups all-purpose flour plus more for dusting

1 tablespoon baking powder

1 teaspoon baking soda

6 ounces (1½ sticks) unsalted butter, at room temperature

1¼ cups sugar

2 large eggs

1 cup whole milk

2 tablespoons anise extract

Confectioners' sugar for dusting

1. Position racks in the upper and lower thirds of the oven and preheat the oven to 400°F. Line two baking sheets with parchment paper. Dust one of the lined pans with flour.

2. In a medium bowl, whisk the flour, baking powder, and baking soda.

3. In a bowl, with an electric mixer, cream the butter and sugar on high speed until light and fluffy, about 5 minutes. Add the eggs one at a time, mixing well after each addition. Beat in the milk and anise extract. With the mixer running on medium speed, add the flour mixture and mix just until the wet and dry ingredients are combined.

4. Turn the dough out onto the floured baking sheet. Lightly flour your hands and dust the top of the dough with flour. Using your hands, shape the dough into a log about 6 inches wide and 1 inch high.

5. Bake the log until it is light golden brown and a toothpick inserted into the center comes out clean, 20 to 25 minutes. Remove the log from the oven and set aside for about 5 minutes, or until it is cool enough to handle.

6. Reduce the oven temperature to 300°F.

7. Transfer the log to a cutting board and use a serrated knife to cut it crosswise into 1-inch-wide slices. Lay the slices cut side down on two parchment-lined baking sheets, spacing them 1 inch apart. Return the cookies to the oven and bake until they are golden brown, 15 to 20 minutes, rotating the pans from top to bottom and front to back halfway through the baking time. Remove the cookies from the oven and set aside to cool completely on the baking sheets.

8. Sprinkle the cookies with confectioners' sugar (skip this step if you are using them to make stuffing for Biscotti-Stuffed Boneless Loin, page 159) and store them in an airtight container at room temperature for up to 1 week.

EATALY'S PORCHETTA

FENNEL RUB

¾ cup fennel seeds

¾ cup black peppercorns

¾ cup kosher salt

PORK

1 (8-inch-long) center cut boneless
    pork loin (about 3½ pounds)

2 (8-inch) pork bellies (about 5
    pounds each)

2 tablespoons extra-virgin olive oil

2 tablespoons kosher salt

BUTCHER'S NOTE:

In order to have the belly wrap around
the loin, you need to be sure your
butcher cuts the loin and the belly to
exactly 8 inches. You will roll and tie
the two together after you've seasoned
them, but they need to fit together.

Traditionally, porchetta is made with a whole saddle of pork with the belly meat still attached, which weighs forty or fifty pounds. For this version, an adaptation of Eataly's, you buy the same meat—the loin and the belly—separately, and then wrap them together to make a much smaller roast. This recipe makes two roasts. Porchetta makes great sandwiches so leftovers are a good thing.

SERVES 16 TO 20

1. For the fennel rub: In a medium skillet, toast the fennel seeds over high heat, shaking the pan to keep the seeds from burning, until they're fragrant, about 1 minute. Transfer the seeds to a plate to cool completely. Working in batches, grind the fennel seeds and the peppercorns in a spice grinder until they are finely ground. Transfer them to a bowl and stir in the salt.

2. For the pork: Cut the loin down the middle to make two long narrow loins. With the blade of your knife parallel with the cutting board (see "Butterflying a Loin," page 144), cut both bellies horizontally through the middle leaving one side attached. Open the bellies like a book and lay them flat, skin side down. Use a rubber spatula to spread the rub evenly over the surface of both bellies. Lay one of the pork loins on each belly so that the long side of the loin is flush with one of the 8-inch sides of the belly. Roll one of the loins tightly so the belly completely covers it. Use butcher's rope to tie the porchetta about 1 inch from one edge (see "Tying a Roast," page 145). Do the same to the other end, then continue tying about 1 inch apart until you reach the center. Roll and tie the second loin in the same way. Rub 1 tablespoon of the oil and sprinkle 1 tablespoon of the salt over each porchetta. Wrap both porchettas tightly in plastic wrap or put them in a resealable plastic bag and refrigerate them for 24 hours or at least overnight.

3. When you're ready to roast the porchettas, preheat the oven to 400°F.

4. Put the porchettas on a rack in a roasting pan and roast until a meat thermometer inserted into the center of the porchettas registers 135°F, about 2½ hours. Remove the porchettas from the oven and adjust the oven temperature to broil. Return the porchettas to the oven and broil until the skin is golden and crispy, about 8 minutes; use tongs to turn the porchettas every 2 minutes so the skin crisps all over. Let the porchettas rest for about 15 minutes before slicing.

5. Slice the porchetta however thick you want. Leave the butcher's rope on; it will help to hold the porchetta together as you cut it. Serve it just like that or put the porchetta on a crusty roll for a delicious sandwich.

BEEF

WHAT THE BUTCHER HAS TO SAY

If there is one part of our success that has always baffled my father, it's the media coverage. We've always had the mind-set that any glory or fame that is to be had is all for the restaurants that we supply, not for us. We've always been the behind-the-scenes guys, there to support them but not to be mentioned in any way. But then that started to change. As we started getting more successful, restaurants began putting our name on their menus. Naming their sources was part of a trend of restaurants, whether it was who made the cheese or what farm grew the vegetables. So our name started to be known not just by chefs, but by their customers—and by the media. When the media started to call for quotes or to write about us, my dad was so intrigued, he asked, "Why do they want to hear what the butcher has to say?"

I explained to my dad that diners were starting to be interested in where their food came from. But who really turned their attention to us was the chefs themselves.

In 2008, one of my customers, Adam Perry Lang, who owns the barbecue restaurant Daisy May's, sent a friend of his to me, Riad Nasr, for this kind of consulting. Riad, along with another chef, Lee Hanson, was getting ready to open a steakhouse, Minetta Tavern. According to Adam, Riad's mission was to serve the best steak he possibly could. It turned out to be perfect timing, because I had just begun to perfect dry-aging.

In the past, when chefs had asked me for aged steaks, I had to tell them no, because it wasn't something we did. My dad had never wanted to get into dry-aging because it was so temperamental—if all the factors aren't just right, instead of the meat aging, it rots. But then, around 2000, suddenly *everybody* was asking me for aged beef. I knew I had to do something about it. When we expanded within our Leroy Street location to take over space that we had previously rented out, I turned one area into an aging room. I put up some walls and rails, and hung up some beef.

I didn't know what I was doing, and in the beginning, a lot of meat rotted on me. I had the temperature right. And since refrigeration is a natural dehumidifier—which I already knew from working in a refrigerated room all day long for my whole life—I thought that would take care of the humidity requirement. But fresh meat has a lot of water in it. So when you put as much meat into a room as I was, the natural moisture from the meat increases the humidity levels to a point where the refrigeration alone can't solve your problems. Suffice it to say that learning to age meat properly was a long, involved, and expensive process, but eventually I got it right. Now, I have a beautiful dry-aging room with over $1.3 million in inventory: a total of about six thousand primals (each of which consists of about twelve portions) of porterhouse, T-bones, rib steaks, rib-eyes, and strip steaks. It's so beautiful. It's my prized possession.

Riad came to see the room, and he was so excited he asked if I could designate a wall of meat that was just for him. I said, "Sure." And I suggested we take it a step further. The restaurant was six weeks from opening, so I said, "Let's pick out your meat now, while it's red." With fresh, red meat, you can see the intramuscular fat, which you can't once the meat is aged, because of the crust that forms on the exterior of dry-aged beef. I told him, "We'll pick out the fresh meat for you, we'll put it up against one wall now, and that will be your wall of meat." He loved the idea. And then for a second I got worried. I said,

"But you're going to take it, right, Riad?" Because here I was, putting tens of thousands of dollars' worth of meat aside for a restaurant that hadn't opened yet. And I'd just met this guy. I had heard of the restaurants where he'd worked, but I'd never been to them. But I liked Riad, and he was so excited about what I was doing, I wanted to do this for him.

A few months after Minetta Tavern opened, I was working at our shop on Leroy Street when I got a call from Riad. It was a Tuesday around midnight. When I picked up the phone, Riad said, "Come to Minetta Tavern *right now*." I said, "What's wrong?" And he goes, "Pat, get your ass over here. Now." I didn't know what had happened. I thought maybe there was something wrong with the meat. I panicked. I threw off my coat and I ran over to the restaurant. Minetta Tavern had quickly become a big celebrity hangout. Basically it was and still is so impossible to get in that you have to either *know* somebody or *be* somebody to eat there. So I walked in, wearing a fleece and work boots, and I noticed Sarah Jessica Parker and Matthew Broderick were there, Gwyneth Paltrow, Madonna . . . I started back toward the kitchen and there was Keith McNally, the owner, and then Riad and Lee came out and they start hugging me in the middle of the dining room. I asked them, "What's going on?" And they said, "Didn't you read Frank Bruni's review?" Frank Bruni was the *New York Times* restaurant reviewer at the time. No matter how many blogs or websites or reviews about a restaurant, one story in the *Times* is all it takes to make or break a place. Riad told me Bruni had written that Minetta was the best steakhouse in New York City. In his review, Bruni talked about the Black Label burger, the steaks, and the aging room. And he mentioned LaFrieda Meats by name. This is very uncommon. Even though restaurants mention purveyors on their menus, reviewers, at least in the *Times*, didn't mention the purveyors. Riad and Lee really felt like LaFrieda Meats had played a part in their success. That was a defining moment for us. From that point on, as far as restaurants wanting our steaks, it was just crazy. I met Frank Bruni not long after that and I thanked him for the review. He said, "No, don't thank me. That was seriously the best steak I ever had."

OPPOSITE: *Minetta Tavern on Minetta Lane in Greenwich Village, New York City.*

ALL ABOUT BEEF

Beef has been consumed by humans since prehistoric times; cave paintings dating back to 8000 BC show images of domesticated cattle. Today, beef is the third most consumed meat in the world. Until recently, beef was the most consumed meat in America, but it has been surpassed by poultry. Nevertheless, America produces 25 percent of the world's beef supply, and cattle production represents the largest single segment of American agriculture. What's more, the culture of beef, whether it's in the image of cowboys, ranches, or hamburgers, is a part of America's identity.

Today, there are essentially two types of beef on the American market: that harvested from "fed" cattle, which means the cattle were raised specifically to produce high-quality meat, and meat harvested from older dairy cows, which typically ends up in low-quality chopped meat. The meat from cattle thirty months or older is specified as "risk material" because of the threat of BSE (mad cow disease). This meat is often seen at retail in chopped meat, and then sold to fast-food chains, which is just one reason I don't feed my children fast food.

The USDA grades beef according to the age of the animal and the amount of intramuscular fat the meat contains. Grade A beef, or "prime," which comes from cattle between nine and thirty months old, is the best, followed by "choice," "select," and "standard." You'll almost never see "standard" or those rated lower than "standard" in stores. The grading of beef is voluntary and done for marketing purposes, which means that low-end beef is typically "no roll," which is the term we use for beef that is not graded.

GRASS-FED VS. GRAIN-FINISHED BEEF

In recent years there has been a lot of misconception about grass-fed versus grain-fed (also called grain-finished) meat due to the information and misinformation in the media. The two most widely held misconceptions are that it is healthier for the animal to eat an all-grass diet, and that cattle fed on an all-grass diet have a lower carbon footprint than those fed grain. Both of these beliefs are wrong.

All beef cattle are raised on grass for the first 85 percent of their lives. But where grass-fed cattle eat the same diet until slaughter, at 120 to 160 days before slaughter, grain-fed cattle are moved from grass to a diet of silage, which is a mixture of primarily corn (both the plant and the kernel), alfalfa, wheat, and barley. The change in diet is done to fatten the animal, which increases marbling, which in turn results in tender, flavorful meat.

Finishing cattle with grain takes a significantly shorter period of time and thus, cattle fed an all-grain diet produce fewer greenhouse emissions than those that are strictly grass-fed. And as for the notion that corn is unhealthy for the animal: It's in no way unhealthy. The idea that corn-fed cattle

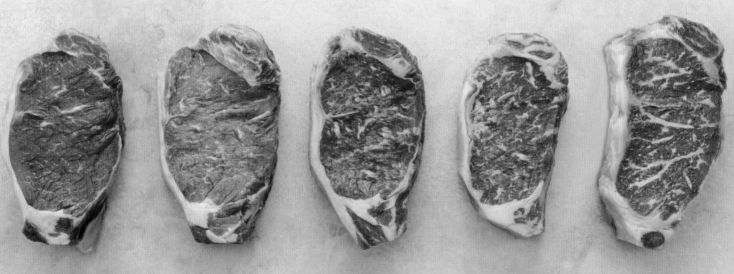

Grass fed   Select   Choice   High Choice   Prime

are unhealthy may come from images of very old cattle being prodded to get them to slaughter. Those are old dairy cows; they weren't raised for meat, so they have no muscle or fat. They are force-fed corn in order to try to develop those things. These are not the animals we deal in. The animals we buy are all healthy and under twenty-four months of age.

Another fact to consider is that the majority of American beef comes from the Midwest, which is also known as the Corn Belt. So you have American corn farmers supplying their product to their neighboring cattle farmers. There is nothing more sustainable than that. Ask a grass cattle farmer what he feeds the cattle in the winter, or what he does when the cattle have trampled all their paddocks and the grass hasn't yet grown back. They all supplement the cattle with grain or corn.

Grass-fed meat is also touted as being healthier for the consumer. The main argument for the health properties of grass-fed meat is that it is high in omega-3 fatty acids, which are known to be good for you. But there is so little of these fats in grass-fed meat that you would have to eat more than you possibly could for it to make any difference. In any case, I am in the business of providing restaurants with the most flavorful meat available, and that is not grass-fed meat.

Grain-fed beef accounts for an overwhelming majority of beef sold in the United States. And with good reason. From an economical standpoint, there is no better way to add weight to the animal; it also results in a better product from a culinary point of view.

There is some consumer interest in grass-fed beef, but that is primarily at the retail level, because customers have read and bought into the hype. Very few chefs ever ask for grass-fed beef, and when they do it's a short run before they switch back to grain-finished beef. It tastes better, and that's what chefs care about.

BUYING BEEF

When buying beef, insist on beef that comes from Black Angus cattle that are under twenty-four months of age; the only way to know this is to ask your butcher. Also look for meat that appears moist, not dried out, and is free of stickiness. Beef should have virtually no odor, unless you are buying dry-aged meat, which can have a sharp smell similar to that of corn. And you want beef that is a light red, almost pink color, and evenly colored throughout. Beef with a dark red or purplish hue comes from an old animal. In the industry, they're referred to as "dark cutters"; the color indicates that meat is at the low end of the quality spectrum.

COOKING BEEF

The most controversial factor when it comes to cooking beef is what temperature you want it cooked to. Whether you want your steak well-done or rare is a matter of personal preference and it's almost impossible to sway people from what they like or are accustomed to. The USDA recommends cooking beef to an internal temperature of 160°F to kill any pathogens that might exist on the surface of the meat, but I don't know a single chef who would recommend cooking a prime steak past medium-rare (135°F). The same holds true for quality roasts, such as a standing rib roast (see Standing Rib Roast with Dried Porcini Rub and Port Wine Reduction, page 216). If you're confident that your meat is fresh, you can eat it raw—think about steak tartare or Carne Crudo (page 100). From my teenage years until this day, anytime I split a top round of beef, I slice a sliver from the center and eat it raw.

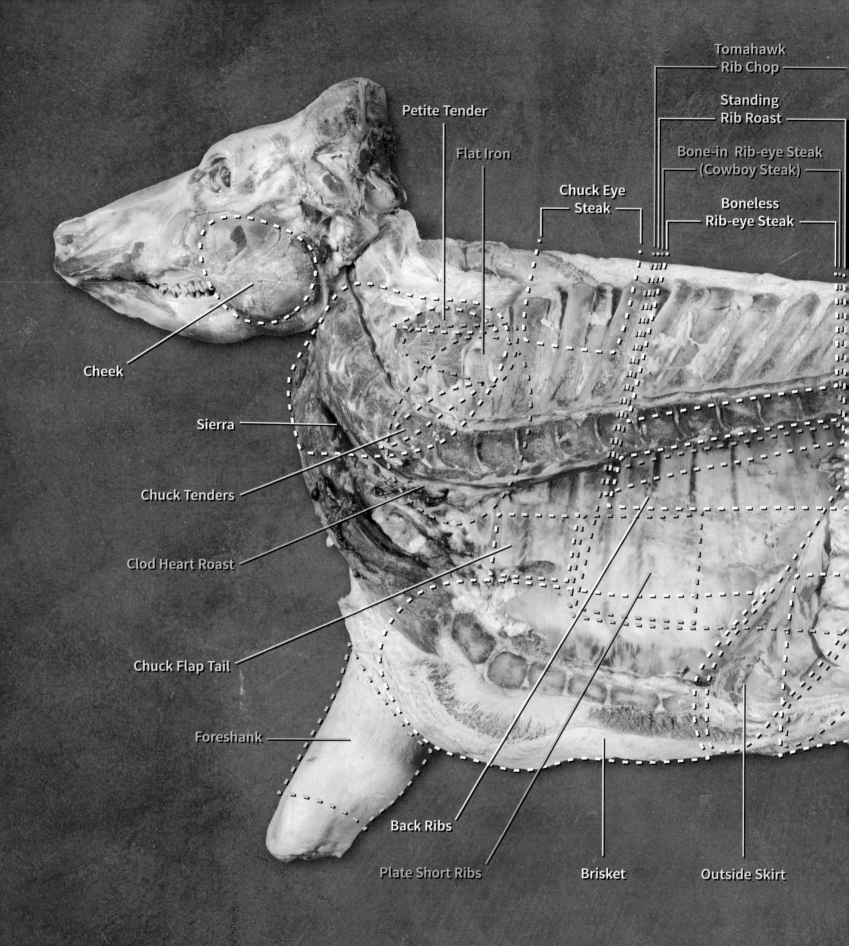

Tomahawk
Rib Chop

Standing
Rib Roast

Bone-in Rib-eye Steak
(Cowboy Steak)

Boneless
Rib-eye Steak

Petite Tender

Flat Iron

Chuck Eye
Steak

Cheek

Sierra

Chuck Tenders

Clod Heart Roast

Chuck Flap Tail

Foreshank

Back Ribs

Plate Short Ribs

Brisket

Outside Skirt

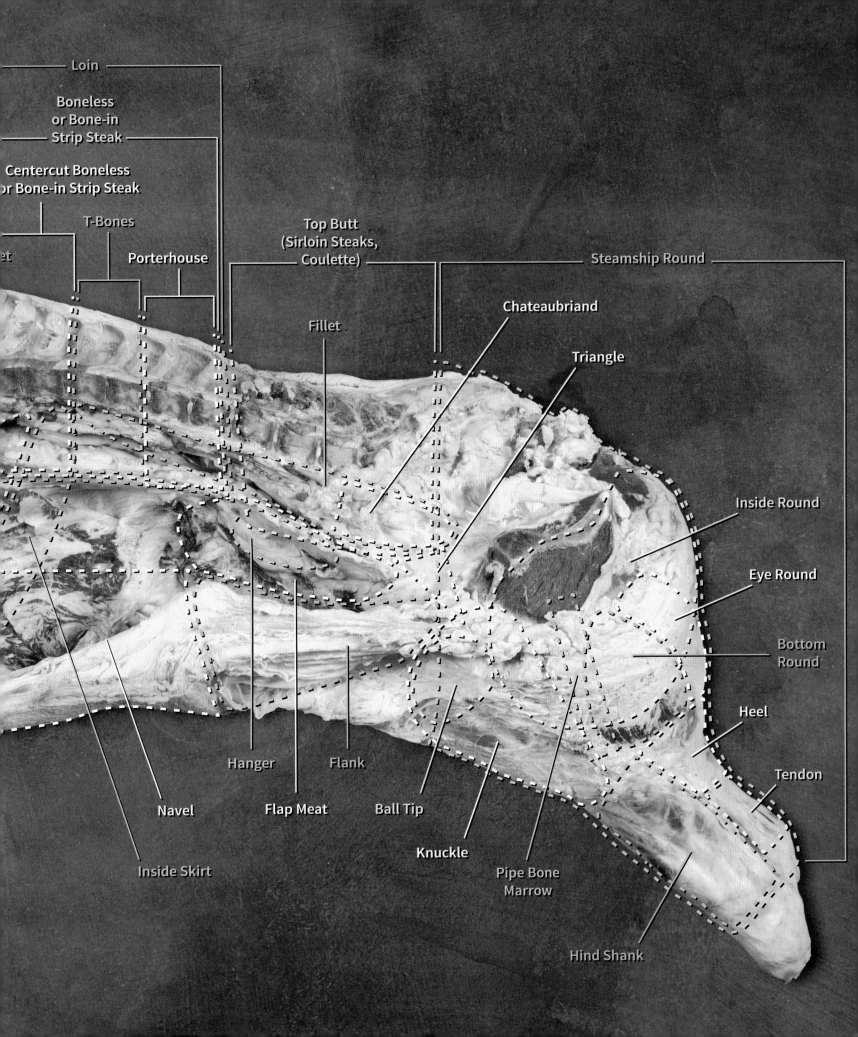

Loin

Boneless
or Bone-in
Strip Steak

Centercut Boneless
or Bone-in Strip Steak

T-Bones

Porterhouse

et

Top Butt
(Sirloin Steaks,
Coulette)

Fillet

Steamship Round

Chateaubriand

Triangle

Inside Round

Eye Round

Bottom
Round

Heel

Tendon

Hanger

Flank

Navel

Flap Meat

Ball Tip

Knuckle

Inside Skirt

Pipe Bone
Marrow

Hind Shank

BEEF CUTS

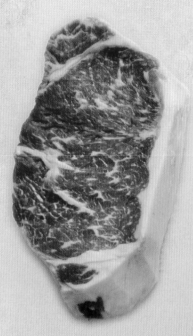

Boneless Strip Loin Steak

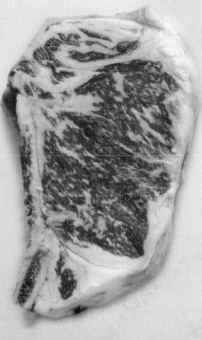

Bone-in Strip Loin Steak

T-Bone Steak

BEEF STEAKS

With the chine bone and spine removed, the bone-in strip loin steak becomes a **boneless strip loin steak**. Some people prefer this because you don't have to cut around the bone; a boneless steak also cooks more evenly, and unlike a rib steak, there is no sparerib meat to gnaw on as with the bone of a strip steak. Both have their fans and with good reason.

The **bone-in strip loin steak**, named because it is "stripped" from the short loin (a primal cut of the animal's lower back), is the iconic steakhouse steak. Also called New York strip, Kansas City strip, shell steak, hotel-cut strip steak, or ambassador steak, it is very tender and juicy. I prefer this to a boneless steak both because a steak looks beautiful and majestic when it comes out with a

bone, and I also like the experience of cutting around a bone when I'm eating a steak. The last steaks along the loin are called "end steaks," or "vein steaks," for the large nerve running along the edge. Restaurants buy the entire loin and cut the steaks from that; they usually reserve those for patrons who order their meat well-done. In a retail shop, end steaks should be labeled as such, but to be sure to specify that you don't want end steaks.

T-bone steak is cut from the short loin across the animal's spine, with sections of both the strip and tenderloin muscles separated by the familiar T-shaped bone. Although the porterhouse is considered a more luxurious cut, I prefer the T-bone because it has only a scallop-size piece of fillet, which for me is just enough.

The **porterhouse steak** is a classic steakhouse steak. It's the same cut as the T-bone, but from farther back on the animal, so it contains a larger portion of tenderloin. This is the favorite steak for a lot of people, who think it offers the best of both worlds: the strip, prized for its flavor, and the tenderloin for its tenderness. It has a nerve that runs through the strip side; that nerve is smaller on the T-bone.

Tenderloin or "**filet mignon**," is the most tender and expensive cut; it is made up of very fine and delicate muscle fibers that account for its characteristic tenderness. It's a long cylindrical muscle that runs along the inside of the spine from the mid-body to the hind leg and tapers as it goes toward the front of the animal. You'll

Hanger Steak

Porterhouse Steak

Filet Mignon

Chateaubriand

occasionally see tenderloin roasted whole, but more commonly you'll see it cut into individual cylindrical steaks about 2½ inches tall, usually referred to as filet mignon, which means "small boneless steak" in French. Because tenderloin has almost no marbling or fat, it doesn't have a lot of flavor, so it is usually accompanied by a rich sauce, such as a wine reduction. Tenderloin isn't as flavorful as other cuts, but I do love Beef Wellington (see Beef Wellington with Mushroom Cream Sauce, page 198), which is made with filet mignon, and it's also delicious in LaFrieda's Original Filet Mignon Steak Sandwich (page 218) because the onions and cheese lend it a lot of

flavor. On an almost nightly basis at work, I take advantage of the buttery texture of tenderloin and slice it very thin and eat it straight from the slicer. If you have access to a meat slicer, you could use tenderloin to make carpaccio, an Italian dish of sliced beef dressed with olive oil, lemon, shaved Parmigiano-Reggiano, and arugula.

The thickest portion of the tenderloin, referred to as the head of the fillet, is cut about 3 inches thick to make **Chateaubriand**, which refers to both the dish of roasted tenderloin for two—served with either béarnaise (see Foolproof Béarnaise, page 213) or mustard sauce— and the cut used to make it.

Hanger steak, cut from the diaphragm, gets its name because it hangs, surrounded by kidney fat, from the loin. The hanger is the only cut that would be damaged if not removed whole when the animal is bisected. It's also the only cut that there is only one of; the rest of the animal is symmetrical. The hanger steak has a tough silverskin in the middle that must be removed before cooking it; in the process, the steak is cut into two pieces, one of which weighs about double the other. The steak is often called "butcher's steak," because in the old days, if the hanger was damaged, butchers would take it home. It's a tough cut; even cut against the grain, it can be chewy, but it has a good, rich flavor.

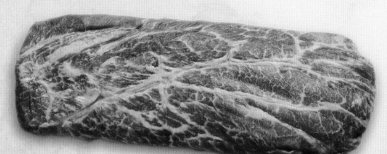

Flat Iron Steak

Chuck Flap Tail

Sliced Chuck Flap Tail

Clod Heart Roast

Chuck Tender

Sierra Cut

Chuck Eye Steak

Petite Tender

FLATIRON

The **flat iron steak**, named for its ironlike shape, is a tender cut that comes from the front shoulder, under the shoulder blade. In a blind taste test some years back, the participants couldn't tell the difference between a New York strip and a flat iron. That was big news for the flat iron; it has since become a popular steakhouse item. The flat iron has a large strip of sinew down the middle that makes it difficult to use as a steak, and for years, we used it only to make chopped meat. To get around that, more recently, the flat iron has begun to be cut into two fillets and the sinew dividing them removed. It's a very good steak, but I also think it's one-third the price of strip steak for good reason.

The **chuck flap tail**, a boneless cut from the chuck, is the very same muscle as short ribs. Flap tail is about the same price as short ribs, but you're not paying for the bone, so it's more economical. Flap tail also makes a flavorful addition to a chopped beef blend (see Pat's Favorite Blends, page 74).

Sliced chuck flap tail sliced thin, is used in Korean-Style Sticky "Short Rib" Sandwiches with Ginger-Sesame Aïoli (page 195). To use flap tail in place of long-bone short ribs, have your butcher cut the meat to the width of a short rib bone, about 1½ inches.

The **chuck tender**, which comes from the shoulder, is similar in shape to tenderloin, which is why it is often called the "mock tender." Unlike the tender, it is a very tough cut, so it is usually cut into "minute" steaks, or sliced and used in stir-fries.

The **petite tender**, also called the shoulder tender, is a flavorful and economical cut from the chuck. It is similar in shape (but much smaller) than tenderloin. Restaurants in New York often sell petite tender as "mini fillets," and prepare them as they would tenderloin; they are tender, but nowhere near as buttery as the real thing.

The **clod heart roast**, cut from the top part of the front shoulder above the shoulder blade, makes a flavorful and economical roast. It can also be ground to make lean chopped beef; we use it along with fattier cuts to lean out our Original Blend (page 74).

The **Sierra cut**, similar in structure and appearance to flank steak, is the largest single muscle from the chuck roll, or shoulder. It's heavily marbled, but in this particular cut, marbling does not translate to tenderness. It is an economy cut, usually sliced into strips for stir-fry meat or what in my father's day they would call pepper steaks.

The **chuck eye steak** has the same tenderness and flavor as the more expensive rib-eye. It consists of the same muscle group as the rib-eye. They are the first two cuts from the shoulder before you start cutting rib-eyes. When a restaurant calls asking for a good, economical alternative to rib-eye, I often suggest this.

Navel

Flank Steak

**Outside Skirt
Steak**

**Inside Skirt
Steak**

Brisket

True New York pastrami is made from beef **navel**, which is a flat, wavy cut that comes from the plate. It's full of fat and flavor. We use it in some of our chopped beef blends.

Flank steak, which comes from the lower belly, is a large, flat muscle with long muscle fibers, which makes it very chewy. It is the steak traditionally used to make London broil, an American dish where the meat is marinated, seared, and sliced that is unknown in England. Asians use flank steak very often.

The **outside skirt steak**, derived from the diaphragm, helps with the inhalation and exhalation functions of the lungs. It's one of my two favorite steaks (the other being rib-eye). Skirt steak is not as tender as what we call "middle meats," but it has a distinct flavor. If I go to my father's house and he's grilling, you can bet he'll be grilling skirt steaks. We both love it rare.

The **inside skirt steak**, so named because it is deeper inside the animal, closer to the lungs than the outside skirt, isn't nearly as tender or flavorful as the outside skirt. The outside is about two-thirds as wide as the inside skirt, and it has more marbling. Inside skirt needs to be marinated to tenderize it; it's often prepared as fajita meat. Both the inside and outside skirts are called Romanian steaks when you see them in old-school diners.

The **brisket**, which corresponds to the animal's chest, consists of the deep pectoral—called the "first cut" or "lean brisket"—and the superficial pectoral—referred to as the "second cut," the "point," or the "nose"— divided by about 1½ inches of fat. The second cut has triple the amount of marbling. Whole brisket is used to make corned beef, pastrami, and Texas-style barbecue; it's also a staple in Jewish-style delicatessens, where it's sliced and made into sandwiches. When I make brisket (see Jewish Deli-Style Brisket, page 197), I use only the second cut. Both sides of brisket have a slightly sweet, rich flavor, which is why we use it in many of our hamburger blends, including Original Blend (page 74).

Plate Short Ribs

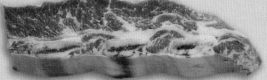

Flanken-Style Ribs

Tomahawk Short Ribs

Boneless Rib-Eye Steak

Bone-in Rib-Eye

Tomahawk Steak

Beef **plate short ribs** are cut from the plate, on the lower part of the animal's rib section, and include three ribs. Short ribs can be butchered in different ways, either cut **flanken-style** across the ribs, so each portion contains three pieces of rib bone with the meat lying across them, or they can be cut parallel to the bone, called "long bone," where the meat sits directly on top of the bone (not pictured). Short ribs are most often braised to tenderize the tough meat, as in Chipotle-Braised Tomahawk Short Ribs (page 207). In Korean barbecue, short ribs are sliced thinly flanken-style, then marinated to tenderize the meat, and cooked quickly on the grill as they are for Korean-Style Sticky "Short Rib" Sandwiches with Ginger-Sesame Aïoli (page 195).

Making **tomahawk short ribs** is something that I came up with. I start with a long-bone short rib, french the meat off the bone (see "Frenching a Rib Bone," page 186), and then roll the meat into a pinwheel. It makes for a beautiful and unusual presentation.

Without the bone, the rib steak is called the **boneless rib-eye steak**; I prefer it with the bone because I like to gnaw the sparerib meat off the bone. The rib-eye is sometimes called the Delmonico, named for the nineteenth-century New York City restaurant that served it.

Ask any butcher what his or her favorite steak is and more often than not they'll tell you it's the **bone-in rib-eye** or rib steak. (For me, it's the second favorite,

after outside skirt.) The rib-eye consists of two very different muscles: the loin, also called the *longissimus dorsi*, or "eye," and the cap, also called *spinalis dorsi* or "deckle." The rib-eye is the most marbled and flavorful meat on the entire animal. This one has the intercostal meat left on the bone, but when the bone is frenched, the same steak is known as a frenched cowboy steak (page 178).

The **tomahawk steak** is a bone-in rib steak with the entire rib bone intact. It is cut based on the thickness of the bone and is typically two inches thick. One tomahawk can easily feed two people.

Back Ribs

Standing Rib Roast

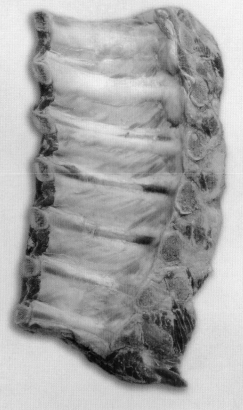

**Frenched
Cowboy Steak**

Beef **back ribs** are the bones trimmed from the rib-eye; they consist of mostly intercostal or "finger" meat, which needs to be cooked low and slow, braised, or smoked. Back ribs are very popular in Texas and Kansas City–style barbecue. We can hardly keep up with demand because of the popularity of barbecue joints in New York City.

A full **standing rib roast** is a rack that consists of the same tender, juicy eye meat that comprises rib-eye steaks. Traditionally it is cooked with the ribs standing straight up; this requires that the chine bone be left intact, which means that you would have to carve this off before slicing the roast. It is often called "prime rib," but that doesn't mean the meat is graded "prime." Standing rib roasts are popular around the holidays, when you want to put a roast in the oven

and forget about it while you prepare everything else, and when you want a large-format roast for a large group (see Standing Rib Roast with Dried Porcini Rub and Port Wine Reduction, page 216). The rib roast pictured is frenched (see "Frenching a Rib Bone," page 186) for presentation.

A **frenched cowboy steak** is a rib steak with the rib bone frenched, which is done purely for presentation. With the rib bone left even longer, it becomes a tomahawk steak (see "Frenching a Rib Bone," page 186). Cowboy steaks have been popular for many years, but tomahawks are a fairly recent phenomenon.

The **hind shank** contains the tibia bone surrounded by a dense, tightly bound mass of muscles. Hind shank is rich in collagen, which converts into gelatin when cooked. We often crosscut it for chefs to make an economical version of veal osso buco; or for an unusual twist on traditional beef bourguignon (see Braised Beef Shank Bourguignon, page 204).

Canoe-cut pipe bone marrow is made of the femur bone with the knuckles cut off at either end, and the bones split down the middle. They are often cut into cross sections, but I prefer the canoe cut, because this way, the marrow doesn't spill out when the bones are roasted.

Hind Shank

Canoe-Cut Pipe Bone Marrow

Heel

Knuckle

Knuckle Bones

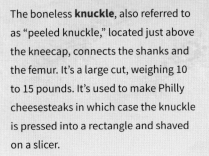

Ball Tip Steak

Roasted bone marrow has become extremely popular in restaurants over the last ten years. The soft marrow runs through the center and becomes custardlike when roasted. It's usually eaten spread on toast.

The **heel** is the outer part of the calf muscle on the hind shank. It's similar in flavor and texture to shank meat. Like shank meat, it's very tough and contains an abundance of gelatin, which makes it a great choice for stew.

The boneless **knuckle**, also referred to as "peeled knuckle," located just above the kneecap, connects the shanks and the femur. It's a large cut, weighing 10 to 15 pounds. It's used to make Philly cheesesteaks in which case the knuckle is pressed into a rectangle and shaved on a slicer.

Knuckle bones are used to make beef stock (see Brown Veal Stock, page 31); they contain a lot of collagen, which makes for a rich, gelatinous stock.

The **ball tip steak** comes from the leg at the tip of the knuckle. It weighs 2 to 3 pounds and can be cooked as a roast, but is more commonly sliced into "baseball steaks," an inexpensive steak often served at inexpensive chain restaurants as part of "surf and turf" specials. Baseball steaks have no fat content, no flavor, and are not very tender. The only reason to buy this cut is for the price; but for the same price I would rather eat a hamburger.

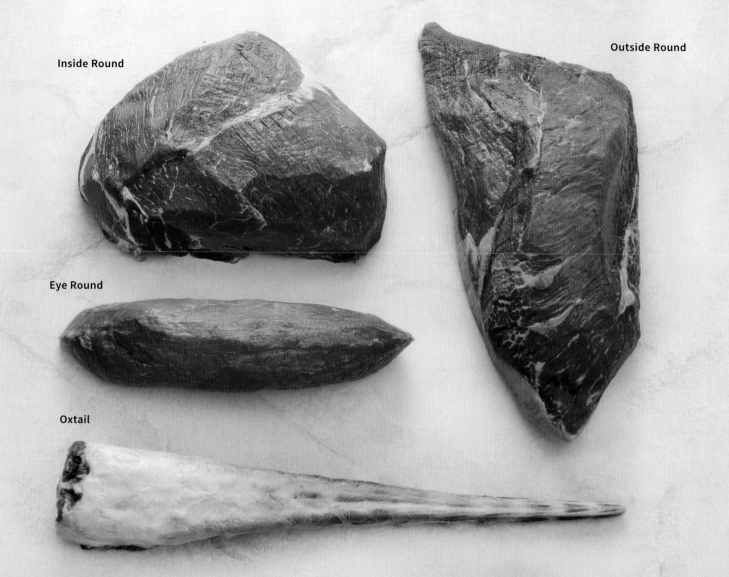

Inside Round

Outside Round

Eye Round

Oxtail

TAIL

The **inside round** (also called top round) is a large (17- to 23-pound) economy roast used to make everything from London broil to Philly cheesesteaks. But it's most commonly used to make roast beef. It is inexpensive, and it doesn't contain bones or nerves. There is no comparison between fresh roast beef and the manufactured product. A roasted inside round makes a delicious, inexpensive meal to put on the table. It's large, but you can slice meat all week long to make sandwiches.

The **eye round** is a single muscle roast, about 4 to 5 pounds, and an almost

perfect cylindrical shape. It is fairly lean so it can be dry, but if you roast it at high heat and don't overcook it, you can make a nice roast beef. Because of its shape, it's great for making carpaccio, sliced raw beef that in Italian cuisine is traditionally drizzled with olive oil and often served with an arugula salad.

The term **oxtail** once actually referred to the tail of an ox, but now it is a culinary term for beef tail. It is a very expensive cut. It is almost all bone and contains very little meat. It is most often used to make oxtail soup, which makes some sense economically because you are

using the oxtails to flavor a whole pot of soup. In Latino cooking, where it is very prevalent, fat is trimmed off crosscuts of oxtail and the meat is then braised and picked off the bone. The gravylike sauce that surrounds it is rich and flavorful, but it takes a lot of work to get a small bit of meat.

The **outside round**, also called the bottom round, is a large cut from the leg that often weighs as much as 16 pounds and is often used to make pot roast. Because it is lean, it is also used for making beef jerky. We grind it to make "ground round" for hamburgers.

Liver

Tongue

Heart

Cheek

Suet

Honeycomb
Tripe

OFFAL

Beef **liver** has a more intense flavor than chicken or calf's liver. But if you soak it in milk, which helps to mellow its flavor, and cook it to medium-rare, it is a good economical alternative to either (see Lidia Bastianich's Seared Calf's Liver with Caramelized Onions and Balsamic, page 30). Beef liver is often sold frozen, whereas calf's liver is too delicate to freeze.

Beef **tongue** is one of the less expensive cuts on the animal. It needs to be braised and then the skin peeled off before searing or grilling it. It has become more popular in recent years.

Beef **heart** is a very tough and lean muscle that is generally braised to tenderize it. It has a lot of veins that have to be trimmed before you cook it. See if your butcher will do this for you. We sell a lot, especially in recent years as chefs and diners have become more adventurous in their choices.

Beef **cheeks**, an extremely tough and fibrous muscle, used to be an inexpensive cut of meat, but that is no longer the case as they have become very popular with chefs who braise them in wine until they are fork-tender. The meat is most often used as ravioli filling, but if you want to enjoy this rich, flavorful meat on its own, use beef

cheeks in place of shanks to make Braised Beef Shank Bourguignon (page 204).

Beef tripe is the lining of the stomach. Cows have four stomachs, each of which has a different texture and a different name. Tripe can be derived from any of these, but the only tripe you will see at the market is **honeycomb tripe**, which is from the second chamber. Tripe needs to be boiled and/or braised to tenderize it as it is in Tripe in Red Sauce (page 192).

Suet is fat derived from the kidney and loin area; it is often rendered and used for deep-fat frying.

Top Butt

Sirloin Steak

Coulette

Triangle

Sirloin Flap

SIRLOIN AND FLAP

The **top butt** is cut from the sirloin and is one of the largest loin cuts, spanning several muscles and weighing up to 15 pounds. You'll rarely see top butt labeled as such at retail; it's usually sliced into **sirloin steaks**, which are low-quality steaks offered as part of surf and turf at lower-end restaurants. You often see "sirloin" or "top sirloin" written on menus as if it's a bragging point, but that is nothing more than a marketing campaign. Sirloin is not terrible, but there's nothing special about it. It has almost no intramuscular fat and therefore isn't particularly tender or flavorful.

The **coulette** refers to the cap of the top butt; it is generally sliced into coulette steaks, which are often sold as "top sirloin." It's a popular cut in Argentine steakhouses. Coulette steaks are more marbled and tender than sirloin steaks, and definitely the preferable of the two.

The beef **triangle**, also known as tri-tip, is a triangular-shaped cut from the bottom sirloin, typically weighing 3 to 4 pounds. It is a popular cut in central and southern California, where it's marinated and grilled whole for Santa Maria barbecue. You rarely see it in New York.

The **sirloin flap**, also called "flap steak" or "flap meat," is derived from the bottom sirloin butt. It has striated muscles similar to skirt steak, and robust flavor like strip steak, but it's chewy. It's usually cut into bavette steaks, which are economical steaks such as those that are offered at restaurants as a bar steak. Flap steaks cut from Wagyu beef are very tender and a good alternative to prime New York strip steaks because they will be less expensive, yet just as great of an experience.

STEAMSHIP ROUND

The single largest cut of beef by far is the 85-pound **steamship round**, which is basically the whole leg, or "round" primal cut from which the inside round, eye round, and bottom round are cut. The steamship round got its name because at one time it was a mainstay on ocean liners; the giant roast could be used to feed a large number of guests. It's an event dish, there's no doubt about it. It makes a great presentation piece with the frenched femur bone sticking out like a handle. If you wanted to cook beef instead of the more common pig in a Caja China, this, coated in Dried Porcini Rub (see page 217), would be the piece of meat to use.

DRY-AGED STEAKS

Dry-aging is a process where steaks are hung or put on racks in a temperature- and humidity-controlled room for 21 to 120 days in order to tenderize the meat and make it more flavorful. Through the process of dry-aging, the moisture is drawn out of the meat, so the flavor becomes concentrated. Also, in the process of aging, the steak's natural enzymes work to break down collagen in the meat, essentially decomposing it. Collagen is what makes muscle tough, so when it starts to break down, the meat becomes tender. An aged steak can be so tender that you could stick your finger right through it. Dry-aged beef has a sweet, cornlike smell similar to that of cooked beer.

7 days: The collagen has just begun to break down, but the steak won't have the flavor or texture qualities that you are looking for in a dry-aged steak. Steak is not sold aged to this stage. The meat is still fairly bright, but it will darken as it ages and becomes drier.

21 days: The steak loses 10 percent of its weight in the first 3 weeks through evaporation. The water seeps out the front and the back of the meat, but the fat and bone on the sides of the steak make the sides waterproof. Because the meat shrinks, the steak will become more concave as it ages. Although the fat doesn't shrink, it does darken in the aging process.

30 days: This is the most commonly requested age in steaks. The steak has developed the flavor and texture qualities associated with dry-aged meat: It is very tender, with a flavor I can best describe as a mix of buttered popcorn and rare roast beef. At this point the steak has lost 15 percent of its total weight.

45 days: The steak has a little bit more funk than one aged to 30 days. The steak has lost only a fraction more weight, and the flavor of the fat changes before the meat does, so it's important not to trim off all the fat before you cook it. (And what you do trim, use to make a condiment of Aged-Beef Lard with Rosemary and Garlic, page 213.)

90 days: The white striations on the surface of the meat are good mold and also salt, which is extracted from the meat along with the water. The crust that develops around the meat protects it in the same way a rind does with cheese. The exterior crust is shaved off before the meat is sold. What you're left with is a steak that is slightly darker and drier in appearance than fresh steak, but to the untrained eye the two might be indistinguishable.

120 days: This is the longest we age steaks, and it's about four times as long as aged steaks you'd find at most restaurants and butcher shops. Only a handful of very high-end restaurants buy it. The steak has lost 35 percent of its original weight. A steak aged this long has a very funky flavor and it's also very expensive, so it is for someone who really appreciates an intense beef flavor.

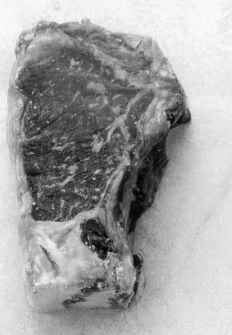

7 Days

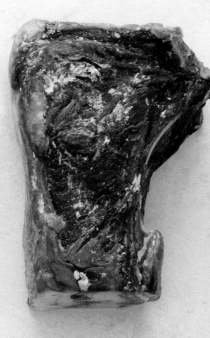

21 Days

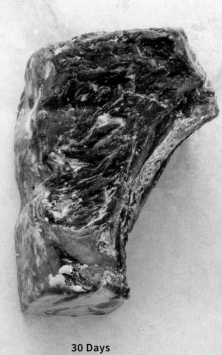

30 Days

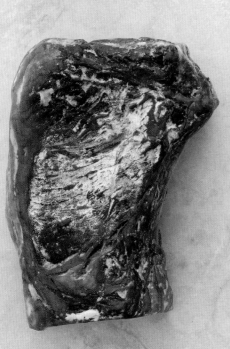

45 Days

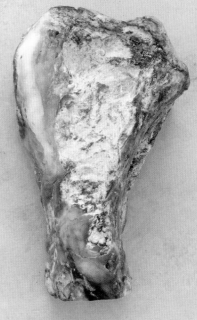

90 Days

120 Days

BUTCHERING TECHNIQUES
FRENCHING A RIB BONE

A "frenched" rib bone is one that has been stripped clean of meat, usually sparerib meat. This is done solely for presentation. A frenched rib steak makes a cowboy steak; and with a longer bone, it becomes a tomahawk steak. It's a fun, dramatic presentation.

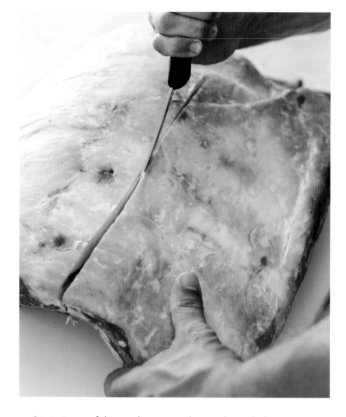

1. To french the bone(s) of a rib steak, rack, or short rib, rest the cut in question with the bone(s) facing down and the fat cap facing up. Insert a boning knife at the point where the meat begins to taper off and mark off each side at the point where the loin eye muscle meets the bone.

2. Start at one of the marks you made, cut through the meat and fat until the knife is resting on the bone, then cut all the way across the rack, chop, or rib to the second mark.

3. Stand the meat with the bone(s) facing up and run the knife along the bone on the side you made the horizontal cut to strip the remaining meat off the bone(s) so the bone is clean.

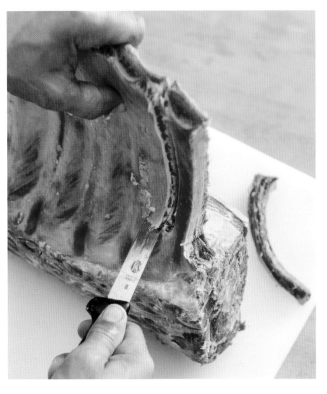

5. Start with the outermost bone, draw the knife down the length of the bone to cut out the intercostal meat—also called "finger" meat because of its shape.

4. Start at the top of the bone(s), make downward movements to shave the meat off the bone(s).

6. Continue cutting between the bones in a U motion, going down one bone and then up on its neighbor until you've removed the finger meat from between all of the bones.

8. One at a time, with the meat facing up, draw your knife across the bone away from your body to scrape off any remaining meat, leaving the bone neat and clean.

7. Unless you are making a crown roast, at this point you can cut the rack into individual chops.

9. When you french the bone of a rib steak with the full rib bone still attached it's called a tomahawk steak.

ROASTED BONE MARROW WITH SHALLOT CONFIT

SHALLOT CONFIT

2 cups finely chopped shallots
(about 1¼ pounds)

2 cups red wine

1 cup port

1 cup packed light or dark
brown sugar

½ teaspoon kosher salt

1 bay leaf

MARROW BONES

6 canoe-cut beef pipe marrow
bones

1 tablespoon plus 1 teaspoon
Maldon or other flaky sea salt
plus more for seasoning

1 tablespoon freshly ground black
pepper (mignonette)

1 tablespoon fresh thyme leaves

1 tablespoon chopped fresh
flat-leaf parsley leaves

TOAST

12 long diagonal slices (½-inch-
thick) baguette

1 clove garlic

¼ pound (1 stick) unsalted butter,
melted

BUTCHER'S NOTE:

Ask your butcher for "canoe-cut"
marrow bones.

This simple bone marrow preparation from Minetta Tavern is seasoned with salt and pepper and roasted, and then served with a rich, sweet shallot confit. It couldn't be easier to make, or more delicious. This recipe makes more shallot confit than you'll need for six marrow bones, but it's great on grilled meats or sandwiches. It will keep for at least a week in the refrigerator.

SERVES 6

1. For the shallot confit: In a medium saucepan, combine the shallots, red wine, port, brown sugar, salt, and bay leaf. Bring to a boil over high heat, reduce the heat, and simmer the shallots, stirring occasionally, until the liquid thickens and the shallots appear glossy, 40 to 50 minutes. Turn off the heat and allow it to cool to room temperature before serving. Refrigerate it in an airtight container. This can be made up to a week in advance. Warm it over low heat before serving.

2. For the marrow bones: Arrange the bones cut side up in two baking dishes. Cover them with water and put them in the refrigerator overnight to soak.

3. Preheat the broiler with the oven rack about 2 inches from the heat source (if it's adjustable).

4. Drain the bones, pat them dry, and arrange them cut side up on a baking sheet. (It may seem like a jigsaw puzzle getting all the bones to fit on one sheet, but you can do it; and if not, cook them in batches.) Season the cut side of the bones liberally with the salt and pepper. Put them under the broiler until they are deep brown and charred in places, 10 to 12 minutes.

5. Remove the bones from the broiler but leave the broiler on. Sprinkle the tops of the marrow bones with the thyme, parsley, and the additional salt.

6. For the toast: Rub each slice of bread on both sides with the garlic clove and brush both sides with melted butter. Lay the slices on a baking sheet. When you take the marrow bones out of the broiler, put the bread slices in and toast them until they are golden and crispy, about 30 seconds.

7. Serve the marrow with the shallot confit and toast on the side.

TRIPE IN RED SAUCE

1½ pounds honeycomb tripe, cut
    on an angle into strips ½ inch
    wide and about 3 inches long

Kosher salt

6 cups Tomato Sauce (page 95; or
    store-bought)

¼ cup sugar

Toasted semolina bread

There's nothing worse for a tripe addict such as myself than thinking you have a piece of tripe on the end of your fork and it turns out to be a potato. What I like about the way we make tripe in our family is that there are none of the distractions that you often see in tripe dishes. No potatoes. No peas. Nothing but tripe and red sauce and toasted semolina bread to sop it all up. Simple as can be. Our favorite bread is a wide, braided semolina loaf packed with sesame seeds.

SERVES 8

1. Rinse the tripe under cold water. Bring a large pot of salted water to a boil (add about 1 tablespoon of salt per quart). Add the tripe and boil it until it's tender, about 1½ hours. Drain the tripe.

2. Meanwhile, follow the recipe for the tomato sauce to the point where you get the first bubble (about 1½ hours after you add the tomatoes). If you're using store-bought sauce, heat the sauce over medium heat, stirring often, until it begins to bubble. Stir in the tripe and sugar and return the sauce to a simmer over medium heat. Reduce the heat to low, cover the pot, and gently simmer the tripe for about 1 hour to tenderize the tripe further and marry the flavors.

3. Serve the tripe with the semolina bread.

KOREAN-STYLE STICKY "SHORT RIB" SANDWICHES WITH GINGER-SESAME AÏOLI

SHORT RIBS

1 Asian pear (about ½ pound), peeled, cored, and cut into 1-inch pieces

½ medium yellow onion, diced (about ½ cup)

1 ounce (about 2 inches) fresh ginger, peeled

4 cloves garlic

1½ cups reduced-sodium soy sauce

1 cup packed dark brown sugar

¾ cup mirin

3 ounces dried shiitakes, ground in a spice grinder (about ¾ cup)

½ tablespoon crushed red pepper flakes

2½ pounds chuck flap tail or boneless short ribs, cut ⅓ to ¼ inch thick

GINGER-SESAME AÏOLI

1 cup mayonnaise

1 tablespoon rice vinegar

2 teaspoons grated fresh ginger

1 clove garlic, minced or grated

½ teaspoon sesame oil

½ teaspoon mirin

½ teaspoon kosher salt

CUCUMBER

1 English cucumber (about 9 ounces), cut crosswise into ⅛-inch-thick rounds

1 tablespoon sugar

1 tablespoon kosher salt

For these sandwiches, I use flap tail in place of short rib meat because it's the same thing. Most people would use short rib meat and then cut away the bone, wasting a lot of money in the process. In either case, I had never seen flap tail or short rib meat cut against the grain the way they are here until I moved into a Korean neighborhood in New Jersey. Once one of my Korean tenants brought me a big bowl of short ribs cut this way (and marinated so all I had to do was throw them on a grill). I was stunned. Here I was in the meat business and I had never had this cut, nor thought of cutting it this way myself. They were so good—sweet and spicy and redolent with scallion. And I loved the idea of taking a muscle that normally needs to be braised for hours and instead, just by cutting it differently, entirely changes the way it's cooked. Cut this way and marinated, the thin slices of flap tail or short rib meat can be thrown on the grill for a few minutes. My brother Chris's mother-in-law, Janet, who is Korean, gave me her recipe, which was the inspiration for the one here. This recipe makes a lot of sandwiches, but they're small. I could eat five or six of them. They make great party food because they're easy to eat standing up.

MAKES ABOUT 40 SANDWICHES

1. For the short ribs: In a blender, combine the pear, onion, ginger, and garlic and puree. With the blender running, add enough water to form a loose puree, about ¼ cup water. Pour the puree into a large nonreactive baking dish. Add the soy sauce, brown sugar, mirin, ground shiitakes, and red pepper flakes and whisk to combine the ingredients. Add the meat, cover the dish, and put the meat in the refrigerator to marinate for at least 8 and up to 24 hours.

2. For the aïoli: In a small bowl, stir together the mayonnaise, vinegar, ginger, garlic, oil, mirin, and salt. Cover and refrigerate until you're ready to use it, or for up to several days.

3. For the cucumber: Put the slices in a bowl and sprinkle them with the sugar and salt. Toss to coat the cucumber with the seasonings and set aside for 30 minutes. Remove the cucumber slices from the liquid that has been released from them and transfer them to another bowl. Cover and refrigerate until you're ready to serve them, or for up to 24 hours.

(continued)

CARROTS

2 medium carrots, cut into thin
    matchsticks

2 cups apple cider vinegar

½ cup sugar

2 tablespoons kosher salt

3 dried red chiles, left whole

1 star anise

SANDWICHES

40 Chinese steamed buns or
    40 (3-inch segment) baguettes
    (about 5 long baguettes)

1 head butter lettuce, leaves torn
    into 2-inch pieces

¼ cup toasted sesame seeds

1 cup chopped kimchi (optional)

4. For the carrots: Put them in a 1-quart canning jar or large bowl and place a fine-mesh sieve on top. In a small saucepan, combine the vinegar, sugar, salt, chiles, star anise, and 1 cup of water. Bring the liquid to a boil. Remove from the heat and pour the liquid through the sieve over the carrots. Let the carrots cool to room temperature. Cover the jar or bowl and refrigerate the carrots for at least 8 hours and up to 1 month.

5. To cook the meat, preheat a grill or grill pan over high heat. Remove the meat from the marinade, scrape off the excess marinade, and grill the meat until it is nicely browned on each side, about 1 minute per side.

6. For the sandwiches: Split the buns or baguettes in half, leaving them hinged on one side. Spread 1 teaspoon aïoli on the bottom of each bun or baguette. Lay a lettuce leaf on top of the aïoli and a few carrot matchsticks on top of the lettuce. Lay 2 slices of meat on each sandwich and a few cucumber slices on each serving of meat. Sprinkle each sandwich with a pinch of sesame seeds and top with 1 teaspoon kimchi, if using. Close the sandwiches and serve.

JEWISH DELI-STYLE BRISKET

1 brisket (about 4 pounds)

1 tablespoon plus ½ teaspoon kosher salt

½ teaspoon freshly ground black pepper

6 cups beef stock (Brown Veal Stock, page 31; or low-sodium store-bought beef stock), or as needed

½ cup packed light or dark brown sugar

½ cup honey

¼ teaspoon ground cinnamon

¼ teaspoon ground cloves

BUTCHER'S NOTE:
Ask your butcher for the "second cut," which is the fattier cut. Since the meat is cooked for several hours, the first cut will dry out.

David Levine was a longtime customer; he owned a couple of restaurants in the Village during the seventies, including One Potato and then another called Two Potato, both very popular. He gave my dad this recipe dozens of years ago and it's been a part of our family repertoire ever since. The only thing I changed from Dave's original recipe is that I make it using only the second cut (a brisket is two separate muscles, and the one known as the "second cut" is the better piece of meat). The two pieces cook very differently and there's a big piece of fat that separates the two that you have to throw out. If you just use the second cut, you're getting a better piece of meat and excluding that chunk of fat. When I make this, I always make a few at a time. When I was growing up in Brooklyn, my dad used to take me for brisket sandwiches at Jewish delicatessens. This meat reminds me of the meat I got on those sandwiches.

SERVES 6

1. Preheat the oven to 325°F.

2. Season the brisket with 1 tablespoon of the salt and the pepper and put it in a large Dutch oven. Add enough stock to just cover the brisket. Cover and bake until the meat is fork-tender, 4 to 4½ hours.

3. Meanwhile, in a small bowl, mix the brown sugar, honey, cinnamon, and cloves.

4. Remove the brisket from the oven and increase the oven temperature to 400°F. Pour out and discard the braising liquid from the roasting pan. Spoon the sauce over the brisket and use the back of the spoon to coat the meat on both sides.

5. Return the brisket to the oven to roast until a candied crust forms on the outside, about 10 minutes. Remove the brisket, sprinkle it with the remaining ½ teaspoon salt, and let it rest for 10 to 15 minutes before slicing it. Cut the brisket against the grain into ¼-inch-thick slices.

NOTE: If you don't have a Dutch oven, use a roasting pan and cover it with foil.

BEEF WELLINGTON WITH MUSHROOM CREAM SAUCE

MUSHROOMS

2 tablespoons extra-virgin olive oil

2 tablespoons unsalted butter

1 pound mixed mushrooms (such as cremini, shiitake, and white), wiped clean, stems discarded, finely chopped

¼ cup finely diced shallots (about 2 medium)

½ teaspoon kosher salt plus more to taste

¼ teaspoon freshly ground black pepper

1 heaping tablespoon minced fresh sage leaves

2 teaspoons truffle oil (optional)

WELLINGTONS

4 beef filet mignons (1½ inches thick, about 4 ounces each)

2 teaspoons kosher salt

½ teaspoon freshly ground black pepper

1 tablespoon canola or another neutral-flavored oil

1 box (17 ounces) frozen puff pastry

2 (8-inch) flour tortillas

All-purpose flour for dusting

2 large eggs

SAUCE

1 cup heavy cream

Beef Wellington consists of a fairly thick piece of tenderloin that is covered in foie gras and sautéed mushrooms and then wrapped in puff pastry and baked. It's my favorite preparation for beef tenderloin. I don't need the foie in mine, but the mushrooms and puff pastry add flavor and moisture to a cut that otherwise doesn't have a lot of either. If you want to include foie in yours, lay a spoonful of Foie Gras Mousse (page 125) on each fillet just before covering them with mushrooms. The flour tortillas in this recipe absorb the moisture from the meat and keep the puff pastry from getting soggy. They will blend into the puff pastry while cooking; you'll never know they're there.

SERVES 4

1. For the mushrooms: In a large skillet, heat the olive oil and butter over medium-high heat for about 2 minutes, until the fats slide easily in the pan. Add the mushrooms and cook until they begin to wilt and brown slightly, 12 to 15 minutes. Add the shallots, salt, and pepper. Reduce the heat to medium and cook until the shallots are softened, about 5 minutes. Remove from the heat, stir in the sage and truffle oil, if using, and season with more salt to taste. Set the pan aside for the mushrooms to cool to room temperature.

2. For the Wellingtons: Season the beef with the salt and pepper. In a second large skillet, heat the canola oil over medium-high heat until it slides easily in the pan, about 2 minutes. Sear the beef on both sides, about 30 seconds per side. Take the beef out of the pan and set aside to cool slightly.

3. Take the puff pastry out of the freezer and out of its package and let it sit at room temperature for 5 minutes before working with it.

4. Fold each tortilla into quarters. Unfold them and use a 2½-inch biscuit cutter to cut one round from each quadrant. Use a ½-inch aspic cutter to cut a small hole in the centers of four of the tortilla rounds to create a vent (or use a paring knife to cut an "X"). Set the tortilla rounds aside.

5. Dust a work surface with flour and lay a sheet of puff pastry down. Use a 6-inch metal ring to cut out a large round. (You can also use a bowl with a 6-inch diameter as a guide and cut it out using a paring knife.) Cut a second 6-inch round out of that sheet. Then use a 3½-inch cutter to cut two rounds out of the same sheet. Repeat with the second sheet of puff pastry for a total of four rounds of each size. Use the ½-inch aspic cutter to cut a hole in the center of each of the smaller rounds to create a vent (or cut an "X" in the pastry with a paring knife). Put the smaller rounds on a baking sheet or parchment paper and put them in the refrigerator while you assemble the Wellingtons. Put the larger rounds on a parchment-lined baking sheet.

(continued)

6. Put a non-vented tortilla round in the center of each of the larger pastry rounds. Spoon 1 tablespoon of the mushroom mixture on each tortilla round and spread the mushrooms to the edges of the tortilla with the back of the spoon, making sure to not get it on the pastry. Place the tenderloins on top of the mushrooms. Spoon another tablespoon of the mushrooms on top of each tenderloin and spread to the edge of the meat. (This will not use all of the mushrooms.)

7. Place the vented tortilla rounds on top of the mushrooms. Remove the 3½-inch pastry rounds from the refrigerator and place one on top of each tenderloin. To close the Wellingtons, lift the edges of the pastry up around the meat to meet the top round of dough. Crimp the top and bottom pastry together with your fingers; you may need to wet your fingers to make the dough sticky enough to crimp. Put the Wellingtons in the freezer until they are very cold, about 30 minutes.

8. Meanwhile, preheat the oven to 450°F.

9. Make four collars out of foil by tearing each sheet about 2 inches wide. Wrap one foil collar around the outside circumference of each Wellington (this will help them to not collapse as they bake).

10. Put the Wellingtons in the oven to bake for 10 minutes.

11. Meanwhile, in a small bowl, lightly beat the eggs to make an egg wash.

12. Remove the Wellingtons from the oven, remove the foil collars, and brush the Wellingtons all over with the egg wash. Put the Wellingtons back in the oven to bake until the pastry is golden brown and a meat thermometer inserted into the beef registers 130°F for medium-rare, 10 to 15 minutes. (For medium or medium-well meat, cook the Wellingtons until the thermometer registers 145° to 150°F, an additional 5 or 10 minutes. If the pastry is browning before the meat is at the desired temperature, tent the Wellingtons with foil to protect them and then put them back in the oven to continue baking.)

13. For the sauce: Put the skillet with the remaining mushrooms over medium heat and cook them to warm through, 3 or 4 minutes. Add the cream and cook until the cream reduces slightly, about 5 minutes.

14. To serve, spoon some mushroom sauce on each plate. Place one Wellington on top of the sauce.

NOTE: To make these, you will need a 3½-inch biscuit cutter and a 2½-inch biscuit cutter; or make do using jars or drinking glasses with the same diameter. You will also need a 6-inch ring (or a bowl with a 6-inch diameter). We used a ½-inch round aspic cutter to make a hole for ventilation, but you can also just cut an "X" in the pastry with a paring knife.

FIVE-MINUTE MARINATED SKIRT STEAK

2 cups Five-Minute Marinade (below)

3 outside skirt steaks (about 3 pounds)

Kosher salt and freshly ground black pepper

Outside skirt steak is my favorite cut of meat. In addition to having great flavor, it's always been my dad's favorite, which makes it even more special to me. I prepare skirt steak often at home, always on the grill, and always with my Five-Minute Marinade.

SERVES 6

1. Put the marinade in a large casserole dish if it isn't in one already. Add the skirt steaks to the marinade and turn to coat them on all sides.

2. Heat a grill or a grill pan to high heat.

3. Remove the skirt steaks from the marinade. Season both sides with salt and pepper and put the steaks on the grill. Cook the steaks until they are caramelized on both sides, about 3 minutes per side for medium-rare. Remove the steaks from the grill and let them rest for 5 minutes.

4. Slice the steaks against the grain and serve.

FIVE-MINUTE MARINADE

2 cups packed light or dark brown sugar

½ cup balsamic vinegar

¼ cup Worcestershire sauce

6 cloves garlic, smashed and roughly chopped

Leaves from 5 or 6 sprigs fresh rosemary (optional)

What I love about this marinade is that it's so thick from all the brown sugar in it that it sticks to the meat. I made it at an event and the TV personality Adam Richman begged me for the recipe. I never got it to him, but here it is. I call this Five-Minute Marinade because you only need to keep steaks in the marinade for five minutes for it to have an impact on the meat's flavor. That isn't to say that if you wanted to leave the meat in the marinade for hours, it wouldn't be just as good or better. I usually use it on skirt steaks, but you could use it on any beef cuts that are fit for grilling.

MAKES 2 CUPS, OR ENOUGH FOR ABOUT 3 POUNDS OF MEAT

Combine the sugar, vinegar, Worcestershire sauce, garlic, and rosemary (if using) in a large casserole dish. The marinade is now ready for your steaks.

Skirt Steak Pinwheels

2 outside skirt steaks (about
   1½ pounds each), trimmed of
   excess fat

2 teaspoons kosher salt

1 teaspoon freshly ground black
   pepper

8 ounces grated Parmigiano-
   Reggiano cheese (about 2 cups)

4 lemons

1½ cups finely chopped fresh
   flat-leaf parsley leaves

This preparation was popular with retail butchers in the 1940s and 1950s. Angelo Bonsangue, a butcher who worked with us on Leroy Street, taught me how to make them. I occasionally teach these at cooking classes and people love them. I often grill them at home.

SERVES 4

1. Lay the skirt steak out on your work surface and season it on both sides with the salt and pepper. Sprinkle the cheese over the steak, leaving a ½-inch border with no topping. Grate the lemon zest from all 4 lemons directly onto the steak and sprinkle the parsley on top of the lemon zest. Starting at one of the short ends, roll the skirt steak from one end to the other. Tie a butcher's knot in the center of the roll. Then tie two more butcher's knots in the center of each side. Cut the roll in half along the first knot (remove that string) to form two wheels of equal size.

2. Preheat a grill or a grill pan over high heat.

3. Place the pinwheels cut side down on the grill or in the pan and cook them until they're browned on both sides, about 8 minutes. Serve one pinwheel per person.

BRAISED BEEF SHANK BOURGUIGNON

6 (1½-inch-thick) beef hind shank slices (about ¾ pound each)

1 tablespoon kosher salt

1 teaspoon freshly ground black pepper

1 tablespoon canola or another neutral-flavored oil

4 ounces bacon (about 5 slices), cut into ½-inch pieces

3 medium yellow onions, thinly sliced

2 stalks celery, thinly sliced

2 large carrots, thinly sliced

2 tablespoons finely chopped fresh flat-leaf parsley leaves, stems reserved

3 cloves garlic, chopped (about 1 tablespoon)

1 can (14 ounces) diced tomatoes

2 tablespoons dark brown sugar

1 tablespoon tomato paste

Grated zest of 1 large orange (about 2 teaspoons)

2 cups red wine

3 cups beef stock (Brown Veal Stock, page 31; or low-sodium store-bought beef stock), or as needed

18 baby carrots, peeled, stems trimmed

2 tablespoons Dijon mustard

¼ cup fresh breadcrumbs

BUTCHER'S NOTE:

Ask your butcher to cut beef hind shanks into 1½-inch rounds as if for veal osso buco.

This recipe was given to us by chef Paul Denamiel, whose family owns Le Rivage on Restaurant Row. My father has been selling meat to his father, Marcel, for thirty or forty years, and now we work with both father and son. Paul uses an osso buco cut to make this classic French braise. You could use this recipe to braise veal shanks, lamb shanks, or beef cheeks.

SERVES 6

1. Season the beef shanks all over with the salt and pepper.

2. Preheat the oven to 375°F.

3. In a large Dutch oven (or another high-sided ovenproof pan), heat the oil over high heat. Add the bacon and cook until it's crisp, about 5 minutes. Use a slotted spoon to transfer the bacon to paper towels to drain, leaving the fat in the pan. Add the shanks to the Dutch oven and brown them on each side, about 3 minutes per side. Transfer the shanks to a plate. Add the onions, celery, sliced carrots, parsley stems, and garlic to the Dutch oven. Cook the vegetables until they begin to soften, 3 to 5 minutes. Return the shanks to the Dutch oven along with any juices that have collected on the plate. Stir in the tomatoes, brown sugar, tomato paste, and orange zest. Add the wine and cook it for 15 minutes to reduce it by half. Add enough stock so the meat is just covered. Bring the liquid to a simmer over high heat. Put the lid on the Dutch oven (if you're using a pan without a lid, cover it with foil). Put the shanks in the oven to cook until the meat is fork-tender, about 2 hours. Remove the meat from the oven, uncover the pot, and let the meat cool in the braising liquid for at least 30 minutes and up to overnight. (To make in advance, allow the shanks to cool completely, then cover and refrigerate them in the cooking liquid. Heat them in the liquid in a 350°F oven for 15 minutes to warm them through before proceeding to the next step.)

4. When you're ready to serve the shanks, preheat the oven to 400°F.

5. Remove the beef shanks from the braising liquid and place them in a baking dish large enough to hold them in a single layer. Strain the braising liquid into the dish, adding only enough to come halfway up the sides of the shanks. (Strain and reserve the rest of the liquid to serve on the side.) Put the baby carrots in with the beef shanks. Spread 1 teaspoon of the mustard on top of each shank and sprinkle 2 teaspoons of breadcrumbs on the mustard. Return the shanks to the oven to bake until the breadcrumbs are golden brown, about 10 minutes.

6. To serve, put a shank and a few carrots on each plate. Ladle the sauce over and around each serving of meat and sprinkle with the parsley.

CHIPOTLE-BRAISED TOMAHAWK SHORT RIBS

SHORT RIBS

6 dried pasilla chiles (about 1 ounce)

6 stalks celery, cut into ½-inch-thick slices

2 large carrots, cut into ¼-inch-thick slices

2 large white onions, halved and cut into ½-inch-thick slices

1 cup garlic cloves (about 3 dozen), smashed

6 long-bone plate short ribs (about 1¾ pounds each)

Kosher salt and freshly ground black pepper

10 bay leaves

¼ cup dried oregano

2 teaspoons black peppercorns

½ cup pureed chipotle in adobo (to puree chipotles in adobo, dump the entire can, including the adobo sauce, into a blender)

Vegetable oil for broiling or grilling the ribs

Rosa Mexicano, the restaurant where we enjoy short ribs the most, was one of the first in the city to introduce regional Mexican cuisine to New Yorkers. My godfather, Jerry, has been eating there since the beginning. Jerry is as close to me and my brothers and sister as anyone can be; he is trusted and admired by the entire family. Jerry introduced me to Rosa Mexicano many years ago, and I've always loved it. Anytime I go, I end up ordering the short ribs. The founder, Josefina Howard, has since passed away and the restaurant has been bought by a corporate group, which is doing a lot of expanding across the country. But no matter what kind of changes they make in their expansion, the original location, on the East Side of Manhattan, is like sacred ground—they do not mess with it. That location is also the only one that serves these short ribs. To make them, the restaurant buys only the two meatiest short ribs from each plate (the primal cut of beef that short ribs are cut from). For this recipe, I alter the original slightly by making tomahawk short ribs (see "Beef Cuts," page 172) because I like the presentation.

SERVES 6

1. For the ribs: Preheat the oven to 350°F.

2. Wipe the pasilla chiles clean with a paper towel. Tear the chiles open and pull out and discard the seeds and stems. In a medium skillet, toast the chiles over medium heat until they are fragrant, about 1 minute per side. Take the chiles out of the pan so they don't keep cooking; if you overtoast them, they will get bitter.

3. Scatter half the celery, carrots, onion, and garlic over the bottom of a large Dutch oven. Generously season the meat all over with salt and pepper and lay the ribs meat side down on top of the vegetables (the bones may stick up out of the pot). Tuck the pasillas and bay leaves between and around the ribs. Scatter the oregano, peppercorns, and the remaining celery, carrot, onion, and garlic over the ribs. In a bowl, stir together the chipotle puree, salt, and 6 cups water. Pour the liquid over the ribs; add more water if necessary to cover the ribs. Cover with the lid or foil and bake until the ribs are fork-tender (the meat will be pulling away from the bone), about 3 hours. Check the ribs for the first time after 2½ hours. Remove the ribs from the oven and remove the lid or foil, being careful not to burn yourself from the steam that will rise. Let the ribs cool to room temperature in the braising liquid. Refrigerate the ribs along with their cooking liquid for at least 6 hours, or up to 2 days.

4. For the salsa: Preheat the oven to 350°F.

(continued)

1½ pounds tomatillos, husks
    removed, rinsed

1 tablespoon canola oil

4 dried chipotle chiles

1 ancho chile

6 cloves garlic

4 whole cloves

2 teaspoons dried oregano

2 teaspoons kosher salt plus more
    for seasoning

¼ teaspoon ground cumin

1½ tablespoons dark brown sugar

2 teaspoons molasses

BUTCHER'S NOTE:
Ask your butcher for 9-inch long, long-bone plate short ribs. French the short ribs three-quarters of the way down (see "Frenching a Rib Bone," page 186). Roll the meat on each bone into a pinwheel and tie each pinwheel with two segments of butcher's rope. The meat is slightly wider than the bone, which makes it possible to bring the rope all the way around the bone.

5. Spread the tomatillos on a baking sheet. Drizzle the tomatillos with the canola oil, toss to coat, and roast them, tossing them occasionally, until they are browned and collapsed, about 1 hour.

6. Wipe the chipotle and ancho chiles clean with a paper towel. Tear the ancho chile open and pull out and discard the seeds and stems. Discard the stem from the chipotles but keep the seeds intact. Toast the chiles in a medium skillet over medium heat until they are fragrant, about 1 minute per side. Pour ⅔ cup water into the pan and remove from the heat. Set the chiles aside to soak until they have softened slightly, about 10 minutes.

7. Drain the chiles and transfer them to a blender. Add the garlic, whole cloves, oregano, salt, cumin, brown sugar, molasses, ½ cup water, and the tomatillos (including their juices) and blend to a smooth paste.

8. Heat a medium heavy skillet over medium heat. Pour the chile paste into the skillet. Rinse out the blender with ¼ cup water and add that to the pan. Bring the sauce to a boil, then reduce to a simmer, and cook, stirring occasionally, until the sauce is shiny, about 30 minutes. Season with more salt as needed. If the sauce becomes too thick before turning shiny, stir in water, adding it a small amount at a time. The sauce can be prepared up to 2 days in advance; cool to room temperature and then refrigerate until you're ready to serve it. Before serving, bring the sauce to a simmer, adding water as necessary to restore it to the right consistency.

9. When you're ready to serve the ribs, scrape the solidified fat from the ribs. Reserve the cooking liquid for another use.

10. To reheat the ribs in the broiler, adjust the broiler rack so it is 2 inches from the heat source and preheat the broiler. (Use a "low" setting on the broiler if you have that option.) Coat a broiler pan with vegetable oil and put the ribs on the pan. Broil the ribs until the tops are browned and sizzling, about 6 minutes. Turn the ribs and broil the other side in the same way.

11. To reheat the ribs on the grill, preheat a gas or charcoal grill to low heat. Brush or rub the grill grates with vegetable oil and grill the short ribs, turning them occasionally, until the outside is browned and sizzling, about 12 minutes.

12. To serve the short ribs, ladle about ⅓ cup of the tomatillo salsa onto each plate and lay a short rib on top.

THE PERFECT STEAK

Rib steaks, rib-eyes, strip steaks, T-bone steaks, or porterhouse steaks

Maldon or another flaky sea salt (about ½ tablespoon per pound of meat)

Freshly ground pepper (black pepper or a blend of red, white, and black)

BONE OR NO BONE

A lot of chefs like to say that cooking meat with the bone in makes the meat taste better. If you want to gnaw on the intercostal meat that you'll find on the rib bone, and nobody is a bigger fan of that than I am, then that's the biggest advantage of the bone. Cooking a bone-in steak also helps the steak hold its shape, and it might even help prevent overcooking the steak, since the bone, which remains cold, protects one side of it. But does it add flavor? You think flavor jumps off the bone into the meat? No way. Impossible.

One of the questions I'm most often asked is how to cook the perfect steak. Obviously, how you like your steak cooked is a matter of personal preference. I like my steak medium-rare, and I'd rather have it err on the side of rare than medium. Regardless of temperature, for me, the perfect steak must have a nice crust on the outside that you get from searing it. And it must be cooked evenly all the way through—not graduating shades of brown until you reach the pink center.

There is a logical reason for each of the steps involved in cooking the perfect steak. Searing the meat initially starts the Maillard reaction, a chemical reaction that occurs as a result of high heat in which amino acids and sugars that are present in the meat recombine, resulting in the brown color and increased flavor. Searing also helps the seasonings adhere to the steak. Resting the steak after searing it helps equalize the temperature across the steak (within 5° to 10°F). It also gives the temperature at the center a chance to rise to above room temperature. Cooking the steaks in a 450°F oven continues to brown the steak, which adds more flavor. And by cooking the steaks at the lower oven temperature, 300°F, a small miracle happens: At the edge of the steak, the temperature stalls somewhere between 140° and 160°F, while the temperature at the center catches up so the steak is evenly cooked throughout. The other advantage to finishing with the lower oven temperature is that the carryover, the degree to which the temperature rises once the steak is out of the oven, is more predictable. When a steak comes out of a 450°F oven, the temperature rises too quickly, which makes you more susceptible to overcooking the steak. The final resting period equalizes the internal temperature of the steak completely, so it doesn't continue to cook once it's served. When choosing the desired temperature to which you cook your steak, note that the internal temperature will rise 7° to 10°F after you've taken it out of the oven. When making steaks, I find I get the best results if I use a flaky sea salt (my preference is Maldon sea salt) and a medium-coarse pepper. I like a blend of red, white, and black peppercorns, but black pepper would also work just fine. You'll need a meat thermometer to achieve a perfect steak, and preferably you will have an infrared thermometer; with this you can check the doneness of the meat and also the readiness of the pan you sear it in.

For steaks that are 1 inch thick:

Pat the steaks dry with paper towels and generously season both sides of the steaks (but not the edges) with salt and pepper. Heat a cast-iron skillet over high heat until it is very hot, 5 to 6 minutes. (It will register 500°F at the center when measured with an infrared thermometer. A drop of water will dance when dropped on the skillet; if the skillet is smoking, it's too hot.) Put the steaks in the pan (no more than two at a time) and cook for 2 minutes, pressing the steaks down gently to help them develop a good sear. Flip the steaks and cook them for 2 minutes on the second side. Check the temperature of the steaks at this point. You want to cook them on each side again for 1 minute, but not if that means overcooking them; if they are at 110°F, remove them from the pan. If they are below that temperature, continue cooking them for 1 minute on each side. (You will have cooked the steaks for 6 minutes total.) Remove the steaks from the pan and set them aside to rest for 5 to 10 minutes before serving.

For steaks that are 1½ inches thick:

1. Preheat the oven to 450°F.

2. Pat the steaks dry with paper towels and generously season both sides of the steaks (but not the edges) with salt and pepper. Heat a cast-iron skillet over high heat until it is very hot, 5 to 6 minutes. Put the steaks in the pan (no more than two at a time) and sear for 2½ to 3 minutes on each side, pressing the steaks down gently to help them develop a good sear, until they are deep brown on both sides. Take the steaks out of the pan and put them on a baking sheet (in a single layer, not stacked) to rest for 10 minutes while you sear more steaks. Put the steaks in the oven for 8 minutes. Reduce the temperature to 350°F and cook for another 5 minutes, or until the internal temperature registers 125° to 130°F for medium-rare (see "Cooking Temperatures for Beef and Lamb," page 76). Remove the baking sheet from the oven and transfer the steaks to a wire rack or another, cool baking sheet to rest for 7 to 10 minutes before serving.

For steaks that are 2 inches thick:

1. Preheat the oven to 450°F.

2. Pat the steaks dry with paper towels and generously season both sides of the steaks (but not the edges) with salt and pepper. Heat a cast-iron skillet over high heat until it is very hot, 5 to 6 minutes. (It will register 500°F at the center when measured with an infrared thermometer. A drop of water will dance when dropped on the skillet; if the skillet is smoking, it's too hot.) Put the steaks in the pan (no more than two at a time) and sear them for 2½ to 3 minutes on each side, pressing down on them with a spatula, until they are deep brown on both sides. Using tongs, pick up the steaks and hold their edges against the pan, turning them in order to sear all the edges. Take the steaks out of the pan and put them on a baking sheet (in a single layer, not stacked) to rest for 15 to 20 minutes while you sear more steaks.

3. When you've seared all your steaks, put the baking sheet in the oven for 10 minutes.

4. Reduce the oven temperature to 300°F and cook the steaks until a meat thermometer registers 125° to 130°F for medium-rare, 8 to 15 minutes; cooking times will vary so use the thermometer as your ultimate guide. Remove the baking sheet from the oven and transfer the steaks to a wire rack or another, cool baking sheet to rest for 8 to 10 minutes before serving.

STEAK CONDIMENTS

Purist food writers think of sauce as a way of covering things up, and that the flavor of, in this case, the meat should stand alone. I disagree. I am a big fan of steak condiments. I know what steak tastes like. And when I go out to eat, I appreciate when the chef offers something to make their steak experience different from others. The condiment is not about covering up the flavor of the steak, but complementing it. It's yet another opportunity for the chef to do something different. Here are some of my favorite steak condiments.

RAOUL'S AU POIVRE SAUCE

1½ teaspoons unsalted butter

⅓ cup finely chopped shallots

¾ teaspoon fine sea salt plus more to taste

1 tablespoon black peppercorns, crushed with the side of a heavy knife

2 tablespoons cognac

3 cups Brown Veal Stock (page 31; or low-sodium store-bought)

½ cup heavy cream

For many years, when we were on Leroy Street, and there was a family issue my mom and I would go for a sit-down meeting at Raoul's, a French bistro in SoHo. Raoul's was and still is legendary in the neighborhood for its great food and lively atmosphere. I used to make deliveries to Raoul's in the mornings. Restaurants love to take care of their suppliers and when we went to Raoul's, the guys in the kitchen sent every dish they could think of to our table. It was an odd feeling knowing that a few hours before, I was dressed in dirty boots and a fleece, lugging boxes of meat down their back steps, and then to be there in the evening, dressed up, eating a luxurious dinner of that same meat. My mom and I always ordered the same thing: steak au poivre. The sauce—made with peppercorns, cream, and cognac— really blew me away. No matter how much food had been brought to our table, I had to have the steak with that sauce.

MAKES 1 ½ CUPS/6 OR MORE SERVINGS

1. In a medium skillet, melt the butter over medium heat. Add the shallots, sprinkle with the salt and crushed peppercorns, and cook, stirring often, until the shallots are softened (you don't want them to brown), about 6 minutes. Add the cognac and cook it until the pan is almost dry, about 2 minutes. Add the stock and cook until the sauce is thick enough to coat the back of a spoon, about 30 minutes.

2. Add the cream and reduce the sauce again until it is thick enough to coat the back of a spoon, about 20 minutes. Remove from the heat and season with additional salt to taste. Serve warm.

AGED-BEEF LARD WITH ROSEMARY AND GARLIC

¼ pound (1 stick) unsalted butter, at room temperature

¼ pound aged beef fat, rendered (½ cup), at room temperature

1½ teaspoons minced fresh rosemary

1 large clove garlic, minced

1 teaspoon kosher salt

1 teaspoon freshly ground black pepper

The chef Michael White serves this steak condiment, which consists of rendered aged-beef lard mixed with butter and other seasonings, at his restaurant Osteria Morini. To serve an aged-beef steak and then finish the steak off with this—it really makes for an intense experience. What I especially love about it is the fact that they took the excess fat from the steak, a by-product that most people would have thrown out, and turned it into a delicious sauce. The first time I tried it was when the chefs were experimenting with it at the restaurant, adding a little more of this or that, and I happened to be there. A bunch of the chefs and I were all tasting it by dipping bread into it. I couldn't stop eating it. Today when I go to Morini, I just ask for this condiment and eat it with bread, regardless of whether or not I order a steak.

MAKES 8 OUNCES/ABOUT 8 SERVINGS

In the bowl of a stand mixer fitted with the paddle attachment, combine the butter, rendered beef fat, rosemary, garlic, salt, and pepper and mix on medium speed to combine the ingredients. (You can also make this with a hand-held mixer.) Turn the mixture out onto a piece of parchment paper and roll it into a log about 1½ inches in diameter. Refrigerate the log to chill until the "butter" is firm, or for up to a week. To serve, slice the log crosswise into ¼-inch-thick rounds and put one round on each finished steak. You can also melt the "butter" and brush it onto a finished steak, or serve it on the side.

FOOLPROOF BÉARNAISE

⅓ cup dry white wine

⅓ cup white wine vinegar

2 tablespoons finely chopped shallots

30 black peppercorns, crushed

1 sprig fresh tarragon plus 1 teaspoon finely chopped tarragon leaves

3 large egg yolks

7 ounces (1¾ sticks) cold unsalted butter, cut into ½-inch cubes

1¼ teaspoons kosher salt plus more to taste

½ teaspoon fresh lemon juice plus more to taste

Béarnaise is a classic steak condiment made of egg yolks, vinegar, shallots, and butter. This version is different from a classic béarnaise in that it calls for cold butter rather than clarified butter. Using cold, solid butter instead of clarified makes for a more foolproof sauce that is less likely to break. To be sure it won't separate, it is still safest to make it just before you're ready to serve it.

MAKES ABOUT 1¼ CUPS/ABOUT 5 SERVINGS

1. In a small saucepan, combine the wine, vinegar, shallots, peppercorns, and tarragon sprig. Add ⅓ cup water and bring the liquid to a boil over high heat. Reduce the heat to low and simmer until the liquid has reduced to 1 tablespoon, about 15 minutes. Discard the tarragon sprig. Remove from the heat.

2. In a separate small saucepan or skillet, combine the egg yolks, butter, 1 tablespoon cold water, and the contents of the first saucepan and whisk to thoroughly incorporate the ingredients. Cook the sauce, whisking constantly, until it is the consistency of mayonnaise, 2 to 3 minutes, moving the pan on and off the heat if the sauce begins to bubble. Do not let the sauce boil or it will separate. Remove the pan from the heat and whisk in the chopped tarragon, salt, and lemon juice. Add more salt to taste. Serve the sauce immediately or pour it into a thermos to keep warm until you're ready to serve it.

PORT WINE REDUCTION

2 cups port

1 cup full-bodied dry red wine

2 cups Demi-Glace (page 31; or store-bought)

Kosher salt, as needed

I love a rich wine sauce like this one on steak or prime rib (see Standing Rib Roast with Dried Porcini Rub and Port Wine Reduction, page 216).

MAKES 1 CUP/12 TO 14 SERVINGS

In a medium saucepan, combine the port and red wine and bring to a simmer over medium-high heat. Reduce the heat and gently simmer the sauce until the liquid has reduced to ¼ cup, 30 to 35 minutes. Add the demi-glace, increase the heat to medium-high, and return the liquid to a boil. Reduce the heat and simmer the sauce until it is thick enough to coat the back of a spoon, 15 to 20 minutes. Taste and season with salt if needed; depending on the demi-glace you use, you may not need to add any salt.

MAYTAG BLUE BUTTER

6 tablespoons unsalted butter, at room temperature

2 tablespoons minced shallots

Kosher salt

¼ pound Maytag blue cheese, at room temperature

2 teaspoons finely chopped fresh flat-leaf parsley leaves

1 teaspoon Maldon or another flaky sea salt

Until I ate this blue cheese butter on a rib-eye steak at City Hall restaurant in the late 1990s, I'd never had anything like it on steak. I didn't even know you could put cheese on a steak, which is pretty significant considering the fact that I'm a butcher and at that time I sold to a few hundred restaurants in New York City—and tried to dine at them all. Once I tasted it, it became my favorite steak in New York City for many years.

MAKES 8 OUNCES/ABOUT 8 SERVINGS

1. In a small skillet, heat 2 tablespoons of the butter over medium heat. Add the shallots, season them with salt, and cook, stirring often, until they are soft, about 4 minutes. (You don't want the shallots to brown. If they begin to brown, reduce the heat.) Turn off the heat and let the shallots cool to room temperature.

2. In a medium bowl, combine the blue cheese, the remaining 4 tablespoons butter, the parsley, sea salt, and shallots. Fold them together with a rubber spatula.

3. Turn the mixture out onto a sheet of parchment paper and form it into a log. Refrigerate to chill until the butter is solid, or for up to 2 weeks. To serve, slice the log crosswise into ½-inch-thick rounds. Put the round of butter on top of a just-cooked steak, then run the steak under the broiler until the cheese begins to melt, about 1 minute.

Raoul's Au Poivre Sauce

Port Wine Reduction

**Aged-Beef Lard with
Rosemary and Garlic**

Maytag Blue Butter

Foolproof Béarnaise

STANDING RIB ROAST WITH DRIED PORCINI RUB AND PORT WINE REDUCTION

1 (7-bone) standing rib roast (15 to 18 pounds)

Kosher salt and freshly ground black pepper

1 cup Dried Porcini Rub (opposite page)

Port Wine Reduction (page 214)

BUTCHER'S NOTE:

Ask your butcher to remove the chine bone and feather bones from the rib roast; this way you will be able to slice straight through the meat, between the bones, once the roast is done.

A standing rib roast is a meat icon. To see that roast come out into a dining room with those bones sticking straight up—it's a major showpiece, especially during the holidays. The only thing I don't like about a roast cooked whole like that is that when you get it at a restaurant, they don't finish it with anything. Usually you get what I call a "wedding cut," because it's the sort of thing you're served at a wedding: a slice of meat, perfectly cooked so it's a beautiful pink color throughout. But that's just not enough for me. I like something other than the taste of perfect meat, which is why I serve this roast with a port wine sauce.

SERVES 10 TO 12

1. Position an oven rack in the lower third of the oven. Remove any racks above it and preheat the oven to 450°F.

2. Season the roast all over with salt and pepper and rub it liberally with the porcini rub; use your hands to pack the rub onto the meat as much as possible.

3. Put the roast with the bones lying down on a roasting rack set inside a roasting pan and roast for 25 minutes.

4. Reduce the oven temperature to 275°F and cook the roast until a meat thermometer inserted into the center registers 115°F, about 2½ hours. Remove the roast from the oven and remove it from the roasting rack. Tent it loosely with foil and allow it to rest for 30 minutes, or until the thermometer registers 130°F.

5. To carve the roast, you can cut along both sides of each bone, creating alternating slices of boneless and bone-in slices. Or cut double slices, each with a bone, to serve two people. Lightly drizzle the meat with the port reduction, and serve the rest on the side.

DRIED PORCINI RUB

4 ounces dried porcini

¼ cup plus 1 tablespoon sugar

1 tablespoon crushed red pepper
flakes

1 tablespoon kosher salt

1 tablespoon freshly ground black
pepper

A few years ago I went to an event at Martha Stewart's house in Bedford, New York, where the inventor of the Caja China box, Roberto Guerra, cooked a whole hog in a giant version of the box. It was the first time I'd seen one. I was so impressed, I took down the design and the dimensions in my head, and when I got home, I sketched out one large enough to cook a whole steer for an upcoming event. The structure needed to be made of steel so it could withstand extreme heat. I gave the drawing to my father who knew a welder and asked him to have one made. My dad took my specifications to the welder and came back with an astronomical price, basically saying we couldn't do it. But I said, "Great! Make it!" My dad tried every angle to get me to not make this box, but I insisted, and a month later, I had my box. It's bigger than an SUV. You need a forklift to move it. Once I had the box, I turned for help to Mike Toscano, the chef at Perla. Mike was the one chef I knew who was very familiar with cooking whole animals. He came into LaFrieda Meats and got to work. I had an 875-pound steer, which is too big to soak in brine, so he injected it and then packed the outside with porcini rub, and he left it like that for several days. We then cooked it at an event in my giant box. It had never been done before, and it's never been done by anyone other than me since, at least not that I know of. The crowd went wild for it. They loved the spectacle of seeing this enormous animal cooked whole, as well as the meat that resulted from it, which was unbelievably juicy and flavorful. If you wanted to do something similar but more manageable in a standard Caja China, use a steamship roast (page 183), which will feed as many as eighty people. This recipe calls for you to grind dried porcini mushrooms in a spice grinder. If you don't have a spice grinder, you can do the same in a food processor, though you will not be able to grind it as fine. Some specialty spice stores sell dried porcini already ground into a powder.

MAKES ABOUT 1½ CUPS/ENOUGH FOR 1 STANDING RIB ROAST; FOR A STEAMSHIP ROUND; DOUBLE THIS RECIPE

Grind the porcini to a powder in a spice grinder. Transfer the ground porcini to a large bowl and add the sugar, red pepper flakes, salt, and black pepper and stir to combine. Store the rub in an airtight container at room temperature for up to several weeks.

PAT LaFRIEDA'S ORIGINAL FILET MIGNON STEAK SANDWICH

4 tablespoons canola or another neutral-flavored oil plus more as needed

2 large sweet yellow onions or Spanish onions, thinly sliced (about 3 cups)

6 ounces thinly sliced Monterey Jack cheese

1 cup beef stock (see Brown Veal Stock, page 31; or store-bought) or Demi-Glace (page 31; or store-bought)

1½ teaspoons balsamic glaze

12 (½-inch-thick) medallions tenderloin (about 1½ pounds)

1 tablespoon kosher salt

½ teaspoon turbinado sugar or light brown sugar

4 demi-baguettes (or 6-inch) segments of a long baguette

A substantial change in dining is happening in a very unlikely place. The days of stale pretzels and old beer are transforming into fine dining at large format sporting venues. Great leaders in this vastly improved food movement are the New York Mets and its owners, Jeff and Scott Wilpon. They have revolutionized the food experience at baseball games by partnering with Aramark to offer amazing dishes from Danny Meyer's Shake Shack and Dave Pasternack's Catch of the Day, among others. The Wilpons had been eating our meat at restaurants for years and were big fans of our product. In 2012, they asked my cousin Mark and me if we had something that they were missing in their lineup, namely a steak sandwich.

My dad had taught me how to make his favorite steak sandwich when I was a kid. We always made it with skirt steak, which is our favorite beef cut, but I quickly realized that I couldn't use this meat for customers because it was too chewy. The last thing I wanted was for someone to take a bite out of our sandwich and have a big piece of meat come out and slap him or her in the chin. I needed something you could bite straight through so I got the idea of using filet mignon. Customers went wild for the sandwiches. We wound up selling more than ten thousand in the last four weeks of the season.

Yet, the most amazing thing about this new milestone for our business was to be able to take my dad to see the stand. He looked up at that big, beautiful sign that read "Pat LaFrieda." His name. His father's name. My name. My son's name. All lit up. My dad cried. He loved it. Seeing his pride was a real gift.

MAKES 4 SANDWICHES

1. In a large skillet, heat 2 tablespoons of the oil over medium heat until it slides easily in the pan, 2 to 3 minutes. Add the onions and cook, stirring occasionally so they don't stick to the pan, until they are soft and caramelized, about 20 minutes. Spread the onions out over the surface of the pan. Remove from the heat and lay the cheese on top of the onions, letting it melt.

2. To make a jus, in a small saucepan, bring the stock to a simmer over medium heat. Remove from the heat and stir in the balsamic glaze. Cover the pan to keep the jus warm.

3. Season the meat on both sides with the salt and sugar.

4. In another large skillet, heat the remaining 2 tablespoons oil over high heat. Add half the tenderloin medallions, or as many as will fit in a single layer, and sear them

until they are caramelized, 1 to 1½ minutes per side. Cook the remaining medallions in the same way, adding more oil and letting it get hot before adding the meat to the pan.

5. Meanwhile, without opening them, toast the baguettes so the outsides, top and bottom, are hot and crispy. Halve the baguettes horizontally, leaving them hinged on one side.

6. To assemble the sandwiches, lay 3 medallions on the bottom of each baguette. Top with the onions and cheese, dividing them evenly among the sandwiches. Drizzle ¼ cup of the jus on the inside top half of each baguette. Close up the sandwiches and you're good to go.

Pat LaFri
ORIGINAL FILET MIGNON STEAK

HOT DOGS SHAKES

Pat LaFrieda's Reserve, 100% Black Angus, Hand Cut Be
Vermont Monterey Jack Cheese, Sautéed Sweet Vidalia On
Beef Au Jus on a Locally Baked and Toasted French Baguett

The Pat LaFrieda's Original Filet Mignon Steak Sandwich stand at the Mets' ballpark, Citi Field

ACKNOWLEDGMENTS

The first person I want to thank is my father, for teaching me to be proud of what I do and for giving me the opportunity to follow my dreams.

This book was made possible by my team at Atria who went above and beyond in their belief that there was even a page one, especially Johanna Castillo, my editor, whose passion and dedication got this book done. And Judith Curr: I had big ideas for this book but as it turns out, she had even bigger ideas. Jeanne Lee, who designed the cover and who, with Johanna, sacrificed a working day to come walk in the mud with us at a farm, all in pursuit of a perfect shot. And the rest of the creative team of experts at Atria, including Dana Sloan and Stacey Kulig, who worked so hard in implementing my vision.

Carolynn Carreño who spent many hours listening to me tell my family's story and asking the right questions, and who worked hard to ensure that everything in the book is accurate and easy to understand for you, the reader.

My untiring recipe testers, Janet Crandall and Michael Sullivan, who stayed up many nights perfecting the recipes. There was never a task that we asked of them that they didn't take on with enthusiasm and skill.

ICC and Candy Argondizza, for allowing my team to cook in their beautiful kitchens and for all their cooking knowledge, which contributed to the success of our recipes.

My photography team, Evan Sung and his assistant, Eric Bissell, who photographed every inch of every animal and made everything look even more beautiful than I could have imagined. Also, food stylist Suzanne Lenzer and her team, Michaela Hayes and Ashley Schleeper, and prop stylist Kira Corbin—the food looks beautiful and delicious because of them.

Kate Neuhaus, my project manager and right hand, who kept everyone together and on task.

To the CAA family of Lisa Shotland, Adam Nettler, Simon Green, and Cait Hoyt, for introducing me to great projects and taking care of all the details along the way.

The Door (Charlie Dougiello, Tara Melega, Peter McManus), for all their love, support, and confidence in the LaFrieda name and what it represents.

Dean Carlson, for allowing us to feature his gorgeous Wyebrook Farm; it is what every farm should aspire to.

Jonathan Waxman/Barbuto, for allowing us to shoot in his wood-burning oven and for all of the support he has given us through the years.

Frank DeCarlo, for letting us shoot our cover in the beautiful, rustic kitchen at his restaurant, Peasant, and his loyalty for more than a decade.

Anna Schmidt, who cooked her way through this book, fine-tuning all the recipes along the way, so that you, the reader, could cook from it with ease.

My brother Chris, for his dedication to the family business and all the hard work he has done.

To my entire family, including my brother Joseph and my sister Michele, for all your love and support. To my mother who passed along the family tradition and importance of cooking. And to my wife and children, Patrick and Giuliana, who appreciate how hard I work. I want them to know: I do it all for them.

INDEX

see also burgers; chopped meat
hanger blend, for burgers, 74
hanger steaks, or butcher's steaks, 173, *173*
Hanson, Lee, 74, 166
hazelnuts, in Biscotti-Stuffed Boneless Loin, 159–60, *161*
heart, beef, 181, *181*
heart, veal, 14, *15*
hens, stewing, 110, *110*
heritage breeds of pigs, 129–30, 131
Heritage Foods, 130
Heroes, Sausage and Pepper, 89
high choice beef, *168*
hocks, pork or ham, 134–35, *135*
hog, whole, cooking, 131
honeycomb tripe, 181, *181*
Honey Mustard, *62*, 64
hotel-cut strip steaks, or bone-in strip loin steaks, 172, *172*
Howard, Josefina, 207

J

Jalapeño, Chorizo with, *81*, 84
Jewish Deli-Style Brisket, 197
Jimmy Bradley's Frenched Chop with Red Onion Soubise, 156–58, *157*
jobbers, 107
Josh Capon's Chicken Lollipops with Ancho Chile BBQ Sauce, 120, *121*
jowls, or jaw muscles (pig's), 134, *135*

K

kale, in Ribollita, 34–35
Kansas City strip steaks, or bone-in strip loin steaks, 172, *172*
kidneys, lamb's, 14, *15*, 134
kidneys, pig's, 134, *135*
kidneys, veal, *6*, 14, *15*, 134
knives:
    boning, xvi, *xvii*
    scimitars, xvi, *xvii*

sharpening steels for, xvi, *xvii*
Korean-Style Sticky "Short Rib" Sandwiches with Ginger-Sesame Aïoli, *194*, 195–96

L

lamb, 39–65
    all about, 42–43
    butchering techniques: making a crown roast, 54–55
    buying, 41
    chopped, 72, *73*
    cooking, 43
    cornering market for, 39–41
    domestic, vs. lamb produced in New Zealand or Australia, 42
    mutton vs., 42
    spring, or baby, 42
    USDA grades of, 43
lamb, condiments for, *62*, 63–64
    Garlic Confit, *62*, 64
    Honey Mustard, *62*, 64
    Mint Chimichurri, *62*, 63
    Red Pepper Walnut Pesto, Spicy, *62*, 64
    Salsa Verde, *62*, 63
    Yogurt Sauce, Tangy, *62*, 63
lamb, cuts of, *47–48*, 47–53, *51–52*
    belly, *52*, 53
    breast, *52*, 53
    center-cut leg chops, *48, 49*
    cheeks, 43, *52*, 53
    Denver ribs, or spareribs, 43, *52*, 53
    foreshanks, *52*, 53
    frenched 8-rib rack, 47, *47*
    head, *52*, 53
    hind shanks, *52*, 53
    leg, *48, 49*
    leg steaks, 43
    loin chops, 43, 50, *51*
    loin crosscut, or English cut loin chops, 50, *51*, 61
    loin roasts, 50, *51*

neck, 43, *52*, 53, 65
porterhouse chops, 50
rack, 47, *47*
rib chops, 43, 46, *47*
shoulder arm chops, *48*, 49
shoulder blade chops, *48*, 49
shoulder eye roast, or chuck eye roast, *48*, 49
skewer meat and stew meat, *48*, 49
tenderloin, 50, *51*
tongue, *52*, 53
top round, *48*, 49
lamb recipes:
    Braised Lamb Neck Moroccan Style, 65
    Braised Lamb Shank Bourguignon, 204, *205*
    Four-Meat Meatloaf, *92*, 93–94
    Lamb Loin Crosscut with Garlic Confit, 61
    Merguez, *81*, 88
    Plum and Sesame Glazed Lamb Denver Ribs, 58, *59*
    Roasted Leg of Lamb with Garlic, *60*, 61
    Stuffed Lamb Crown Roast, LaFrieda Family, *56*, 57
Lang, Adam Perry, 166
Lard, Aged-Beef, with Rosemary and Garlic, 213, *217*
large format cooking, xviii
Leroy Street, stretch of, renamed for LaFrieda Meats, xiii, *xiii*
Levine, David, 197
Lidia Bastianich's Seared Calf's Liver with Caramelized Onions and Balsamic, 30
liver, beef, *181*, 181
liver, calf's, 14, *15*
    Seared, with Caramelized Onions and Balsamic, Lidia Bastianich's, 30
liver, chicken, *112*, 113